Introducing Genre and English for Specific Purposes

Introducing Genre and English for Specific Purposes provides an overview of how genre has been conceptualized and applied in ESP, as well as the features that distinguish ESP genre research and teaching from those of other genre schools. The macro and micro aspects of ESP genre-based pedagogy are also analyzed and include:

- different possibilities for planning and designing an ESP genre-based course;
- the concrete, micro aspects of materials creation;
- how genres can be learned through play.

Featuring tasks and practical examples throughout, the book is essential reading for students and pre-service teachers who are studying genre, English for Specific Purposes or language teaching methodologies.

Sunny Hyon is Professor of English at California State University, San Bernardino, USA.

Routledge Introductions to English for Specific Purposes provide a comprehensive and contemporary overview of various topics within the area of English for Specific purposes, written by leading academics in the field. Aimed at postgraduate students in applied linguistics, English language teaching and TESOL, as well as pre- and in-service teachers, these books outline the issues that are central to understanding and teaching English for specific purposes, and provide examples of innovative classroom tasks and techniques for teachers to draw on in their professional practice.

SERIES EDITOR: BRIAN PALTRIDGE

Brian Paltridge is Professor of TESOL at the University of Sydney. He has taught English as a second language in Australia, New Zealand and Italy and has published extensively in the areas of academic writing, discourse analysis and research methods. He is editor emeritus for the journal *English for Specific Purposes* and co-edited the *Handbook of English for Specific Purposes* (Wiley, 2013).

SERIES EDITOR: SUE STARFIELD

Sue Starfield is a Professor in the School of Education and Director of The Learning Centre at the University of New South Wales. Her research and publications include tertiary academic literacies, doctoral writing, writing for publication, identity in academic writing and ethnographic research methods. She is a former editor of the journal *English for Specific Purposes* and co-editor of the *Handbook of English for Specific Purposes* (Wiley, 2013).

TITLES IN THIS SERIES

Introducing English for Academic Purposes
Maggie Charles and Diane Pecorari

Introducing Needs Analysis and English for Specific Purposes
James Dean Brown

Introducing Genre and English for Specific Purposes
Sunny Hyon

Introducing English for Specific Purposes
Laurence Anthony

Introducing Course Design and English for Specific Purposes
Lindy Woodrow

For more information on this series visit: www.routledge.com/series/RIESP

Introducing Genre and English for Specific Purposes

Sunny Hyon

Routledge
Taylor & Francis Group

LONDON AND NEW YORK

First published 2018
by Routledge
2 Park Square, Milton Park, Abingdon, Oxon OX14 4RN

and by Routledge
711 Third Avenue, New York, NY 10017

Routledge is an imprint of the Taylor & Francis Group, an informa business

© 2018 Sunny Hyon

The right of Sunny Hyon to be identified as author of this work has been
asserted by her in accordance with sections 77 and 78 of the Copyright,
Designs and Patents Act 1988.

All rights reserved. No part of this book may be reprinted or reproduced
or utilised in any form or by any electronic, mechanical, or other means,
now known or hereafter invented, including photocopying and recording,
or in any information storage or retrieval system, without permission in
writing from the publishers.

Trademark notice: Product or corporate names may be trademarks or
registered trademarks, and are used only for identification and explanation
without intent to infringe.

British Library Cataloguing-in-Publication Data
A catalogue record for this book is available from the British Library

Library of Congress Cataloging-in-Publication Data
A catalog record has been requested for this book

ISBN: 978-1-138-79341-5 (hbk)
ISBN: 978-1-138-79342-2 (pbk)
ISBN: 978-1-315-76115-2 (ebk)

Typeset in Sabon
by Taylor & Francis Books

Contents

Acknowledgements

I am grateful to various people who supported this project in multiple ways. My heartfelt thanks to Brian Paltridge and Sue Starfield for approaching me about writing the book and for their cheerful encouragement and patience during the extended writing process; to the proposal reviewers for their thoughtful, useful, and kind comments; to Helen Tredget of Routledge for her gracious emails, gentle nudges, and readiness to help; to Jessica Lee for her excellent feedback on the manuscript through the eyes of a former MA student and for her ingenious system of tracking my citations and references; to Lisa Bartle and Stacy Magedanz—CSUSB reference librarians extraordinaire—for their ability to find *anything* and for setting up my personalized source-finding page (I use it constantly!); and to Juvette McNew of Interlibrary Loan, who cheerfully helped with hard-to-get sources. Thanks also to my awesome CSUSB English Department colleagues and to my friends and family for encouraging and supporting me through this long process. I continue to be deeply grateful to John Swales—for being a superb dissertation advisor and mentor, for inspiring and engaging the field of ESP all of these years, and for teaching me the art of the task. Finally, I wish to thank my students—past, present, and future—for their energy and desire to learn. As I wrote this book, I tried to imagine what you might find useful.

Part I

Introduction

Chapter 1

Introducing genre in English for Specific Purposes

It does not take long to realize that genre is a central concept in English for Specific Purposes (ESP). As of this writing, a keyword search on *genre* in two of the field's leading journals, *English for Specific Purposes* and the *Journal of English for Academic Purposes*, generates 653 and 426 article hits, respectively. Genre is also referred to in 24 of the 28 chapters in the recent *Handbook of English for Specific Purposes* (Paltridge & Starfield, 2013); and multiple other ESP book titles reflect the field's fascination with genre: *Genre and the Language Learning Classroom* (Paltridge, 2001), *Research Genres* (Swales, 2004), *Genre and Second Language Writing* (Hyland, 2004b), *Worlds of Written Discourse: A Genre-Based* View (Bhatia, 2014), *Academic Writing and Genre* (Bruce, 2010), *Building Genre Knowledge* (Tardy, 2009), and *Genres across the Disciplines* (Nesi & Gardner, 2012), among others. What is it about genre that is so beguiling to ESP? I will return to this question in a bit, but first let's consider what a genre is.

What is a genre?

In simple terms, a genre is a type of spoken or written text. We recognize it as a type, or category, because the various instances of it share similarities in purpose, content, form, and/or context. Wedding invitations, for example, comprise such a category, or genre. They occur in the same context—a couple is getting married—and they share a common function: to ask people to the wedding. They are also characterized by certain linguistic tendencies, including formal, elevated syntax and word choice, as illustrated in the invitation below.

Mr. and Mrs. Dwight Peter Hill
request the honor of your presence
at the marriage of their daughter
Miss Sandra Evelyn Hill
to
Mr. Jonathan Stephen Richards
Saturday, the seventh of May

> Two thousand and one
> At three o'clock in the afternoon
> Ashland Methodist Church
> 869 South Canyon Road
> Ashland, Montana

It is also important to point out that although genres such as wedding invitations (and others) are typically recognized by their recurring elements, they may also encompass variation among their textual members. Johns (1997), for example, discovered that wedding invitations range significantly in content and design according to "social forces" in their contexts of use (p. 41). These texts may also serve varied purposes beyond asking people to the wedding, such as directing guests on where to buy gifts or expressing the marrying couple's personalities and values. Indeed, a highly innovative invitation that Tardy (2016) received illustrates the flexibility possible within this genre. Among its other inventive features, the invitation had the question "Where Have Pat and Yoongju Gone?" on its front panel, and then opened up to a "visual puzzle" where the bride and groom were "hidden in a mélange of cartoon characters, animals and city structures" (pp. 14–15).

To sum up then, a genre can be thought of as a category of texts characterized by similarities as well as—to some extent—differences across its members. The degree of internal difference and creativity particular genres allow is a point taken up further in Chapter 7.

Why genre in ESP?

Genres, their typified features, and their internal variability have proven of great interest to ESP researchers. Why is that so? One reason is that genres are related to ESP's core mission of preparing students to use English in their *target contexts*—that is, the situations in which they hope to study, work, and/or live. All of these target contexts inevitably involve genres, whether they be research proposals in a sociology course, nursing care plans in a hospital, business meetings in a telecommunications company, or safety manuals in a factory. As such, it makes sense that ESP as a field is interested in researching students' target genres and developing effective ways to teach students how to understand and use them. Genre may also be popular in ESP because of its nice "size" for language teaching (Paltridge, 2001, p. 4). A specific genre—for instance, a book review—lends a coherent, meaningful focus to a curricular unit, more so than might, say, a broad concept like textual organization. But such genre-focused units are still 'large' enough to encompass attention to elements like organization, vocabulary, grammar, audience, and purpose. And perhaps even more importantly, a genre unit allows students to see how these elements interact with each other in a specific genre. Finally, genre units also have relevance appeal in ESP courses because they are categories that students see themselves as needing to understand and use.

This book explores ESP's interest in and approaches to thinking about genres and genre-based teaching. The rest of this chapter offers some historical context for this interest, beginning with early ESP work on scientific English and, subsequently, John Swales' groundbreaking analysis of the research article genre. The chapter also considers ESP's connections to and distinctiveness from the work of two other major genre traditions, Rhetorical Genre Studies and the Sydney School of genre studies. The rest of the chapters in the book then offer you opportunities to explore and apply key elements of ESP genre approaches. You will learn how to analyze genre moves and lexicogrammatical features of genres, as well as how to investigate genre contexts and purposes. In addition, you will explore ways that genres can be learned and taught within ESP contexts.

Throughout the book I will refer to both ESP 'genre analysis' and ESP 'genre-based teaching'. Genre analysis includes investigations of genres and their contexts. Genre-based teaching, on the other hand, involves course designs, lessons, and activities that help students learn genres in their present or future target contexts. Genre analysis and teaching have often worked hand in hand. For example, ESP researchers have studied the organizational structures of scientific research papers, and their findings have then been applied to activities that teach students about these structures. In addition, teachers wishing to develop materials on a particular genre may conduct research on that genre or on how students learn it. Thus, ESP researchers and ESP teachers (or 'practitioners') are often the same people.

Early genre work

Pre-genre studies in English for Science and Technology

To understand ESP's work on genre, it is helpful to appreciate what came before it in the first two decades of ESP. During this 'pre-genre' period of the 1960s–1970s, ESP focused mainly on researching and teaching scientific English, also known as English for Science and Technology (EST). As Hutchinson and Waters (1987) put it, "for a time ESP and EST were regarded as almost synonymous" (p. 7). Similarly, Swales (1985a), in chronicling early landmark EST research and teaching developments, noted that "With one or two exceptions ... English for Science and Technology has always set and continues to set the trend in theoretical discussion, in ways of analyzing language, and in the variety of actual teaching materials" (p. x). Since then, other branches of ESP have become influential, yet EST at the time was certainly a central site of new approaches to language research and teaching that later led to genre-based research and teaching. The reasons for this strong EST-focus included the growth of English as an international language of scientific research as well as technological industries, and the related increasing demand for English instruction of international university students pursuing technological fields. Although EST remains an important area of genre work in ESP today, it now is often subsumed within a larger ESP branch concerned with academic English (including scientific English) known as English for Academic Purposes (EAP).

Although EST research of the 1960s was not focused on specific genres per se, it did attend to scientific texts in a general way, with particular attention to their vocabulary and syntactic patterns. The rationale behind this work was that if you could identify the word- and sentence-level features of scientific English, you could teach them to students, who would then be better able to read the English-language textbooks required of their science courses (Swales, 1985a). An important EST investigation along these lines was Barber's 1962 article "Some measurable characteristics of modern scientific prose." Acknowledging the many non-native English-speaking students "who rely wholly or largely on books published in Britain or the United States" (p. 21), Barber set out to identify frequently occurring language patterns in technical texts. Among other things, Barber found that scientific writing contained a high rate of present simple active and present simple passive constructions, as well as a notable number of non-finite verbs, including -ing forms, past participles, and infinitives. In terms of looking forward to later genre work, Barber's focus on counting syntactic patterns was a precursor to corpus linguistics studies of salient genre features, discussed further in Chapter 3.

The teaching materials that grew out of Barber's and other early EST investigations centered, not surprisingly, on sentence-level grammar and vocabulary. The methods reflected in these materials were also what we would now call traditional: Students were explained grammatical rules and then applied those rules in pattern-practice exercises. The segment below on "Infinitive of Result" taken from Herbert's (1965) EST textbook, *The Structure of Technical English*, illustrates the kind of approach used.

[handwritten margin note: Trad. Teaching focus on grammar + what students study]

Infinitive of Result

[handwritten margin note: Ex.]

This is a peculiar construction of only limited use. The *to* + *infinitive* is used to indicate the result of the action previously stated, and is used with only a few verbs, of which the commonest are *form* and *produce*.

'The wires are bound together to form a single strand.'

The idea here is one of *result* rather than *purpose*: '... with the result that a single strand is formed'.

Exercise

Link these statements in the same way

1   The anions unite with the copper of the plate. New copper sulphate
     is produced.
2   Hydrogen and oxygen combine chemically. They form the molecule
     H_2O.
3   The unstable isotopes undergo radioactive decay. Other isotopes
     are formed as a result.

(Excerpt from Herbert, 1965, pp. 189–190;
some changes to format)

Although such exercises may seem old-fashioned, they are sometimes still
incorporated in current genre-based curricula that, for example, ask students
to imitate a sentence pattern (e.g., passive voice) common to a particular
genre (e.g., scientific articles).

Contemporary ESP genre-based teaching materials also reflect other
methodologies that have roots in early EST work. Beginning in the early
1970s, for example, EST text analysis and teaching applications shifted to
describing why and in what contexts English grammatical patterns were used.
Some of the scholars working within this more 'rhetorical' focus were from
U.S. universities in the Northwest and came to be referred to as the
"Washington School" of ESP (Johns, 2013). Among this group, Lackstrom,
Selinker, and Trimble (1972) wrote a seminal article in *English Teaching
Forum*, in which they argued that grammatical elements, such as verb tense,
could only be understood in the context of the surrounding text. Such
"rhetorical considerations," they said, "include judgments concerning the
order of the presentation of information, within the paragraph and within
the total piece of which the paragraph is a part" (p. 4). This attention to the
why and *when* of scientific grammar was a prelude to later focuses in genre
scholarship on how a genre's "communicative purposes" shape its formal
features (Swales, 1990, p. 58)

With this move to thinking rhetorically about texts, EST work of the
1970s began to focus on language patterns beyond the sentence level, such as
paragraph structures—laying a foundation for later research on organization
of whole genres. Swales' 1971 EST textbook, *Writing Scientific English*, for
example, attended in part to the *sequencing* of sentences within scientific
descriptions, for which he offered the following advice:

a   Always begin with a general statement (often of a defining nature).
b   Follow complicated general statements with examples.
c   Explain the meaning of certain technical expressions. Here is a simple
     example:
     *Liquids possess fluidity. In other words, they do not take any definite
     shape of their own.*
d   Always move from the simple to the complex.
e   Leave statements of use (if any) until towards the end.

f   Do not contrast what you are describing with anything else until you have established clearly what you are describing in the first place.

g   Remember that key-phrasing often makes a description easier to understand.

(Swales, 1971, p. 114)

In later reflection on this textbook, Swales (1985a) noted that his focus on "information structure of scientific paragraphs" was born out of his experience working with Arab engineering students. These students, he observed, "had been brought up in a different rhetorical tradition" and therefore would benefit from "some explicit work on how scientific writing in English was organized" (p. 38). With a similar orientation, Lackstrom, Selinker, and Trimble (1973) published a *TESOL Quarterly* article that asked the field to consider even larger patterns of textual organization. They proposed that the most important unit in scientific writing was not the sentence nor the physical paragraph (signaled by indentation and spacing) but rather the "conceptual paragraph," a textual unit that developed a key point, or what they called a "core generalization," potentially across several physical paragraphs (p. 130).

It was also in this later period of early EST work that the term *discourse* was used to refer to larger text segments. The conceptual paragraph, for example, was argued to be "the basic unit of discourse" (Lackstrom, Selinker, & Trimble, 1973, p. 130). Bley-Vroman (1978) also referenced "the total discourse purpose" that is achieved through a scientific text's organization (p. 286). Now in retrospect, this focus on 'macro' discourse structures previewed subsequent work on genre moves, discussed in Chapter 2. In these earlier days of ESP, however, the term *genre* was not much in circulation and the textual categories studied for organization were often quite broad, like description, recommendation, and classification, rather than the more specific categories, like scientific journal articles, characteristic of ESP genre studies.

With the emerging focus on discourse organization, EST teaching materials also changed. They moved beyond sentence pattern drills to exercises that asked students to examine how different elements functioned within the larger text. The excerpt below from Swales' (1971) *Writing Scientific English* illustrates this more analytical approach: Students are presented with a passage (on water taps) and asked to identity what the purposes of the paragraphs and their sentences are (or are not) within the context of the whole passage.

A water tap is a device for turning on and off a flow of water. Its most important parts are a rod with a handle on the top and a washer which is fixed to the bottom of the rod. The metal parts of a water tap are usually made of brass because brass resists corrosion. The washer is made of a flexible material such as rubber or plastic.

[diagram of a water tap]

When the handle is turned the rod either rises or descends because of the spiral thread. The column descends until the washer fits firmly in its 'seat'. (This position is shown in the diagram.) The tap is now closed and no water can flow out of the pipe.

Exercise 8(a) Cross out the wrong alternatives (S=sentence)

1 This description consists of 1/2/8 paragraphs.
2 The first paragraph describes a tap/explains how it works.
3 The second paragraph describes a tap/explains how it works
4 Each paragraph contains 1/3/4/6 sentences.
5 The first sentence (S1) is/is not a definition.
6 S2 describes the main moving parts of a tap/the main fixed parts.
7 S3 explains why brass resists corrosion/why brass is used.
8 S4 explains/does not explain why rubber is often used for a washer.
9 S5 begins with a subordinate clause/a main clause.
10 S6 explains/does not explain why the column goes down.
11 S7/S8 links the description to the diagram.
12 S7 must come before S8/it doesn't matter which sentence comes first.

(from Swales, 1971, pp. 103–104)

Such exercises are not unlike later 'consciousness-raising' activities used in genre-based pedagogies (see Chapter 6).

Genre is in the air: Swales, moves and CARS

ESP's explicit shift toward genre came in the early 1980s. It was at this time that EST scholarship and teaching materials began focusing on quite specific genre categories, as seen in, for example, Tarone et al.'s (1981) analysis of two astrophysics research articles, and specifically, how passive voice functioned within them. Appearing in the inaugural issue of *The ESP Journal* (now *English for Specific Purposes*), Tarone et al.'s article was indeed groundbreaking in more than one way. It was among the first ESP publications to use the term *genre*. And it did so to emphasize that scientific English was not monolithic but rather could vary across genres. As the authors wrote in their conclusion: "It should not simply be assumed that the passive is generally used more frequently in EST … . Is the passive used more frequently in all *genres* of EST? If not, why do we find variation in its usage?" (p. 136, italics added).

Interestingly, it was also in 1981 that John Swales, then a member of the Language Studies Unit at the University of Aston in Birmingham, published a seminal report on the genre of research articles (RAs). Entitled *Aspects of Article Introductions*, Swales' monograph differed from Tarone et al.'s study of whole astrophysics RAs in that it focused specifically on the structure of

RA introductions from various disciplines (Swales, 2011/1981). Swales' investigation was groundbreaking in that it analyzed discourse organization in terms of *moves*, an approach that became (and remains) highly influential in ESP genre analysis (Samraj, 2014). In a later work, Swales (2004) defines a move as "a discoursal or rhetorical unit that performs a coherent communicative function in a written or spoken discourse" (Swales, 2004, p. 229). In this view, therefore, a move is "a functional, not a formal, unit" (p. 228) and can be as short as a word or as long as several paragraphs. Inside each move, there can also be multiple 'steps' (or sub-moves) through which the move is actually performed.

Swales (2011/1981) saw moves and steps of article introductions as especially challenging for RA writers (and therefore for EST students), in part because they involved decisions about how to get the attention of their readers. From his sample of 48 RA introductions in several science and social science fields, he found that the introduction tended to follow a four-move sequence:

Move 1 Establishing the Field
Move 2 Summarizing Previous Research
Move 3 Preparing for Present Research
Move 4 Introducing Present Research

About a decade later, Swales (1990) removed "summarizing previous research" as a separate move because, as he observed, authors often engaged in this strategy throughout their RA introduction rather than in a discrete section. In this three-move model, Swales also renamed the moves in "ecological" terms (1990, p. 142), *Establishing a Territory, Establishing a Niche, Occupying the Niche*, reflecting the idea that RA authors compete for space in a scholarly ecosystem. With this orientation, Swales called his updated moves model "Create a Research Space," or CARS, shown in Figure 1.1.

In Move 1, Swales noted, RA authors may begin to carve out their research space by establishing their general research area or territory as "central in some way to the discipline" (Swales, 2011/1981, p. 33), such as in the following examples:

> In recent years, applied researchers have become *increasingly interested in* …
> Thus, the study of these has become *an important aspect of* …
> The *well-known* … *phenomena* … have been favourite topics for analysis both in …
>
> (Swales, 2011/1981, pp. 33–34, italics added)

In Move 2, RA authors directly create a niche for themselves in the existing research territory by highlighting a limitation, gap, or remaining question in previous research, or by indicating they are extending current scholarship in

Move 1 Establishing a Territory
Step 1 Claiming centrality
        and/or
Step 2 Making topic generalization(s)
        and/or
Step 3 Reviewing items of previous research

Move 2 Establishing a niche
Step 1A Counter-claiming
        or
Step 1B Indicating a gap
        or
Step 1C Question-raising
        or
Step 1D Continuing a tradition

Move 3 Occupying the niche
Step 1A Outlining purposes
        or
Step 1B Announcing present research
Step 2 Announcing principal findings
Step 3 Indicating RA structure

Figure 1.1 CARS moves model for RA introductions
Source: Adapted from Swales (1990, p. 141, Figure 10).

some way. The linguistic signals of this move often include negative sentence connectors, verbs, and adjectives, as in the following sentence:

> *However*, the previously mentioned methods *suffer from* some *limitations*.
> (Swales, 1990, p. 154, italics added)

Swales (2004) later added an optional step of "Presenting Positive Justification" to Move 2 (p. 230) based on Samraj's (2002) finding that, after pointing out what is lacking in previous research, authors may state a positive reason for doing their research. In other words, it is not just because others have *not* done something that it should be done but also because it may actually be useful to do it.

Finally, in Move 3, authors announce how they will occupy the research niche by describing their own study, its purposes, and/or findings. Typical of this move are present tense verbs and deictic expressions like *this* preceding a noun referring the authors' project, as in:

> In *this paper*, we give preliminary results of ...
> (Swales, 1990, p. 160, italics added)

Although the three CARS moves may prototypically follow the 1-2-3 order above, Swales (1990) also indicated that they can be cyclical; that is, they may re-occur at different points in an RA introduction. Task 1.1 gives you a chance to take the CARS moves out for a drive.

Task 1.1 Trying out CARS

1   Find three different peer-reviewed academic journals. They can be from the same field or from different fields.
2   In each journal, find an RA; that is, collect three RAs in total.
3   Read the introduction of each of your three RAs. Mark in the introduction wherever you see one of Swales' CARS moves and label it. Circle words or phrases that signal the moves.
4   To what extent does each introduction conform or deviate from his CARS model?

Genre, communicative purpose, and discourse community

In addition to introducing the field to moves analysis, Swales established a sort of ESP theory of genre through definitions of key genre-related concepts. Below is Swales' oft-cited 1990 description of genre, which built on his 1981 ideas and which he later revisited and took in different directions.

> A genre comprises a class of communicative events, the members of which share some set of communicative purposes. These purposes are recognized by the expert members of the parent discourse community, and thereby constitute the rationale for the genre. This rationale shapes the schematic structure of the discourse and influences and constrains choice of content and style. Communicative purpose is both a privileged criterion and one that operates to keep the scope of a genre as here conceived narrowly focused on comparable rhetorical action. In addition to purpose, exemplars of a genre exhibit various patterns of similarity in terms of structure, style, content and intended audience. If all high probability expectations are realized, the exemplar will be viewed as prototypical by the parent discourse community. The genre names inherited and produced by discourse communities and imported by others constitute valuable ethnographic communication, but typically need further validation.
>
> (Swales, 1990, p. 58)

Genre as a class of communicative events

In this statement, Swales calls genre a *class* of communicative events, reminding us that a genre is not itself a text but rather a category of texts. For example, the email message that you wrote this morning is not a genre but rather one member of the textual class (i.e., genre) known as email messages. In this way, in fact, a genre is an abstraction: We cannot actually see, hear, or produce a genre. Rather, we see, hear, and produce instances

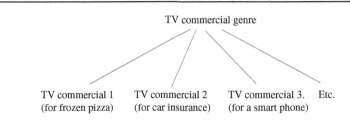

Figure 1.2 A genre and its communicative events

(or what Swales calls "communicative events") of a genre. The simple graphic in Figure 1.2, using the example of television commercials, illustrates this concept further: The genre (class) of TV commercials is comprised of all of the TV commercials in the world (communicative events in this class); we do not watch that genre, but instead watch the individual TV commercials, and from observing their commonalities become aware of the genre, or category, to which they belong.

Task 1.2 Genre as a category of events

Assuming Swales' view of genre as a class of communicative events, which statement (a or b) is more accurate? Explain your answer.

a   Betty writes within the research article genre.
b   Betty writes the research article genre.

Genre and communicative purpose

Another key concept in Swales' 1990 genre definition is *communicative purpose*. Indeed, Swales has called it a "privileged criterion," given that it is through sharing "some set of communicative purposes" that texts are identified as belonging to the same genre (Swales, 1990, p. 58). These genre members' shared purposes, said Swales, also "constitute the rationale for the genre," which in turn shapes its discourse structure (i.e., moves), style, and content characteristics. Returning to our simple example of TV commercials, we see how communicative purpose might work in this way. The short segments in between TV programs—whether they be for frozen pizza, car insurance, or a smart phone—are recognized as members of the TV commercial genre in part because they have a common communicative purpose: to persuade viewers to buy the advertised project. Given this purpose (or "rationale"), commercials employ similar forms and content to make their product appealing to viewers, including attractive colors, happy people, humor, catchy music, and positive claims.

Communicative purpose would seem to operate in this fashion in many situations. However, about a decade after the 1990 definition, Askehave and Swales (2001) offered a reconsideration of whether communicative purpose should occupy such a central, genre-defining role. They highlighted the fact that in a number of situations, a text's communicative purpose may be difficult to determine and therefore perhaps not be the ideal criterion for determining the text's genre. Drawing on a study by Witte (1992), for example, they pointed out that genres we assume have an obvious purpose, such as shopping lists, can actually vary in their functions: Shoppers, for example, might use their lists to prevent impulse purchases, to organize their shopping by the store aisles, or to convince a romantic interest at the deli counter of their "fitness as a domestic partner"! (Askehave & Swales, 2001, p. 201).

Given the slipperiness of nailing down a text's communicative purposes, Askehave and Swales proposed two alternatives for identifying a text's genre: a *text-first*, "linguistic" approach, which begins by observing the text's structural and content features (e.g., a vertical listing of food items) and, based on these features, making a first guess at the text's genre and purpose (e.g., a shopping list to aid the shopper's memory). Afterward, through a deeper look at the text's context, observers may revise their first impression of the genre's purpose (i.e., "repurposing" it), and make adjustments to their original identification of the text's genre (i.e., "reviewing genre status") (p. 207). The second way is a *context-first*, "ethnographic" approach, which begins instead by examining the community that uses the text, including their values, goals, activities, and genre "repertoires," and finally, through deep understanding of the community context, considers the purposes and genre of the text (p. 208). In either the text-first or the context-first approach, identifying with certainty a text's communicative purpose comes late in the analytic process, which acknowledges that all the texts of a particular genre—like shopping lists—may vary in their purposes depending on situation. Thus, rather than being a starting point for identifying genre as it was in Swales' earlier definition, understanding a text's communicative purpose, for Askehave and Swales, is a "reward or pay-off for investigators" after a thorough investigation of textual and/or contextual elements (p. 210).

Task 1.3 Identifying communicative purpose and genre: two approaches

This task gives you an opportunity to try out Askehave and Swales' (2001) *text-first* and *context-first* approaches for identifying a text's communicative purpose(s) and genre; see discussion of these approaches in the section above.

Consider the following text, and then answer the questions that follow.

Melody Carpenter and Pat Sidney Reyes were married on January 9 at Heritage Hall in Redlands, Massachusetts. Pastor Janet Tobias officiated. The bride, 38, is keeping her name. She is a senior attorney for the Redlands District Attorney's office. She received a JD from Yale Law School after graduating with a BA in English from California State University, San Bernardino. She is the daughter of Dr. Rebecca Longacre and Dr. Malcolm R. Carpenter, both pediatric surgeons at Community Hospital. The groom, 36, is the founder of GoUp, a non-profit provider of social services for parolees. He graduated from the University of Michigan with a Master's in Public Health and a Bachelor's in Social Work. He is the son of Sara Reyes (née Jones), principal for the Lakeview School for Girls, and Gene Reyes, lead planner for the Redlands Office of Urban Redevelopment. The couple met at Likeminded.com.

1   Explain how you would determine the communicative purposes and genre of this text using a *text-first approach* (see above).
2   Explain how you would do this using a *context-first approach* (see above).
3   Which of these two approaches—text-first or context-first—most appeals to you as a way to understand the communicative purposes of this or other texts? Why?
4   What communicative purposes did you identify for the genre represented by this text?
5   What would you call the genre of this text?
6   How might this genre be "re-purposed" in ways you would not think of initially?

Genre and discourse community

Also central to Swales' 1990 genre thinking is *discourse community*. As Swales defined it, a discourse community is a network of people with a "set of common public goals" that uses (and sometimes creates) genres to further these goals (p. 24). To illustrate, we can think of a church group—a fairly prototypical discourse community—that employs the genres of sermons, newsletters, budget proposals, and prayer request cards to support the interests and goals of its membership. This relationship between discourse communities and genres is a possessive one: "[G]enres are the properties of discourse communities," argued Swales (1990, p. 9). And as such, discourse communities differ from *speech communities*, which, rather than being defined by common goals and genres, are bounded by a shared language, dialect features, or geography. Thus, while a group of comet followers (hailing from various languages and parts of the globe) could constitute a discourse community, residents of Hokkaido, Japan would be better characterized as a speech community.

In his later re-thinking of such arguments, Swales (1993; 2016) has acknowledged that the concept of discourse community may not be so clear-cut, or necessarily distinct from that of speech community. A geographically defined group of people, for instance, could still have common interests. As Swales writes, "we have university towns (Oxford, Ann Arbor, Madison); sporting towns (St. Andrews, Newmarket, Saratoga), government towns (Ottawa, Canberra), religious towns (Assis, Mecca)" (1993, p. 695). There also exist at least semi-geographical "local discourse communities" defined by particular physical places where people work, "as in a factory or a university department" (2016, p. 5). In addition, with regard to genre, Swales (2016) now suggests that *use* rather than possession better captures the genre-discourse community relationship. He writes that genres are "rarely owned" but rather can be "utilize[d]" by a discourse community "in the furtherance of its sets of goals" (2016, p. 8). In addition, some genres appear to transcend discourse communities. In their study of suicide notes, for example, Samraj and Gawron (2015) suggest that this genre belongs to a broader, perhaps even global, speech community rather than a specialized discourse community.

Genre metaphors

Part of Swales' genre re-thinking has involved not only a nuanced reconsideration of genre's relationships to communicative purpose and discourse community, but also a demurring on whether a genre definition is useful at all. In 2004, Swales writes that he is "less sanguine about the value and viability of such definitional depictions" in part because they do not hold up in all circumstances (as we have seen above) and because they prevent us from seeing all there is to see in genres (2004, p. 61). In lieu of a singular definition, then, Swales (2004) proposes that the genre concept be explored in terms of various metaphors, each illuminating something different about genre. His six metaphors are *genre as frame* that facilitates social action; *genre as standard* that constrains what is appropriate in a given text; *genre as biological species* that can "evolve, spread, and decline"; *genre as families* where members have "a common genealogical history" yet vary in degree of family resemblance; *genres as institutions* that embody community values; and *genres as speech acts* that perform actions as called for by the situation (pp. 61–68).

Applying several of these metaphors to, say, the obituary genre, we see that each highlights a particular way this genre works in the world. For example, an obituary is a *frame* that we use to remember the deceased, and it performs this *speech act* of remembrance as directed by certain circumstances. This genre also has some *standard* moves and conventions of expression; yet, like a *biological species*, it has evolved in unique ways in particular communities such that its *family members*, although sharing some common origins and features, also exhibit variation. Regarding this latter point, Nwoye (1992) found that Nigerian, German, and English (U.S. and British) newspaper obituaries displayed linguistic differences that pointed to the influence of their cultural contexts. The Nigerian obituaries, for example, had much more frequent use than the German or English ones of "expressions with strong religious connotations" (p. 21), including *departed this sinful world, transformed into eternal glory*, and *joined the saints triumphant*, which evolved out of strong beliefs in the afterlife in Nigerian cultural and religious traditions.

From Swales to an explosion of ESP genre research

It is hard to overstate the influence of Swales' genre theorizing, re-theorizing, and analyses on ESP genre research and teaching. Even in just narrow terms, Swales' CARS model illuminated in groundbreaking ways the rhetorically complex introductions of published RAs, a "gargantuan," knowledge-producing genre for many academic fields (Swales, 1990, p. 95). More broadly, Swales' work, particularly his style of moves analysis, has inspired many, many analyses of other genres relevant to ESP students, including lectures, seminar discussions, book critiques, blogs, sales letters, legal case studies, tourist brochures, suicide notes, and research reports of various kinds, as a keyword search on *genre* in ESP-related journals will reveal. Bawarshi and Reiff (2010), in fact, observe that "[i]t is largely due to Swales' work and the research it has inspired over the last twenty years that ESP and genre analysis have become in many ways synonymous" (p. 41). Swales has also changed how text analysis is done, leading ESP researchers not only to study discourse structure via moves analysis, but also to consider how moves are shaped by a genre's communicative purposes and by the communities that use the genre.

The impact of Swalesian genre analysis is seen in ESP teaching materials as well, including several popular graduate writing textbooks that engage students in investigations and productions of various academic genres (Swales & Feak, 2011, 2012; Feak & Swales, 2009). Swales' genre re-thinkings also have applications for ESP classrooms. His work with Askehave on communicative purpose, for example, suggests that teachers (and students) ought to take time to explore a genre's contexts, uses, and forms before (re)defining its purposes. In addition, Swales' genre metaphors provide a sense of how a genre can be taught from different angles, focusing on, for example, its standard conventions, or the social action it accomplishes, or its evolution over time, and so on. Indeed, Tardy (in Johns et al., 2006) has argued that teaching just one such dimension at a time makes genre learning less overwhelming, allowing ESP students to start with a single element and then gradually integrate others.

Task 1.4 Teaching different dimensions of genres

This task asks you to consider how Swales' genre metaphors might inform your own teaching of a particular genre. Imagine that you plan to teach a group of non-native English-speaking graduate students about the genre of *biostatements*, those descriptions of authors (often written by the authors themselves) found at the end of an article, chapter, or book (see discussions of this genre in Hyland, 2012; Swales & Feak, 2011; Tardy & Swales, 2014). Here is one such biostatement from a 2015 article:

> Jean Mark Gawron is Professor of Linguistics at San Diego State University. His research interests include Statistical Parsing, Distributional Semantics, and Formal Semantics. He has used distributional semantics to analyze the language of white militant, climate change, and anti-vaccine websites, focusing on the discovery of linguistic group membership markers.
>
> (Samraj & Gawron, 2015, p. 101)

1   Find three or four sample biostatements at the end of a journal article, chapter, or book.
2   What different aspects of biostatements could possibly be explored with your ESP students? For ideas here, think about Swales' (2004) different metaphors for genre.
3   Which of these aspects of genre would you start with in a unit on biostatements? Which would you conclude with? Why?
4   Design an activity to help students understand one of these dimensions of biostatements.

ESP and other genre traditions

Thus far, this chapter has offered a thumbnail sketch of the evolution of genre studies within ESP's 50-year history, as summarized in the box below.

Evolution of ESP genre studies

1960s–1970s: pre-genre EST (foundation for future genre work)

- EST analyses of scientific texts

  - Early analyses: Frequently occurring grammatical items
  - Later analyses: Rhetorical purposes of grammar and discourse organization (Washington School)

- Teaching materials

  - Early materials: Grammatical pattern practice
  - Later materials: Analysis and production of larger discourse segments

1980–1990: early genre work

- Analyzing grammar in a specific genre

  - Passive voice in astrophysics research articles (Tarone et al.)

- Analyzing genre organization and content as moves

  - CARS moves in research article introductions (Swales)

- Initial theories of genre

  - Genre, communicative purpose and discourse community (Swales)

1990s–present: centrality of genre

- Explosion of ESP genre studies
- Ongoing revisions of genre theory

  - Complexity of communicative purpose
  - Genres in relation to speech communities and discourse communities
  - Multiple metaphors for genre

- Genre-based teaching materials

This 'story' helps us not only to appreciate the progression of genre-related ideas in ESP but also to understand ESP's points of connection and divergence with two other traditions of genre work: Rhetorical Genre Studies, also known as 'New Rhetoric', and Australian genre approaches, also referred to as the 'Sydney School'. Although in recent years some of the differences among these three traditions (and particularly those between ESP and Rhetorical Genre Studies) may have become less sharp (Artemeva & Freedman, 2015; Swales, 2009b), each has had and continues to have distinctive emphases. Comparing the three can illuminate both the uniqueness of ESP genre work and its intersections with other bodies of genre work.

ESP and RGS

Rhetorical Genre Studies (RGS) refers to genre scholarship in the fields of rhetoric, composition (i.e., first-year undergraduate writing), and professional writing. This work has tended to focus on genres within North

American university and workplace contexts, and RGS consequently shares ESP's interest in advanced academic texts such as RAs (e.g., Bazerman, 1988) and professional genres (e.g., Schryer, 1993, 2002; Winsor, 2000). ESP and RGS have diverged somewhat, however, in their approaches to analyzing these genres. In broad terms, ESP genre analysis employs what Flowerdew (2002, 2011) calls a "linguistic approach," while RGS has favored a "contextual approach." That is, although genre context is not unimportant in ESP, researchers working in this tradition have generally given greater 'space' to describing genres' discoursal and linguistic characteristics, including their organizational moves, vocabulary, and grammatical features. This linguistic orientation is in keeping with ESP's history of explicating textual features. RGS work, on the other hand, has been more concerned with analyzing what rhetoric scholar Carolyn Miller (1984) describes as the *social actions* that genres perform in their situational contexts. The following statement in Miller's (1984) seminal article captures this orientation: "[A] rhetorically sound definition of genre must be centered not on the substance or the form of discourse but on the action it is used to accomplish" (p. 151).

In the RGS view, a genre's social actions also have an important shaping relationship to their contexts. As Bawarshi and Reiff (2010) describe, "RGS has tended to understand genres not only as situated within contexts ... but also as constitutive of contexts" (p. 54). That is, genres, through the actions they perform, are seen as helping to create, or at least participating in and influencing, the contexts in which they are used. One RGS study with such an approach is that of Winsor (2000) who investigated how an agricultural equipment company's 'work order' genre actually helped shape the company environment by reinforcing political hierarchies between engineers and technicians. And in a healthcare setting, Schryer et al. (2012) as well examined the impact of a 'dignity interview' genre on palliative care contexts, particularly in relation to patients' sense of well-being.

ESP and Sydney School genre studies

ESP has also had points of connection and divergence with Sydney School genre work, a tradition grounded in systemic-functional linguistics (SFL). Developed by British-born linguist Michael Halliday, SFL is concerned with relationships between language forms and their meanings in social contexts (Martin, 2015; Rose, 2015). Within SFL-oriented Australian school-based projects (Martin, 2015), genre has been described as a "staged, goal oriented social process" that cultures use to carry out various functions (Martin, Christie, & Rothery, 1987, p. 59). Such a definition resembles the ESP concept of genres as having both communicative purposes and structural moves (stages), as well as the RGS view of genres producing social actions.

Also like ESP, as Flowerdew notes (2011), Sydney School genre work has tended to take a linguistic approach to genre analysis, producing fuller descriptions of the organizational and linguistic properties of genres than of the contexts where they carry out their social processes. One area where this work has diverged from ESP (and from RGS), however, has been in the categories of genres analyzed. Sydney School genre labels tend to be quite broad, such as *narrative, report, explanation, discussion, exposition*, and *procedure* (Macken-Horarik, 2002; Rose & Martin, 2012; Rose, 2015). Broad categories like narrative have been called "pre-genres" in ESP (Swales, 1990, p. 61) rather than genres in their own right. Sydney School genre projects, on the other hand, have viewed these broader categories as "elemental genres" (or 'micro-genres') that combine within 'macrogenres', i.e., ESP's genres.

Views on genre-based teaching

ESP and Sydney School genre scholars have shared a strong belief in the value of teaching students about genres, while RGS has been more ambivalent about such instruction or at least certain manifestations of it (see discussions in Hyon, 1996; Bawarshi & Reiff, 2010). ESP's and the Sydney School's similar worldviews here may relate in part to their target student populations. In ESP, these include non-native English speakers acquiring English language skills for their current or future life paths. Likewise, some Australian genre teaching projects have been geared for non-native English speakers in the Adult Migrant English Program (Feez, 2002), as well as for economically disadvantaged children in Sydney primary and secondary schools (Cope et al., 1993; Rose & Martin, 2012). Because of their language learning and literacy needs, these populations have been argued to benefit from explicit teaching about academic and professional genres. Indeed, in Australian school contexts, genre-based instruction developed as a direct reaction against progressive, 'process' pedagogies, which genre scholars argued did not explicate for students the genres they needed for academic success (Cope et al., 1993; Rose and Martin, 2012).

Some RGS scholars, on the other hand, have expressed skepticism about the value of classroom genre teaching. Freedman (1993, 1994) for example, argued that direct teaching of genre features is unnecessary because genre knowledge can be acquired unconsciously through exposure to and practice using texts within natural contexts. Furthermore, although Freedman acknowledged that instruction in genre features may have some limited value "for students with the appropriate learning style," she argues that such teaching may also be "dangerous" if the instructor, who is likely an outsider to the students' target fields, has incomplete genre knowledge or if students misapply the knowledge presented (Freedman, 1994, p. 206).

Such concerns about genre-based teaching may be linked to RGS' "contextual approach" to genre (Flowerdew, 2011). Because genres are perceived in the RGS tradition as so closely tied to their contexts and because contexts are constantly changing, genres are also believed to be "fluid and dynamic"

(Freedman, 1993, p. 232; see also Miller, 1984). As such, teaching genre features accurately might be seen as impossible because "we may never be able to specify or to articulate with assurance the rules for ... genres" (Freedman, 1993, p. 232). While ESP and Sydney School scholars also recognize the changeability of genres and their contexts, they tend to assume a greater degree of stability (and thus teachability) of genre characteristics. RGS's skepticism about genre teaching may also be due to the fact that some of its scholars have focused on native-English-speaking university students, who might be assumed to acquire genres more unconsciously than, say, ESP populations.

Coalescence of traditions and remaining distinctions

Although I have presented distinctions among ESP, RGS, and Sydney School approaches, as noted earlier, some have observed them to be coalescing to a certain extent (Swales, 2009b). Among the three traditions, it is perhaps ESP and RGS that have drawn closest to each other in both genre analysis and pedagogy. Askehave and Swales' (2001) "context-first" analysis option, for example, reflects an RGS-style contextual orientation. Flowerdew (2011) has also highlighted benefits for ESP of complementing linguistic analysis with contextual analysis, as illustrated in his investigations of tax accountant and auditor genres (Flowerdew & Wan, 2006, 2010). Johns (2015a) also notes that although "much of ESP pedagogy and research remains text internal," in her own EAP teaching she advocates giving students multiple opportunities to reflect "on the ecology of the situation" of genres, probing with such questions as "Why was this text written?", "What events were going on when this text was written ...?", and "Was it successful in achieving what the writer wanted to get done?" (pp. 367, 369–371).

As well, some RGS scholars have expressed belief in genre-based pedagogy in terms not unlike those used in ESP. Even in an early essay, RGS scholar Richard Coe (1994) suggested, via a swimming analogy, that for at least some students, direct genre teaching enhances genre learning (p. 159):

> People learned to swim for millennia before coaches explicitly articulated our knowledge of how to swim, but kids today learn to swim better (and in less time) on the basis of that explicit knowledge ... Might it be true for writing as well?

One RGS undergraduate writing textbook, *Scenes of Writing: Strategies for Composing with Genres* (Devitt, Reiff, & Bawarshi, 2004) also assumes the usefulness of genre-based teaching, with multiple activities guiding students to analyze genres in terms of their contexts, forms, and social actions and to produce their own texts within various genres.

Distinctions among the three traditions remain, however. For example, Sydney School and ESP projects still generally differ in the level of specificity of the genres analyzed and taught. Between ESP and RGS, the differences seem to be more of degree than of kind. Both fields attend to linguistic and contextual aspects of genres, though ESP tilts linguistic and RGS leans contextual. Also, as discussed earlier, the goals of genre analysis and genre-based pedagogy in these two fields are differently weighted: In ESP, importance is still placed on examining genre forms so that students can use them appropriately in the contexts that call for them. RGS emphasizes students understanding genres not only so that they can use them but also so that they are aware of the social actions that genres perform and how these actions empower or disempower their participants (Devitt, Reiff, & Bawarshi, 2004).

I would also like to point out that genre work has not been limited to these three (Anglophone) traditions. There is a long-running body of genre work in Brazil, for example, characterized by its own theoretical and pedagogical approaches. As Motta-Roth and Heberle (2015) point out, Brazilian genre work is a mélange of ESP, Sydney School, and RGS orientations, and also integrates 'socio-discursive interactionism', a Swiss-originated paradigm on discourse and teaching (see also Cristovão, 2015). In its hybridity, Brazilian scholarship has also "rearticulate[d]" these various genre traditions to meet its local educational concerns (Motta-Roth & Heberle, 2015, p. 24). For ESP teachers, understanding these multiple genre fields is helpful in appreciating the unique ways that ESP continues to evolve, as well as to intersect with and depart from the work of genre colleagues around the world. For more on various traditions of genre work, see Artemeva and Freedman (2015); Bawarshi and Reiff (2010); Flowerdew (2002, 2011); Hyland (2004b); Hyon (1996); Johns (2002); Motta-Roth and Heberle (2015).

Preview of the rest of this book

This chapter has considered the evolution of ESP approaches to genre and the relationship of these approaches to those of other genre traditions. The remaining six chapters invite you to explore further various aspects of ESP genre work. Part II focuses on several dimensions of ESP genre analysis, beginning with analysis of genre moves (Chapter 2) and lexicogrammatical features of genres (Chapter 3), and then complementing these 'linguistic' methodologies with examination of genre contexts (Chapter 4). Through these chapters, you will not only learn about previous ESP genre investigations but also gain experience doing textual and contextual analyses on your own. Part III of the book then turns to ESP perspectives on and applications for genre learning and teaching. Chapter 5 considers several 'macro' (big picture) issues involved in designing a genre-based course so that it addresses students' needs and interests. Chapter 6 then turns to more 'micro' aspects of genre-based teaching, discussing ways of creating and assessing specific classroom activities to enhance students' awareness of and ability to use genres. As in Part II, these two pedagogy-oriented chapters have a practical bent, with opportunities for you practice planning your own genre-based courses and classroom materials. Finally, Chapter 7 considers future directions for ESP genre work, including the analysis of playful, convention-defying genres and ways genre play can be used in ESP classrooms to promote students' long-term genre learning.

Part II

ESP genre analysis

Chapter 2

Analyzing genre moves

A major focus of ESP genre analysis has been on moves, those textual segments that make up a genre's organizational structure and help the genre achieve its purposes. One reason for moves analysis' popularity is that its findings can be translated into genre moves models, such as Swales' CARS, for use in ESP classrooms. Of course, one fear about such models is that they will be applied by ESP teachers or students as formulas rather than as flexible guidelines. As we will see in this chapter and in Chapter 6, however, move analysis and moves-focused teaching materials are also capable of addressing genre variation and flexibility. In offering an overview of ESP moves analysis, this chapter begins by considering what moves are and then describes processes for examining them. These processes include text-focused moves identification, consultation with expert informants, and comparison of genre moves across different cultural contexts. At various points in the chapter you will also have opportunities to practice moves analysis on your own.

What are moves?

A dance analogy

For those new to genre analysis, moves as a concept can be a bit challenging to grasp, at least at first. I have found that a dance analogy borrowed from my graduate student intern, Florelei Luib, helps newcomers ease into understanding what moves are. Think of some dances that you know or have heard of—perhaps the waltz, the jitterbug, a Chinese folk dance, the Korean 'Gangnam Style' dance, a Bollywood dance, and so on. What most readily differentiates these dances from one another? The likely answer is their moves. Consider, for example, the distinctive three-step of the waltz, or the Gangnam dance's lasso movements. In a similar way, a spoken or written genre, whether it be a business presentation, weather report, journal article, or election ballot, is also distinguished by its moves—those pieces within the genre that give it its characteristic shape. In addition, genres, like dances, allow for variation across individual performances of their moves.

We see such variation, for example, in two videos of 'The Hustle', a popular American dance during the 1970s disco era (see screenshots below). Watching the two Hustle performances, one notices that they share several common moves, such as walking forward and backward, which suggests that these may be obligatory moves for this dance. But the second version also contains different moves such as 'the Travolta' and 'the chicken'; and in both versions, each of the individual dancers brings a unique spirit to executing the moves. Likewise, genres, such as those you might teach in an ESP course will exhibit regular, even obligatory, move patterns. At the same time, they may allow for move omissions or additions, as well as individualized expressions of speakers' and writers' styles and personalities.

Moves as functional units

If you now have a rough sense of what moves are, you may still wonder what they look like—are they words, sentences, paragraphs? Actually, genre moves vary in size and are identified by what they do in a text rather than by their exact form. Emphasizing this function-over-form criterion, Swales (2004) writes:

> A 'move' in genre analysis is a discoursal or rhetorical unit that performs a coherent communicative function in a written or spoken discourse. Although it has sometimes been aligned with a grammatical unit such as a sentence, utterance, or paragraph … , it is better seen as flexible in terms of its linguistic realization. At one extreme, it can be realized by a clause; at the other by several sentences. It is a functional, not a formal, unit.

(Swales, 2004, pp. 228–229)

Figure 2.1 "Do the Hustle" (screenshot)
Source: meerrd08, YouTube (30 Nov. 2008). Available at www.youtube.com/watch?v=0ZyQlh0sH5A.

Figure 2.2 "(how to) do the hustle" (screenshot)
Source: Ousama Itani, YouTube (27 July 2006). Available at www.youtube.com/watch?
v≈7TsRdkrxl4g.

One might even extend Swales' boundaries further and speculate that some moves can be as small as a word or two (e.g., a "Sincerely" at the end of a business letter) or as large as several paragraphs (e.g., assessment of food in a restaurant review).

This idea that moves are *functional units* is important to keep in mind when doing your own moves analysis or helping your students do one. Genre analysis neophytes sometimes incorrectly describe moves in terms of what certain text parts are saying rather than what they are *doing*. This may be because they are more used to talking about a text's content than about the purposes of its different parts. When analyzing a restaurant review, for example, students might label a move as 'the waiter's friendliness' rather than as 'evaluating the service'—the latter being a more productive and functionally oriented move label, extendable to other instances of the restaurant review genre (even when the waiter was not friendly!).

Moves, genres, and communicative purposes

Moves can also be understood in terms of their relationship to a genre's overarching communicative purposes. As we saw in Chapter 1, communicative purpose is a key dimension of ESP conceptions of genre (Askehave

& Swales, 2001; Bhatia, 1993; Swales, 1990). Given that individual moves in a genre perform particular functions, we can think of them as fulfilling 'mini communicative purposes' that together serve the genre's larger communicative purposes. The CARS moves in an RA introduction (Establishing a Territory, Establishing a Niche, Occupying the Niche), for example, collectively achieve the global communicative purpose of creating a research space for RA writers. Or, to take a spoken genre example, the moves in a wedding toast, such as describing the bride and groom's positive qualities, illustrating them with anecdotes, and wishing them future happiness, help to achieve the toast's broader goals of honoring the couple and entertaining the guests.

To sum up then, moves are textual segments that help classify a text as a member of a particular genre; they perform specific functions that contribute to the genre's overarching purposes; and, although they often exhibit conventional patterns, they may vary in their shape and style depending on the text, situation, and individuals 'dancing' them.

How to do a moves analysis

Few published ESP genre studies describe the processes that the authors used to identify genre moves. Instead, the researchers often only include a statement like "an analysis of move patterns was undertaken" or "the macro-structure of the texts in the corpus was investigated." (The term *macro-structure*, by the way, is another way to describe the move patterns in a text.) Some authors, however, have offered details of their move analysis processes— useful information for beginning genre analysts. Swales (2011/1981), for example, notes that he made his initial CARS moves discoveries by applying to his collection of RA introductions "a system of neutral color-coding using a range of marker pens" (p. 21), likely with a different color used for each move. Ding (2007) also tells us that, after her initial move coding of 'personal statements', a genre often required of applications to academic programs, she re-coded her texts five months later (a good strategy for bringing a fresh perspective to one's analysis).

A more systematic description of move analysis how-tos has been offered by Upton and Cohen (2009). Drawing on Biber, Connor, and Upton's (2007a) moves analysis framework, Upton and Cohen propose a multi-stage, recursive process for identifying and describing moves. They illustrate how this approach worked in their analysis of a very interesting genre—that of 'birthmother letters', texts written to expectant mothers by couples wishing to adopt the birthmothers' babies. Their corpus, based on Cohen's (2007) original study, consisted of 46 texts: 20 'successful letters', which resulted in consent by the first or second birthmother to whom they were sent, and 26 'unsuccessful letters', sent out at least 15 times before the authoring couples were selected by a birthmother (p. 590). Although this is not a typical ESP genre, it illustrates in a clear, accessible fashion the concept of moves as functional units; and, given the rhetorical delicacies of asking for someone's child, it usefully demonstrates how moves work together to achieve particular communicative purposes. In Task 2.1 below, you get a chance to think about the moves in this interesting genre.

Task 2.1 Moves in a birthmother letter

Read through the following excerpts from a successful birthmother letter in Upton and Cohen's (2009) study and then answer the questions that follow.

Dear Expectant Mother:

We are Joe and Barbara. It is hard to put into words what we really want to express to you. We want you to know who we really are, what we think, and how we feel from our hearts ...

We wanted you to hear both of our voices in this letter. We thought it would be fun to use italics when I (Barbara) am speaking, and regular type when it's me (Joe). There will be times when we both want to say the same thing, so when it appears in bold black type, we're both talking to you ... [Note: The italics, regular type, and boldface were not indicated in Upton and Cohen's (2009) analysis, but in the excerpted portions below it is still generally clear which member of the couple is speaking when.]

[...]

Like most families today, Joe and I both work. I'm lucky to have a job that I enjoy, and a boss that understands how important it is to spend time with your children. I work as a dental assistant with advanced skills and responsibilities. I am home most days between noon and 2:00 pm, so that leaves a lot of time to spend with baby. I still work for the same Construction Company as a union bricklayer. I have good benefits, a nice income and I enjoy what I do. I take pride in my work.

[...]

As we stated earlier, summer is our favorite season ... . We take great pleasure in sitting on the porch swing, on warm summer nights, and listening to the frogs and crickets sing. On hot days we take Jack (our dog) to my grandparents['] pool to cool off and visit with the family. There are always kids (big and little) splashing around and having fun.

[...]

We have a very extensive family consisting of grandparents, parents, uncles, aunts, and cousins. The whole family welcomes the opportunity of giving their love and support to a new child.

[...]

I'm one of the luckiest ones to have found my soul mate on the first try. I knew I loved Joe after our first date, and I wanted to marry him on our second. Joe is the kind of person you strive to become close to. He has an honest, forthcoming feel about him.

[…]

We want to thank you for taking the time to learn a little bit about us. We would very much like to talk to you in person. You can reach us through our toll free number at … . Please know that if you call, no one will try to pressure or influence you in any way. We want to provide you with as much information as possible.

We wish you and your child the best,

[Signatures]

(Excerpts taken from Upton & Cohen, 2009, Appendix 2, pp. 602–603)

1   What moves do you notice in these excerpts? To answer this question, think about what the writers (a couple named Barbara and Joe) are *doing* in particular sections of the text.

2   How do these moves together help to achieve the ultimate purpose of convincing the birthmother to let Barbara and Joe adopt her child?

3   The birthmother letters in Upton and Cohen's study, including the one above, were all written by white, middle-class, heterosexual couples. How might the moves in birthmother letters in a different cultural community (perhaps one you are familiar with) be similar to or different from the moves in this letter?

Now that you have a feeling from the task above of what it is like to look for moves in a text, we can consider the formal process for doing so that Upton and Cohen (2009) describe. I have outlined eight stages of this process below, changing some of Upton and Cohen's original stage labels in order to consolidate some sub-stages, and including a few additional thoughts of my own. This eight-stage process is quite useful for a detailed moves analysis study, although, as I suggest below, it can also be simplified for other purposes.

1   **Collect a set of texts to analyze.** You will need to gather a set of texts from a particular genre to analyze. Upton and Cohen (2009) suggest that the larger the sample, the more you will be able to generalize with confidence your findings to other texts of this same genre. If you are new to moves analysis, however, it is also okay to start out with a few texts (even just one or two) to make discoveries about possible moves in the genre. The sample texts that you collect constitute the *corpus* for your analysis.

2   **Get an initial sense of the texts, their genre, and the genre's purposes.** Before launching into segmenting the texts into moves, it is useful first to gain an understanding of the larger purpose(s) of the whole genre to which these texts belong. That way you can better identify moves that contribute to that/those larger purpose(s). As discussed in Chapter 1, it may not be possible to pinpoint all of the purposes of the genre at the beginning of your analysis, but go ahead and jot down your initial impressions about the texts' genre and purposes.

3   **Gather your first impressions of the texts' moves and steps.** You should now take a first pass at identifying moves in the texts. First, read through your texts once in an informal way to get a feel for them and their patterns; and then read through the texts once again, this time marking moves that you see via the following process:

- *Marking and labeling moves.* Wherever you observe a segment of a text performing a clear or interesting function, highlight that segment and write a note next to it briefly describing its purpose. For example, if you are analyzing film review texts, you might notice a certain part of the text gives a plot summary. Write 'plot summary' or 'summarizing plot' next to that section. As you are doing your move labeling, you may already start thinking about how these moves serve the larger overall functions of the text's genre, which you considered in Stage 1 of this process.

- *Marking and labeling steps.* If you see sub-parts to the moves, mark those as possible 'steps' within the moves. For example, *within* the plot summary move, you may notice that film reviewers perform such steps as 'describing the setting' and 'noting a conflict'. One thing to keep in mind is that not all moves analyses need to go to the level of steps. And if you are a moves analysis beginner, it is fine just to stick to moves for now and skip the internal steps.

- *Do not worry about being perfect.* At this early stage of your moves analysis, do not worry about getting the moves and steps 'right'. As Upton and Cohen (2009) note, "Multiple readings and reflections on the texts are needed before clear move types, with their defining function(s), emerge" (p. 591).

4   **Establish a working set of moves (and steps) categories.** Read back through the move (and possibly step) labels you marked in your texts on your first read through and list them on a piece of paper. Look at your list and see if there are any move or step categories you wish to revise; perhaps where you notice overlaps, you can

combine categories, or, conversely, split a category where differ-entiations are needed; alternatively, you may wish to rename some of your categories to better capture their functions. Make the revisions needed to your list of move/step categories. You now have a working set of categories for again marking—that is, *coding*—the moves and steps in your texts.

5   **Pilot code the moves and refine the categories as needed.** Go through a few of your texts again and code their moves/steps once more, using your list of working moves and steps developed above in Stage 4. This is your 'pilot-coding' stage to see how well your move/step categories work to capture the functions of different parts of your text. Try to segment each of your small sample of texts into moves/steps. In other words, there should not be any stranded chunks of text that are unla-beled. If you are really not sure what move a text portion belongs to, label it 'unknown'. Take notes on how you want to further revise your categories, if at all. Upton and Cohen (2009) also recommend that for each of your move/step categories you write a clear definition of it and have a representative example, which you can refer back to as you code the rest of your texts in the next stage.

6   **Code the moves/steps in your full set of texts.** Using the revised move/step categories you have developed so far, code your full set of texts for their moves and, if applicable, steps. Do not be surprised if you discover "additional steps or even move types" through this process (Upton & Cohen, 2009, p. 594); these discoveries will help you refine your move/step categories further so that they better capture the functional units in the genre you are studying. Upton and Cohen also recommend at this stage asking a colleague to code the full set of texts and then checking your *inter-rater reliability*, i.e., the degree of agreement on the coding of your moves/steps. You can then discuss any discrepancies and adjust your coding of the texts accordingly.

7   **Note patterns in move/step frequency and organization/sequencing.** After coding all of your texts, you may have noticed that some moves/ steps occur more frequently than others. Calculate the frequency of occurrence of the various moves/steps and note which ones seem to be more obligatory, or core, and which ones more optional. Also make note of patterns in the order in which the moves occur. For example, do certain moves tend to occur in a particular place in the text? Do some moves tend to appear before or after other moves? How much variation is there in the move sequencing?

8   **Analyze linguistic features of the moves.** Upton and Cohen (2009), drawing on Biber, Connor and Upton (2007a), recommend analyzing the lexical and grammatical features of the various move types, pre-ferably using corpus linguistics analysis software if you have a large set

of texts. We will discuss processes of lexicogrammatical feature analysis in Chapter 3.

Simplified moves analysis process

After reading through the stages above, you may have concluded that moves analysis is a lot of work. Well, it definitely can be but need not always be. The very detailed process above, for instance, might be appropriate if you were undertaking a formal moves study for publication or developing comprehensive teaching materials on a genre. The process could be considerably scaled down, however, if you just wanted a preliminary sense of a genre's moves, perhaps for an informal research study or for an initial moves lesson in an ESP class. In such cases, instead of going through the recursive stages of developing, piloting and refining move categories, you could make relatively quick move observations, which you and your ESP students would discuss and try out on additional texts they find for homework. In other words, the thoroughness of your moves analysis could be adjusted depending on your purposes.

Task 2.2 Practice with moves analysis stages

1   Select a genre related to your research or teaching interests.
2   For this genre, go through several of the eight moves analysis stages above, deciding on which stages to pursue or not depending on your interests. At the very least, you will need to do Stage 1, and a few others.
3   Write a brief reflection on what this moves analysis experience was like for you.

Analyzing moves in spoken genres

Although there have been fewer ESP studies of spoken genres than of written genres, spoken moves analysis is nevertheless important, given that many of the genres that ESP students need to understand are spoken, including lectures, office hour interactions, business meetings, grocery store exchanges, TV news programs, and others. Analyzing moves in these oral texts often involves some additional stages that you can add to our eight-stage process above:

- Recording and transcribing the spoken texts that you will analyze.
- If it is an interactive spoken genre (e.g., a meeting or discussion of some kind), analyzing the moves of all of the participants contributing to the text.

Two published investigations illustrate possible processes and products of spoken move analysis—one of academic lecture introductions

(Thompson, 1994) and the other of bargaining in a marketplace (Orr, 2007).

Academic lecture introductions

In many university courses, lectures remain a key genre by which students are expected to learn class content. ESP students, however, often have difficulty comprehending lectures, particularly if the lecturer does not provide extensive written aids such as handouts or slides for following their real-time spoken delivery. In order to develop teaching materials for helping ESP students with lecture listening and comprehension, Thompson (1994) examined moves in academic lecture introductions, which she said provide "an interpretive framework for the audience to use as they listen to the rest of the lecture" (pp. 174–175). She collected 18 lecture introductions from various disciplines and coded their moves. Thompson also asked a second rater to analyze a sample of the lecture transcripts, and then made adjustments to her codes accordingly. From her analysis, Thompson found that lecture introductions contain two major moves and sets of steps (or what she called "functions" and "subfunctions") to orient the listening audience to the focus, format, and importance of the lecture content: *setting up the lecture framework* (through announcing the topic, structure, and aims of the lecture) and *putting the topic in context* (through showing the relevance of the topic and relating the topic to earlier lectures), as listed below (Thompson, 1994, pp. 176, 178).

Function: Set up lecture framework

Sub-function: Announce topic, e.g., *what I'm going to do in this section is*
Sub-function: Indicate scope, e.g., *I'm not going to dwell very long on this side of things*
Sub-function: Outline structure, e.g., *I move on to*
Sub-function: Present aims, e.g., *I want to talk a bit about the problems of measurement because*

Function: Putting topic in context

Sub-function: Show importance/relevance of topic e.g., *the implications of this are enormous*
Sub-function: Relate 'new' to 'given', e.g., *we've all seen slides like this before*
Sub-function: Refer to earlier lectures, e.g., *if you cast your mind back to Friday and the lecture I gave*

Thompson argued that teaching students to listen for these introductory moves and steps could help them predict and follow the rest of the lecture's content. See if you agree with Thompson after doing Task 2.3.

Task 2.3 Listening for moves in a lecture introduction

Listen to the introduction (the first 3 minutes, 26 seconds) of the following psychology lecture on language given at Yale University: http://oyc.yale.edu/psychology/psyc-110/lecture-6. As you listen, keep Thompson's functions and sub-functions (i.e., moves and steps) above in mind, and then answer the following questions:

1   Which of Thompson's lecture introduction moves and steps do you hear the psychology professor use? What order do you notice that these moves and steps occurred in?
2   Based on the introduction, what do you predict about the structure and content of the rest of the lecture?
3   Do you think that having attended to these introductory moves you would better recognize and comprehend key points in the rest of the lecture? Why or why not?

Thompson's study also illustrates another aspect of moves analysis: its potential to reveal variability in a genre's moves. Specifically, she found that the 18 lectures from her study did not exhibit a consistent ordering of functions and sub-functions. For example, while one lecture might begin by outlining the structure of a lecture and then indicating its scope, another would first announce the topic, present the lecture aims and connect to previous lectures before outlining the structure. Indeed, in Task 2.3, you may have noticed that the psychology lecturer used several of Thompson's moves but not in the order she listed in her model. This variation, Thompson observes, may be in part because spoken genres, such as lectures, are not as planned and revised as most written genres and are thus subject to the speaker's "spontaneous decisions about 'what to put where'" (p. 181). Lecturers may also switch up their planned order depending on what they perceive the audience needs at that moment. As you analyze the moves in spoken genres, therefore, keep in mind that you may find less constancy in their move structures.

Bargaining moves in a Chinese street market

Interactive spoken genres may be particularly unpredictable, given that participants are each making their own moves choices in the interaction. In her study of bargaining in Chinese street markets, Orr (2007), for example, describes various move patterns in customer (C) and salesperson (S) negotiations over an item's price. The example price negotiation below (from Orr, 2007, p. 79) shows one type of offer–counteroffer–acceptance moves sequence. (The numbers in the Cantonese transcription indicate tones, and the English translation is in single quotations.)

1. C: (Pointing to a kettle) Ni l go3 gei2 cin4 aa1?
'How much is this?'
2. S: Jaa6 man1.
'Twenty dollars.'
3. C: (Picks up the kettle and examines it) Sap6 ng5 man1 laa1.
'Fifteen dollars.'
4. S: Hou2 laa1.
'Okay.'
5. (S puts kettle in a bag. C pays and leaves)

As the next example demonstrates (from Orr, 2007, p. 82), however, salespersons do not always respond to the customer's counteroffer with an acceptance move.

1. C: (Points at some bamboo trivets) Gei2 cin4 aa1?
'How much are these?'
2. S: Ng5 man1 go3
'Five dollars each.'
3. C: Sei3 man1 laa1. Dak1 laa1. (Opens up purse to take out some money)
'Make it four dollars. Okay.'
4. S: Hou2 peng4 gaa3 laa3. Mou5 zaan6 nei5 gaa3 laa3.
'It's already very cheap. I'm not making any money off of you.'
5. C: (Picks two trivets up) Naa4. (Hands the trivets and ten dollars to S)
'Here.'
6. S: (Puts the trivets in a plastic bag and hands it back to C).

Badarneh, Al-Momani, and Migdadi (2016) have also examined bargaining interactions in women's clothing stores in Jordan, paying particular attention to salesmen's and female customers' uses of mock conflict talk, sociability talk, and flirtation talk.

In academic contexts as well, interactive genres can have variable move patterns, as Basturkmen (1999) found to be the case with MBA seminar discussions, where students' moves for questioning their peers had wide-ranging structures, and varied in how polite or challenging they were.

Seeking input from specialist informants

Sometimes in studying a genre's moves it is helpful to get the input of *specialist informants*, that is, members of the community that actually uses the genre. Although an ESP researcher may be expert at identifying textual moves, a specialist informant may understand better how those moves come across to 'real' readers or listeners in the community, which moves are most important to these audiences and why, and how well these moves are working in particular instances of the genre.

Specialist informants have offered insights into a number of genres, including *personal statements*, a genre that individuals often perform when applying to academic or professional programs (Chiu, 2016). Personal statements are challenging to write, requiring applicants to skillfully frame their individual histories, achievements, and/or interests in terms of the values of the program to which they are seeking entrance. Given that few models of successful personal statements are publically available (Samraj & Monk, 2008) and that the stakes of writing a poor one are high (e.g., possible rejection from the program), several researchers have sought to uncover valued moves in this genre, using a combination of textual move analysis and specialist informant commentary (Barton, Ariail, & Smith, 2004; Brown, 2004; Samraj & Monk, 2008). Samraj and Monk (2008), for example, interviewed faculty reading personal statements for master's program applications about their "priorities" when "read[ing] statements from applicants" (p. 210); they also presented these reviewers with authentic personal statements written for their particular programs and asked them to evaluate the statements' content, organization, and language. The informant input revealed move preferences particular to certain fields and programs. A linguistics program informant, for instance, spoke favorably of an applicant's description of his/her language teaching experience, while an electrical engineering informant particularly liked another applicant's comments about his interest in sports and volunteer work with earthquake victims, which, the informant said helped him to get the know the applicant "as a well-rounded person" and spoke to the program's interests in "leadership" and "team involvement" (p. 207). The MBA program informant, on the other hand, affirmed that for their program it was important that a personal statement address what the applicant is still "lacking" and "why [they are] going back to graduate school" (p. 204).

In a similar study, Barton, Ariail, and Smith (2004) used a technique known as a *think-aloud* with their specialist informants, reviewers of applications to U.S. medical residency programs. Specifically, they asked residency selection committees members to verbalize their reactions while they read applicants' personal statements in real time. The informants' responses revealed that the statements' opening moves, in which the applicants explain their decision to enter medicine and/or tell a story from their personal experience, were important in shaping evaluators' judgments about the candidate. Task 2.4 gives you a chance to reflect on the informants' think-aloud reactions to two different applicants' opening moves.

Task 2.4 Informants' views of moves in medical residency personal statements

In the chart below, Column A includes opening moves from two medical residency personal statements in Barton, Ariail, and Smith (2004). Column B shows the think-aloud responses of two surgery residency selection committee members to these moves. The same two committee members commented on each of the two applicants' moves. Read the material in both columns and then answer the questions below.

Column A: Two sample opening moves	Column B: Residency selection committee members' think-aloud reactions
Two of my patients died today, while two of my patients who were about to die were given a second chance at life. The deaths were not unexpected, for even before our paths had crossed, these individuals had ceased to exist in any sort of meaningful way. It is those who have been afforded the chance to greet another tomorrow who are, in my mind, nothing short of a miracle. You see, I am currently participating in a rotation in transplantation surgery. The last 24 hours of my education have been marked by the incomparable poignancy of witnessing two human beings exit this world, as well as the unbound joy and hopefulness of seeing the organs of these deceased individuals provide the gift of life to two once terminally ill patients. It is this specialty's phenomenal melding of intri-cate surgical procedures and extensive medical knowledge that propels me toward the study of surgical medicine.	"I am not impressed" "My response is not strong" "stilted, too formal" "attempt at philosophy" "This personal statement gives no experiences that set the candidate apart"
After transferring to the University of Virginia to begin my third year of college, I decided to join the track team as a javelin thrower. Despite the fact that I had never thrown a javelin in my life, I was given a trial period by the coaching staff. I showed up for practice day after day, arriving early and staying late, trying my hardest and making improvements in areas in which I was deficient. None-theless, I was expecting each practice to be told that I was not good enough to remain on the team. But that never happened. At the end of the semester, the coach took me aside and apologized for not speaking to me earlier. He explained that I had no natural talent and would never be a competitive thrower, especially starting so late in my eligibility. But he also explained that he did not cut me because I made the rest of the team better. He stated that my infectious enthusiasm, work ethic, dedication, and persistent sense of humor pushed everyone around me to excel.	"I am really interested. He has me hooked" "That is a good start, sort of concrete and starts to tell a story" "Now that's a very clever use of a per-sonal story to really blow your trumpet without blowing your trumpet" "exactly the stuff you need in order to be a good surgeon" "We like people who profess not to be afraid of hard work" "The first paragraph is helpful in that that would separate him from other candidates"

Source: Material excerpted from Barton, Ariail, and Smith, 2004, pp. 103–106, and organized into chart format.

1   What do the informants' responses reveal about successful opening move elements for these medical residency personal statements?

2   What surprises you, if anything, about the informants' reactions?

3   Can you imagine incorporating specialist informant responses to other genres in an ESP course you are teaching? If so, how?

Cross-cultural moves comparisons

In addition to consulting specialist informants, one can integrate other dimensions into a moves analysis. Some ESP researchers, for example, have taken a cross-cultural approach and compared a single genre's moves across different cultural contexts. Such comparisons are particularly useful for illuminating variability in move forms and functions. These cross-cultural moves analyses may be across two or more national or ethnic contexts, or what Holliday (1999) has called *large cultures*, while others may focus on narrower communities, or *small cultures* (Holliday), that exist within and across large cultures. By these terms, Samraj and Monk's (2008) analysis of personal statements in three academic programs would be a small-culture comparison. A study comparing personal statements in Korea and the U.S., on the other hand, would be large-culture in orientation. For ESP researchers and teachers, both types of comparisons may reveal a range of move possibilities for a particular genre. This section illustrates how such comparisons may be done at both large-culture and small-culture level.

Moves comparisons across 'large' cultures

A number of studies have compared genre moves across national cultures, focusing on such genres as letters of recommendation in the U.K., the U.S., and Germany (Precht, 1998), PhD defenses and vivas in Sweden and the U.S. (Mezek & Swales, 2016), RA abstracts in the U.S. and Iran (Friginal & Mustafa, 2017), and newspaper editorials in Mexico, the U.S., and Spain (Pak & Acevedo, 2008). This work has straddled the interests of ESP and of Contrastive Rhetoric, also known as Intercultural Rhetoric, a field concerned with discourse patterns across cultures of various types (Connor, 2011; Connor & Rozycki, 2013).

Vergaro's (2002) study of Italian and British 'money-chasing letters' is one such example of a contrastive, large-culture analysis of moves variation. Through studying the discourse patterns of 47 letters that Italian and British companies sent to customers delinquent on their payments, Vergaro found that this genre shared common moves in both Italy and Britain. These moves included Subject (of the Letter), Address the Issue, Solicit Payment, Warn or State Consequences, End Politely, and Closing

Salutation. Differences across the two letter sets, however, were also evident and contributed to very distinct tones in the letters. The British letters contained an Express Availability move that offered assistance to the customer, thus softening the payment solicitation and creating a sense of solidarity with the customer, as illustrated in the British letter excerpts below.

> We request you to settle the account in the next 7 days.
>
> If there is any particular reason why payment has not been made, and this may include your company's financial policy, we will gladly assist if it is possible for us to do so, but, in that event, please do notify us immediately by telephone or fax.
>
> (from Vergaro, 2002, p. 1221)

This polite Express Availability move was absent in the Italian letters, consistent with their overall more distant and direct tone. All of the Italian letters, in fact, opened immediately with an Address the Issue move, without any preceding salutation, as illustrated in one letter's opening below:

> *Riesaminando la Vs. partita contabile rileviamo che risultano tuttora scoperti, salvo pagamenti in corso, i documenti riportati in allegato.*
>
> (Upon examining the balance of your account we notice that, unless payment has been recently made, the enclosed items remain unpaid)
>
> (from Vergaro, 2002, p. 1217)

Vergaro withholds judgment on whether the British or Italian letter moves are more effective, stating that "as in food tastes, each style is appropriate within a given culture" (p. 1223). For the purposes of collecting money, she suggests that "[a]n Italian style letter apparently works best with Italians, although it would appear terse and bureaucratic to an English reader, and an English style letter apparently works best in England, although it would appear strangely solicitous and probably hypocritical to an Italian" (p. 1223). For ESP practitioners and their students, then, a possible take-away from this and other large-culture moves studies is that "being aware of similarities and differences in the writing practices of particular cultures, i.e. adopting a contrastive stance, will help students learn to write effectively for a given audience" (p. 1212).

Moves comparisons across 'small' cultures

Other genre investigations have compared genre moves across small cultures, described by Holliday (1999) as "any cohesive social grouping" that is

characterized by "a discernible set of behaviours and understandings connected with group cohesion" (pp. 237, 248)—a similar concept to that of
discourse community discussed in Chapter 1. Under this definition, a workplace, an academic discipline, a religious organization, or even an individual
classroom of students could be considered a small culture, as its members
engage in particular actions (such as creating products, conducting research,
completing class assignments, and so on) that connect members to each
other. Holliday argues that small-culture investigations are more revealing
than large-culture studies. While the latter often reduce national or ethnic
cultures to stereotyped differences, or "pre-defined characteristics" (p. 245),
a small-culture analysis, says Holliday, does not assume that differentiating
characteristics of the culture(s) already exist but rather explores whatever
behaviors actual occur in the group(s) being examined: "Small culture is …
more to do with activities taking place within a group than with the nature
of the group itself" (p. 250).

In the rest of this section, I illustrate some approaches to small-culture
comparisons of genre moves, through three studies: one on RAs in two
academic disciplines, another on non-traditional student theses, and a third
on legal opinion writing by law students and expert barristers.

RA introduction moves in two fields

Samraj (2002) was one of the first to compare RA introductions across
two academic fields, a type of small-culture study that has since become
frequent in ESP genre research. She specifically contrasted introductory RA
moves from two related environmental science disciplines—Wildlife
Behavior and Conservation Biology—and found that even between these
two connected fields, there existed move differences that pointed to distinctions in the disciplines' interests and concerns. In Move 1 (Establishing
a Territory), for example, Samraj found that the Wildlife Behavior and
Conservation Biology RA authors made different sorts of "centrality
claims" about the importance of their research areas (p. 5). Task 2.5 asks
you to compare these claims and what they say about the two disciplinary
cultures.

**Task 2.5 Small culture influences on research article
introduction moves**

The chart below includes excerpts illustrating the *claiming centrality* step of
Move 1 from two RA introductions in Samraj's (2002) study. Excerpt A is
from a Wildlife Behavior (WB) RA, while Excerpt B is from a Conservation
Biology (CB) RA. Read these two excerpts and consider the questions
below.

Excerpt A: Wildlife Behavior RA Move 1	Excerpt B: Conservation Biology RA Move 1
Since the results of Burley (1981, 1985, 1986) and Burley et al. (1982) on the effects of colour bands on mate choice, reproductive success, and survival in zebra finches, *Taeniopygia guttata*, there have been a number of studies on birds both in captivity and the wild attempting to evaluate the impact of colour bands. Results have varied, some showing no effects of colour bands (e.g., Watt 1982; Ratcliff & Boag, 1987; Beletsky & Orians, 1989) and others demonstrating effects (Brodsky, 1988; Hagan & Reed, 1988; Metz & Weatherhead, 1991).	Tropical-forest nature reserves are experiencing mounting human encroachment, raising concerns over their future viability even in remote areas. Long-term maintenance of nature reserves in economically marginal areas of the tropics is particularly problematical because protection is based on severely restricted funding from politically and administratively weak governments. Many tropical forest reserves consequently operate on skeletal budgets, are chronically understaffed, lack the most basic infrastructure, and cannot count on effective institutional support to enforce conservation legislation. Such frailties render reserves susceptible to a wide range of illegal activities—hunting, fishing, logging, mining, land clearing—carried out by both individuals and corporations. Worse, the frequent inability of guards, who are often unarmed and lacking authority to make arrests, to prosecute violators leads to a general disregard of reserve boundaries and regulations.

Source: The excerpts are from examples in Samraj, 2002, pp. 4–5, organized into chart format for the purposes of this comparison task.

1   Regarding these Move 1 centrality claims, what differences do you notice in how WB and CB authors emphasize the importance (i.e., centrality) of their research topics? In answering this question, consider Samraj's observation that CB RA introductions express their studies' centrality "more in terms of the phenomenal world than the epistemic world" (Samraj, 2002, p. 5).

2   Samraj (2002) shares with us the following information about Wildlife Behavior (WB) and Conservation Biology (CB) as disciplines:

- WB is a long-established discipline whereas CB is a relatively new field.
- Compared to WB, CB is more interdisciplinary, drawing on fields such as resource economics and policy, ecology, and environmental ethics.
- WB is a theoretical, more traditional academic field, while CB is an applied field, with a focus on finding solutions to real-world conservation problems.
- CB has been described as a crisis discipline.

How might one or more of these distinctions in the history and activities of CB and WB as small cultures help to explain the different Move 1 RA strategies seen in the excerpts above?

Doctoral theses in the visual and performing arts

Small-culture studies can also involve comparing what is already known about a genre's moves in certain community contexts with new discoveries about these moves in other communities. Such an approach was taken by Paltridge et al. (2012), who contrasted previous findings about doctoral thesis moves with patterns they observed in 36 visual and performing arts theses produced by Australian university doctoral students. About half of these visual and performing arts theses departed from the conventional dissertation macro-structure of introduction-method-results-discussion, and instead had a looser "topic-based" form, whereby each chapter addressed particular topics relevant to the students' project (p. 337). Moreover, within these chapters, students performed thesis-type moves in non-traditional ways. Consider, for instance, the following excerpts from the introductory chapter of a painting doctoral thesis, in which the student author unconventionally contextualized her painting project (a sort of Move 1) by narrating experiences in her mother's garden.

> My mother's garden in Dianella has a lemon tree at the edge of the back patio ... My father started this garden but he died a year after we moved in ... I have a habit of sitting on the back step ... Enclosure and connection are important senses I relate to in both the works and in the photographs ... The invisible thing I want from gardens has not been constant ... Through the journey of this doctoral project I began to see, or desire, differently ... it is difficult to write about such things in a doctoral exegesis ...
>
> (Excerpts from student's thesis introduction, quoted in Paltridge et al., 2012, p. 340)

Compared to traditional dissertation introductions in other disciplines, this art student's moves seem atypical. Indeed, even the student suggests that the conventional "doctoral exegesis" genre is not well suited for what she wants to express about her project. Yet, as Paltridge et al. argue and as their comparison to previous thesis research reveals, much thesis move variation is allowed in visual and performing arts doctoral theses. That is, for students in these disciplinary (small) cultures, "there are multiple and valid options for presenting their work, and ... it does not necessarily have to fit a pre-conceived template, or indeed 'straight-jacket', for this kind of writing" (Paltridge et al, 2012, p. 342).

Legal opinions in academic and professional communities

Genre moves can also be compared between academic and professional small cultures within the same general field. In the area of law, for example, differences have been observed between legal opinions written by law students and by working attorneys. The version of the opinion genre taught in law schools is sometimes called the *legal problem-question-answer* and involves a response to a legal case in which law students are asked to "identify legally material facts in the simulated situation, describe and interpret applicable law, and through a process of 'legal reasoning' reach a decision about the likely legal outcome of the dispute" (Hafner, 2013, p. 132). This format has also been described in terms of a four-move pattern known in British-influenced common law and U.S. law schools by the acronym IRAC, or *Issue, Rule, Application*, and *Conclusion* (Bhatia, Langton, & Lung, 2004; Tessuto, 2011). The IRAC move pattern is explained well by Professor Eugene Kim of the University of San Francisco School of Law in his YouTube video www.you tube.com/watch?v=qNW31cLKcLU. Before watching the video, you can read through the sample opinion text that Kim provides and listen to his explanation of this text's IRAC moves (Figure 2.3).

In the culture of professional law, Hafner (2013) found that the genre of *barrister's opinion* has somewhat similar moves to that of legal

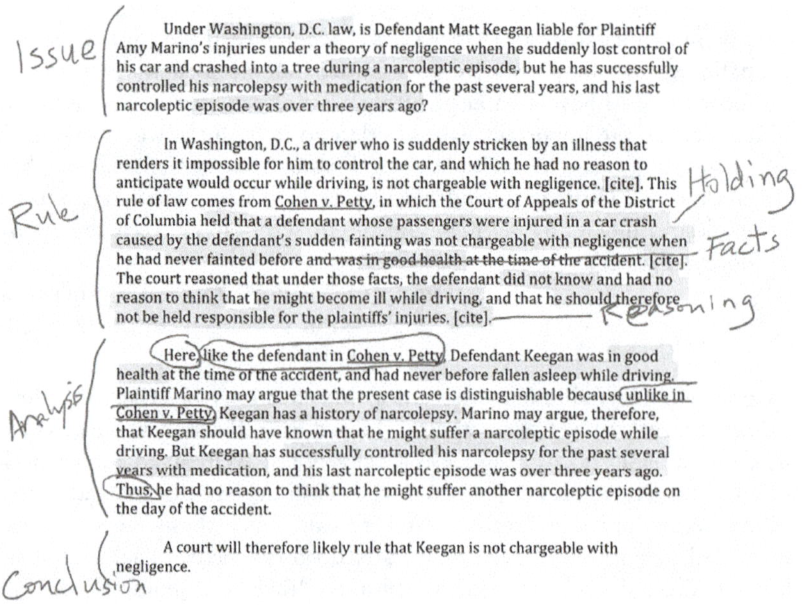

Issue

Under Washington, D.C. law, is Defendant Matt Keegan liable for Plaintiff Amy Marino's injuries under a theory of negligence when he suddenly lost control of his car and crashed into a tree during a narcoleptic episode, but he has successfully controlled his narcolepsy with medication for the past several years, and his last narcoleptic episode was over three years ago?

Rule

In Washington, D.C., a driver who is suddenly stricken by an illness that renders it impossible for him to control the car, and which he had no reason to anticipate would occur while driving, is not chargeable with negligence. [cite]. This rule of law comes from Cohen v. Petty, in which the Court of Appeals of the District of Columbia held that a defendant whose passengers were injured in a car crash caused by the defendant's sudden fainting was not chargeable with negligence when he had never fainted before and was in good health at the time of the accident. [cite]. The court reasoned that under those facts, the defendant did not know and had no reason to think that he might become ill while driving, and that he should therefore not be held responsible for the plaintiffs' injuries. [cite].

Holding
Facts
Reasoning

Analysis

Here, like the defendant in Cohen v. Petty, Defendant Keegan was in good health at the time of the accident, and had never before fallen asleep while driving. Plaintiff Marino may argue that the present case is distinguishable because unlike in Cohen v. Petty, Keegan has a history of narcolepsy. Marino may argue, therefore, that Keegan should have known that he might suffer a narcoleptic episode while driving. But Keegan has successfully controlled his narcolepsy for the past several years with medication, and his last narcoleptic episode was over three years ago. Thus, he had no reason to think that he might suffer another narcoleptic episode on the day of the accident.

Conclusion

A court will therefore likely rule that Keegan is not chargeable with negligence.

Figure 2.3 "IRAC with cases—sample memo" (screenshot)
Source: Eugene Kim, YouTube (29 Aug. 2013). Available at www.youtube.com/watch?v=qNW31cLKcLU.

problem-question-answer but are approached differently by barristers (a type of lawyer) than by students. In his comparison of opinions written by seasoned barristers and by new law school graduates on the same cases, Hafner observed that barristers used considerably fewer words than did the graduates in describing the applicable law (or, in IRAC terms, the Rule move), possibly due to the fact that with their greater experience, the barristers were more oriented to the case facts than to referencing the law to bolster their authority. Also, because the barrister's opinion is primarily a lawyer-to-lawyer genre, it may not require extensive law explanations. In contrast, the recent law school graduates may have still been in the academic mindset of displaying their knowledge in detailed law moves (Hafner, 2013). Hafner concludes that for novice lawyers "the process of developing professional expertise means going beyond the role of legal expert to take on the roles of fact finder and practical adviser" (p. 141). Extrapolating this idea more generally, it seems that transitioning between even closely related small cultures often requires writers or speakers to adjust their previous moves knowledge and their orientations to performing these moves for relevant audiences.

[handwritten margin note: Conclusion / Wordiness / is]

Considering large-culture and small-culture influences

It is also possible to consider the simultaneous interplay between large- and small-culture influences on genre and their moves, or what Atkinson (2004) has called the complex "interactions of different cultural forces" (p. 286). Ahmad (1997) addressed such intersecting forces in her study of RA introduction moves in Malaysian journal articles. She found that the Malaysian article authors frequently omitted Move 2, the Establishing a Niche move where authors often point out a gap in previous research (Swales, 1990). And when the Malaysian authors did include a Move 2, it rarely mentioned weaknesses of other researchers' studies. Although not specifically referring to small and large culture, Ahmad suggests that this pattern may be due to the dynamics among academic researchers in science and engineering (small culture) specifically in Malaysia (large culture). In particular, she argues that because this Malaysian academic community is relatively few in membership and the possible needed research activities vast, "Malay research article writers do not feel the pressure of competing for a research space, especially when writing for a small local readership audience in Malay" (Ahmad, 1997, pp. 296–297). Fredrickson and Swales (1994) similarly found an absence of competitive Move 2s in RA introductions written for a Swedish linguistics journal, which they also attributed to the relatively limited size of the Swedish linguistics research community (again, a combination of large culture and small culture). Indeed, rather than focusing on carving out a research space, these Swedish linguists were most concerned with making their introductions as engaging as possible, given their limited number of readers!

Using and revising existing move models

In doing a moves analysis, you may also wish to begin with a previous set of moves identified for the genre you are interested in (or a closely related genre), and adjust them as needed to fit the texts in your study. For example, some have applied Swales' CARS model to their own corpora of RA introductions and proposed revisions to its moves and steps (e.g., Samraj, 2002; Swales, 2004). Similarly, in comparing lecture introductions in small and large university classes, Lee (2009) started with Thompson's (1994) lecture moves framework and added another move, *warming up*, where he observed lecturers took care of "housekeeping" matters about the course or, especially in smaller classes, told rapport-building anecdotes and asides (p. 47).

✗ Summary of moves analysis steps

In the box below, I summarize the moves analysis stages we have covered in this chapter, including consultation with specialist informants and cross-cultural comparisons.

> ### Possible stages of moves analysis
>
> 1   Collect a set of texts of a particular genre to analyze. If you are doing a cross-cultural moves study, include texts from more than one small and/or large cultural context.
> 2   For spoken genres, audio or video record the texts and transcribe them.
> 3   Read or listen to the texts to get a sense of their genre and of the genre's purposes.
> 4   If desired, consult existing moves frameworks for this genre or similar genres.
> 5   Gather your first impressions of the texts' moves (and steps, if desired), by:
>
>   a   marking and labeling moves;
>   b   marking and labeling steps;
>   c   not worrying about being perfect.
>
> 6   Establish a working set of moves (and, optionally, steps) categories. If you are using an existing moves framework, feel free to delete, add, or revise the moves or steps to better capture patterns in your data.
> 7   Pilot code the moves/steps in a small sample of your texts.
> 8   Refine the move/step categories as needed.
> 9   Code the moves/steps in your full set of texts. Optionally, have a colleague code the texts as well and check your inter-rater reliability.
> 10 Note patterns in moves/steps frequency and sequencing.
> 11 Identify linguistic features of the moves (see Chapter 3).

12   Consult specialist informants about their views on the moves in your texts
     and what makes them more or less important or effective.
13   If your data set allows, identify similarities and differences in how the
     moves are realized in different small and/or large cultural contexts.

As I emphasized earlier, a researcher or teacher may choose to follow only some of the moves analysis stages above, depending on their interests or purposes.

Tying it all together: analyzing moves in a TED Talk

In this concluding section you get to apply what you have learned about moves analysis to a relatively new genre: the TED Talk. TED Talks are short (less than 18 minutes), quasi lecture-like presentations that cover a range of topics in science and technology, arts, politics, business, education, social justice, and other areas. They are delivered by experts (some famous, some less so) and are video-recorded at the annual conference for TED, a non-profit organization whose acronym stands for Technology, Entertainment, and Design; as well as at independently organized 'TEDx' events in countries around the world. This is an influential genre. In the last decade or so, many of these talks have been posted on the TED website (www.ted. com/talks), extending their reach well beyond attendees at TED events. Strikingly, by northern hemisphere fall (autumn) 2012, the TED Talks website had reached its billionth view (History of TED, n.d.), and every day, the talks receive approximately 1.5 million views (Gallo, 2014). This genre has also made a substantial mark on post-secondary education; Sugimoto and Thelwall (2013) found that nearly all of the more than 1,000 TED Talk videos in their study were included in at least one course syllabus online. Interestingly, the authors also observed that TED Talks received more general views than they did academic citations, suggesting that they "have a much greater impact on the public than within the scholarly community" (p. 671). Part of what has made TED Talks so appealing to general listenerships is that they are both informative and enjoyable. Partington (2014) in fact has characterized this genre as "enlightentainment" (p. 144).

For ESP classrooms, TED Talks can also be useful teaching fodder. The over 2,400 TED Talk videos (as of 2017), cover a wide range of topics relevant to different students' academic, professional, or personal interests, as reflected in the titles below of some frequently viewed TED Talks:

*   "How to spot a liar" (Speaker: Pamela Meyer)
*   "The thrilling potential of SixthSense technology" (Speaker: Pranav Mistry)
*   "The power of introverts" (Speaker: Susan Cain)

- "What's so sexy about math?" (Speaker: Cédric Villani)
- "Doctors make mistakes. Can we talk about that?" (Speaker: Brian Goldman)

Many TED videos have an accompanying written transcript, which students can use to enhance and/or to check their listening comprehension. They are also often excellent models of well-constructed spoken presentations, and, as such, examining their moves can help ESP students learn how to present specialized information to non-specialist audiences, a skill they may need in their target professions.

This final task gives you an opportunity to work through some of this chapter's moves analysis stages with the TED Talk genre.

Task 2.6 Move analysis of TED Talks

1   Go to the TED Talks webpage at www.ted.com/talks and select two or three TED Talks that look interesting to you. To help you with this process, you can browse the talks by their subject area or speaker and then also sort them by most recent or by most viewed.

2   Listen to your selected talks and, optionally, read along in the transcripts if available.

3   Try applying some of the stages of moves analysis summarized in the box earlier. At a minimum, do Stages 3 and 5.

4   How challenging was it to identify moves in these TED Talks? How similar or different were the moves in each of the talks? How much variation do you think there is across TED Talk moves, and why?

I hope that you have enjoyed this chapter and from it have learned ways of examining moves in genres relevant to your research or teaching interests. In the next chapter (Chapter 3) we will consider how to examine the linguistic elements, also known as lexicogrammatical features, that make up moves.

Analyzing lexicogrammatical features

In the last chapter we examined ways of analyzing genre moves, those functional text segments that define a genre's overall, or 'macro', shape and organization. At a more 'micro' level, genres can also be examined for their *lexicogrammatical features* (Bhatia, 1993), that is, the vocabulary and grammatical patterns that help to express the genres' moves. These patterns may include recurring words, phrases, and parts of speech; tense, aspect, and voice; and various syntactic constructions. ESP students are often particularly interested in these features, as they offer them linguistic options for communicating particular meanings within specific genres and situations.

In order to integrate attention to lexicogrammar in an ESP course, teachers may first wish to investigate the linguistic features in genres relevant to their students. This chapter explores some different approaches for doing such investigations. These include *manual approaches*, whereby a genre analyst codes, counts, and interprets lexicogrammatical features 'by hand'; and *corpus linguistics approaches*, which rely, at least in part, on electronic software and online corpora to uncover linguistic patterns in a set of genre exemplars. These approaches are not mutually exclusive, and you may decide to use both in a genre analysis. The chapter also illustrates how these approaches have been applied in ESP studies of 'linguistic politeness' in spoken and written genres. As in the previous chapter, there will be opportunities for you to practice the analytical techniques covered, which you also might encourage your students to use as they explore the linguistic features of new texts on their own.

Methods of lexicogrammatical analysis

Manual approaches

In a manual approach to lexicogrammatical analysis, the genre researcher, sometimes with little more technology than paper and colored pencils, follows a similar protocol to that discussed in the previous chapter for moves analysis: S/he reads or listens to the texts carefully, notices features that seem interesting, develops a scheme for categorizing and coding them, and then identifies and counts (perhaps with only a calculator) instances of the focal features in the genre exemplars.

Such an approach was used by Samraj (2013) in her comparative analysis of source citations in eight graduate student MA theses and eight published RAs, all in the field of biology. Samraj examined both the forms and rhetorical functions of the citations in these research genres. For her formal analysis, she located, through her own close reading of the 16 texts, citations that were "integral" (i.e., with the source author woven into the sentence) and "non-integral" (i.e., with the source author cited outside of the sentence grammar proper) (Samraj, 2013, p. 301), illustrated in the examples below.

1   Integral citation: "Selander (1964) suggested that the ancestral cactus wren is most closely represented by *C. b. affinis* of Baja California Sur." [from an MA thesis]
2   Non-integral citation: "The presence of hilly terrain between foodplant patches has been suggested as a factor inhibiting the colonization of new patches for *E. editha bayensis* (Harrison, 1989)." [from an MA thesis]

(Examples from Samraj, 2013, p. 304)

Samraj's investigation revealed that, compared to the RA writers, the student thesis writers had more frequent use of the integral citation type, which, Samraj observed, pointed to students' preference "for granting prominence to individual authors" (p. 303). Similarly, the students, again in comparison to the published writers, had more frequent use of "verb controlled" integral citations (p. 303), whereby the source author took on the "agent" role as the subject of the verb in the student's sentence (as in example A above) rather than just being "named" in a less prominent position in the sentence (p. 301). To arrive at these findings, Samraj carefully read the MA and RA discussion sections and counted and categorized the citations according to their integral and non-integral forms. This manual approach was do-able given the relatively modest size of the corpus (16 texts altogether) and the fact that the citations could be fairly easily spotted in reading through the texts (Samraj, personal communication, November 20, 2016). Samraj's close reading also allowed her to distinguish whether the citations were verb controlled (functioning as the agent of the verb) or named, as well as to interpret the various rhetorical *functions* of the citations within the thesis and RA discussion sections. These functions were actually the central focus of her project, which you can read about further in her article.

In another study of graduate students' source citations, Pecorari (2006) also used a manual approach, which this time revealed ways that the students' citation language *transgressed* norms of source use for research genres. She collected a total of 17 MA theses and PhD dissertations (all written by non-native English speakers) and 363 source texts used in some way by the students in their texts (with or without acknowledgement). In instances where students cited a source, Pecorari checked 'by hand' to see whether the students had actually incorporated language and information from that original source or instead had taken them from another source (i.e., a secondary source that used the original source). What she found was quite interesting: The students often used wording and ideas from secondary sources to present information from the original sources *without* citing the secondary sources. Consider, for example, the following two texts from Pecorari's study; the first was from a student's text and the second from the secondary source text: Datta, Ganesan, and Natarajan (1989); the similar portions of the passages are italicized.

Student text:

Mannan which is *a major constituent of the cell wall in C. albicans, inhibits a Candida antigen-induced in vitro proliferation of normal lymphocytes and also blocks the antigen-presenting ability of macrophages (Fischer et al., 1982).//*In addition, the *polysaccharide fractions from C. albicans stimulate T-cells to produce a suppressor factor, which inhibits interleukin 1 and interleukin 2 production (Lombardi et al., 1985).*

Source text:

Manna, a major constituent of the cell wall in C. albicans, was detected in the serum of some patients with mucocutaneous candidiasis (Fischer et al., 1978). Mannan *inhibited a Candida antigen-induced in vitro proliferation of normal lymphocytes and also blocked the antigen-presenting ability of macrophages (Fischer et al., 1982).//*In another study, *polysaccharide fractions* (containing mostly mannose and glucose residues) *from C. albicans stimulated the T-cells to produce a suppressor factor, which* in turn *inhibited interleukin 1 and interleukin 2 production (Lombardi et al., 1985).* [Excerpt is from Datta, Ganesan, & Natarajan, 1989, p. 70, which was not acknowledged in student text above.]

(Examples adapted from Pecorari, 2006, p. 15)

It appears, on the surface, that the student has cited sources using appropriate forms (e.g., Fischer et al. and Lombardi et al.). However, as Pecorari points out, the close similarities between the student's text and Datta, Ganesan, and Natarajan (the secondary source) indicate that the student incorporated, without citation, these secondary source authors' synthesis of Fischer et al. and Lombardi et al., using much of these authors' language as well. Pecorari's manual analysis was particularly useful for revealing this fact. It allowed Pecorari to observe similarities in language, organization, and argument between the students' citation moves and the secondary source passages. Although a computer-based comparison of the texts, using, for example, a Google search or plagiarism-detection software like Turnitin would have shown what words were identical across the passages, it would not have revealed the extent to which the students followed the logical presentation of the original source material offered by the secondary source (Pecorari, August 2014, personal communication). This approach therefore allowed Pecorari to discover students' "occluded" (i.e., hidden) lexicogrammatical-level and discourse-level borrowing from secondary sources, which transgressed research genre norms for source citations. From these findings, Pecorari is quick to point out that students' violations might not be intentional but rather are likely due to the fact that the rules of secondary-source citation are rarely seen by students in the published articles that they read. That is, because established researchers do not frequently cite secondary sources (presumably drawing on the original sources instead, or going back to the original sources once they had read the secondary sources), the conventions for doing such citation—or of how to avoid needing it—are invisible to students, and are thus a needed focus in EAP writing courses when teaching research genres.

Corpus linguistics approaches

Although, as Samraj's and Pecorari's studies suggest, a manual approach can be very useful depending on what textual elements one is examining and for what purposes, computer technology can also offer much assistance in revealing lexicogrammatical genre features, particularly those that we would not notice on our own. For doing such assisted analyses, ESP researchers have used tools of *corpus linguistics*, which, broadly speaking, is an approach to language study that uses electronically stored collections of spoken and/or written texts (i.e., *corpora*, or *corpus* in the singular) and software that allow corpora to be searched for a wide variety of features. One advantage of using computerized corpora and corpus tools for lexicogrammatical analysis is that they allow you to discover patterns that you would not expect in the texts you are studying (Baker, 2006; Biber, Connor, & Upton, 2007a). As such, a corpus-assisted approach can mitigate against researcher biases about the discourse being analyzed (Baker, 2006), revealing what words and grammatical patterns are *actually* present in examples of a genre, rather than only *assumed* to be there. Another clear benefit of corpus tools is that they radically reduce the amount of time (and tedium) involved in identifying the presence of particular lexicogrammatical forms. Instead of you counting by hand all of the nouns in a set of 58 newspaper editorials, for instance, electronic corpus tools can complete this task in a few seconds and tell you the frequency of each individual noun and what other words each noun occurs with.

Some corpora are publically available to search online, including "mega-corpora" (Koester, 2010, p. 45) like the Corpus of Contemporary American

English (COCA) and British National Corpus (BNC), each made up of millions of words of spoken and written discourse from various genres (e.g., news texts, fiction writing, sermons, academic journal articles, lectures, letters, and radio broadcasts). There are also smaller and more narrowly focused corpora such as the Michigan Corpus of Academic Spoken English (MICASE) comprised of spoken academic genres such as lectures, student presentations, office hour interactions, and dissertation defenses; the British Academic Written English Corpus (BAWE) of undergraduate and graduate student papers of various genres; the British Academic Spoken English (BASE) Corpus of university seminars and lectures, and the Hong Kong Corpus of Spoken English (HKCSE), which includes four sub-corpora of speech produced in academic, business, conversational, and public settings. An internet search on any of these corpora names will lead you to the websites. For a list of several freely available corpora, see Nesi (2013). You can also purchase corpora or develop your own, as a number of ESP researchers have done, compiling and scanning texts from such genres as RA abstracts (Hyland, 2004a); business meetings (Handford, 2010), and fundraising letters (Connor & Gladkov, 2004).

In an electronic corpus, you can readily search for lexicogrammatical features with corpus analysis tools. Some of these tools are available on the websites of the corpora themselves. Others are included in free or for-purchase software, such as *Antconc* (Anthony, 2014), or *WordSmith Tools* (Scott, 2017), that you can apply to your own corpus of texts. In the sections below, I describe several time-saving analyses that corpus tools can perform on lexicogrammatical genre features. (See also descriptions of these and other analyses in Flowerdew, 2009; Hyland, 2004b; Koester, 2010; Nesi, 2013.)

Word frequency

One of the most common uses of corpus software is the identification of frequent words in a set of texts. For example, in the freely available Antconc software (Anthony, 2014), the Word List tool will generate a frequency-ranked list of all of the words in your corpus. The following (Table 3.1), for example, is a list this tool created of the 40 most frequent words in three letters of recommendation I wrote for former graduate students (omitting the students' names, department, and classes).

As you will notice, and as is the case in most texts, the most frequent words are grammatical function words like articles, prepositions, and conjunctions. A bit further down the list, however, are recurring content words like *teaching, class, completed, exam, position*, and *recommend*. In terms of the evaluative words in my recommendations, the list reveals that I use *well* and *excellent* multiple times, and further down on the list, not shown here, *insightful, skillfully, asset*, and *impressed* also appear more than once in my letters. Although these lexical patterns from this very small corpus (three

Table 3.1 Most frequent words in a corpus of three letters of recommendation

Frequency rank	Number of occurrences	word
1	56	and
2	52	in
3	43	the
4	30	of
5	29	a
6	28	his
7	22	he
8	22	to
9	18	for
10	14	as
11	14	I
12	14	on
13	14	with
14	12	an
15	11	teaching
16	10	also
17	10	class
18	10	that
19	10	well
20	9	ESL
21	9	program
22	9	students
23	9	their
24	8	our
25	7	English
26	7	MA
27	7	was
28	6	at
29	6	be
30	6	completed
31	6	exam
32	6	excellent
33	6	has
34	6	him
35	6	is
36	6	language
37	6	my
38	6	one
39	6	position
40	6	recommend

short texts from only one writer) are not representative of the whole recommendation letter genre, they illustrate the usefulness of what a word frequency tool can do (and with much larger corpora as well).

If the words in a corpus are coded electronically for their parts of speech, a process known as *tagging*, more specified frequency lists can be generated, such as all of the verbs in the corpus, and so on. COCA is one such tagged corpus. If you wanted to identify the most common adjectives in this list, for example, you would select "adj.All" from the Part of Speech (POS) menu and the code [j*] would appear in the search box. When you submit this search, within a few seconds, you would see a list showing that the top ten adjectives in this large, mixed-genre corpus of American English are, in this order, *other, new, good, American, great, big, old, high, different*, and *national*, which might suggest some interesting things about American culture. COCA also allows a tagged search in specific genres. For example, if you select "Mag: Religion" for our [*j] adjective search, you will see that the top ten adjectives in American religious magazines are, in this order, *other, Catholic, new, religious, Christian, good, human, social, spiritual*, and *American*.

Keywords

Besides generating word frequency lists, corpus tools can also identify which words in your corpus are *keywords*, that is, words whose frequency is notably greater in your specific corpus than in a general corpus of the language, also known as the 'reference' corpus (Scott & Tribble, 2006). Keywords can thus reveal what concepts or values are especially important in a particular genre and the community that uses it. From just a casual comparison of the two adjective frequency lists above, for example, it appears that the words *social, human*, and *Christian* might be keywords of the American religious magazine genre, an observation that could be checked with a keyword tool. Antconc allows you to load a reference corpus and a specific corpus, and then, with the Keyword List, to generate a list of words in your specific corpus sorted by their 'keyness' strength, that is, their degree of unusual frequency in your specific corpus compared to their frequency in the general reference corpus.

In one keyword analysis, Handford (2010) identified business meeting keywords by comparing a reference corpus of everyday British speech with a corpus of spoken business meetings in the Cambridge and Nottingham Business English Corpus (CANBEC). Perhaps not surprisingly, business meeting keywords included such nouns as *customer, meeting*, and *sales*, along with time words like *January, month*, and *moment* (pp. 107–108). Particularly interesting, however, were differences between keywords in "external meetings" (i.e., between a business employee and outside client), and "internal meetings" (i.e., among employees within the same business). Handford found that although *we* was the most frequent keyword in both types of meetings, it was notably more common in external meetings, likely due to employees' use of "corporate *we*" when talking about their business with outside people (pp. 108–109), as in a statement like "We should be able to accommodate your request." In addition, some business nouns like *issue, price*, and *problem* were found to have greater keyness in internal meetings than in external meetings, possibly because, as Handford points out, these words "have potentially negative connotations," and thus might be avoided in external meetings, where speakers, understandably, are attending to "the relational aspects of communication" more so than in internal meetings (p. 110).

Concordance lines and word collocations

Corpus tools are also useful for analyzing the linguistic contexts in which a particular word appears in a set of genre exemplars. A *concordance* tool, for example, generates concordance lines showing the words that precede and follow a particular word in each of its occurrences in the corpus. Below, for example, are some concordance lines for the word *significant* in university students' critique texts (e.g., book reviews, product evaluations, academic paper reviews) in the British Academic Written English Corpus (BAWE) (Nesi & Gardner, 2012). These lines, which show several words before and after *significant*, were ones I generated using Sketch Engine, the online corpus tool linked with BAWE.

the durability and lifetime were also a *significant* factor to consider since
  racing cars might
that absolute fiscal savings may not be *significant* enough to provide fast
  payback on a potentially
although it is necessary to remember that a *significant* minority of noble
  families did still participate
its focus, the book is probably the most *significant* work on international
  relations in his
organic horticultural systems, by importing *significant* amounts of manure,
  showed the greatest
with insurance-based benefits playing a *significant* role, and in terms of
  gender—with the
work of Ostner and Lewis (1995) points to *significant* differences between
  two welfare states

Some concordance lines for *significant* in critique genres in BAWE

Reading through these lines allows you get an initial impression of some types of words, such as *differences* and *enough*, that *significant* occurs within academic critique genres. These word co-occurrences are known as *collocations*.

The most frequent collocations for a particular word can also be generated through corpus tools. The Sketch Engine collocation function, for example, produced the following list of frequent collocates of *significant* in the critiques (Table 3.2). As you can see, nouns like *difference(s)*, *change(s)* and *impact(s)*, and *role* were among the most common word partners (collocates) of *significant*.

Table 3.2 Frequent collocations with *significant* in critique genres in BAWE

Collocate	Frequency of occurrence with significant
difference	11
in	16
differences	6
impact	6
changes	6
role	6
change	6
increase	6
figures	5
reduction	5
enough	5
effect	5
impacts	4

Using the wildcard * symbol

To generate concordance lines and/or collocates not only for *significant* but also for its related word forms, you can use the wildcard symbol * at the end of the root *significan* (i.e., *significan**). Concordance lines and collocates will then be shown for *significant, significantly*, and *significance*. As well, you can use the wildcard symbol to identify phrases with particular structural frames, such as *it * that*, signifying a phrase that begins with *it* and ends with *that* and has any word(s) in between. Hyland (2004b) found that a concordance search on this pattern in RA abstracts generated lines with phrases including *it is likely that, it shows that, it is claimed that, it is clear that*. Examining these occurrences more closely in the abstracts revealed that "academic writers use this phrasing extremely frequently to express their evaluation of whether the following statement is likely to be true or not" (Hyland, 2004b, p. 218). Thus, as Hyland's analysis suggests, concordancing and the wildcard function are useful not only for identifying instances of words, phrases, or structures in a corpus but also for giving the researcher substantial data from which they can infer possible functions of these items in the corpus.

N-grams

Another way that corpus software can identify word combination patterns is through N-gram analysis. Also referred to as lexical bundles, clusters, or chunks, *N-grams* are "strings of words that frequently recur in a corpus"

(Nesi, 2013, p. 418). Given that 'gram' in corpus studies typically means word, a 3-gram would be a three-word string (e.g., *under these circumstances*), a 4-gram would be a four-word string (e.g., *while I agree with*), and so on. N-grams are another lexicogrammatical element that can help distinguish certain genres from others (Bednarek, 2012; Stubbs & Barth, 2003). Bednarek (2012), for example, found that key "trigrams" (i.e., 3-grams) in a corpus of seven American fictional television series marked the series' language as heavily emotional. These key phrases, which included *out of here, I told you*, and *need to talk*, appeared significantly more frequently in the television series than in the reference corpus of general spoken American English and often "in the context of negative emotions associated with conflict, confrontation or other problematic issues that characters face" (Bednarek, 2012, p. 56). In this way, the N-gram analysis revealed something of the nature of speech in the TV series discourse, and helped lead Bednarek to conclude that "emotionality emerges as *the* key defining feature of the language of television" (p. 59, italics original).

Task 3.1 gives you a chance to practice with several corpus tools that we have discussed above: word frequency lists, concordances, collocate lists, and N-grams.

Task 3.1 Using corpus tools

Do one or both of the following options.

Option A: Using online tools in a corpus website

1   Go to the British National Corpus search engine at http://corpus.byu.edu/ bnc/, a corpus that includes 100 million words of various spoken and written texts of British English.

2   In the Sections menu, select a spoken genre of interest to you, such as arts lectures, public debate, sermons, courtroom discourse, or another genre.

3   In the open box, type a word that might be useful to examine in this genre. For example, if you selected the genre of sermons, you could type in the word *well*, and the website will generate a concordance of all of the sentences contexts where *well* appears.

4   Scan through the concordance lines (at least the first 30 lines) and jot down some notes on the contexts in which your word seems to occur. What words often appear before or after it? What functions does the word seem to serve in the texts where it appears? For example, if you are looking at *well* in sermons, how does *well* function at particular junctures in a sermon?

5   Now, go back to the Search page and click on Collocates. In the Collocates box, type * (the wildcard symbol, meaning any), select how many 'words away' you would like to search for Collocates (for example, "1" on the left

would mean all collocates immediately before the word, and "1" on the right would mean all collocates immediately after the word). Then click Find Collocates. Look at what words that your focus word collocates frequently with. Which collocates confirm what you might expect about this word? Which surprise you? Why do you think these collocations with this word might appear frequently in this particular genre?

Option B: Using corpus software to analyze your own corpus.

1   Find several texts from one genre that you would like to analyze for its lexicogrammatical features (e.g., online dating profiles, newspaper editorials, eulogies, birth notices, company brochures, shareholder reports, transcripts from comedic TV shows, political speeches). Make sure that you have the texts in an electronic text file format that you can analyze with corpus software. You can also download text examples of particular genres for free from BAWE, BASE, MICASE, and the OANC. See their websites to find out how to do so.

2   Go to the Antconc website at www.laurenceanthony.net/software.html, and download the Antconc software. You may wish to watch Lawrence Anthony's excellent YouTube videos, particularly those on Getting Started, Word List, Concordance, Keyword List, Collocates, and N-grams. Once you have opened the software, select the files on your computer that you wish to load into Antconc. These files will serve as your corpus.

3   Use the Antconc Word List tool to generate a word frequency list for your corpus. What strikes you about the most frequent words in the texts— particularly the content words?

4   Use the Concordance tool to create concordance lines for one of the frequently occurring content words in your text. Read through the concordance lines and notice what words frequently precede your word and what words often follow it.

5   Select the Collocate tool and create a collocations list for your focus word. Does this list confirm your impressions from reading the concordance lines in step 4 and/or does it reveal other collocation patterns that you had not noticed before?

6   Select the N-gram tool and search for 4-grams (i.e., 4-word clusters) in your corpus. What N-grams are frequent in your texts?

7   What have you learned about your selected genre and its lexicogrammatical patterns through the analyses above?

Combining manual and corpus linguistics approaches

We have thus far seen benefits of a manual, close reading approach as well as of a corpus-assisted approach to studying lexicogrammatical features in texts. In order to capitalize on what both can show you about a genre, it is often useful to combine them. Fernández-Polo (2014) used such a mixed-methods approach in investigating the phrase *I mean* within the genre of conference presentations produced by non-native English speakers at international conferences in Finland. His data set of 34 presentations came from the English as a Lingua Franca in Academic Settings (ELFA) corpus, a publically available corpus of spoken texts (see Mauranen, 2006). In his analysis, Fernández-Polo first used Antconc to identify the instances of *I mean* across the presentations, and then examined on his own each of the 48 useable *I mean* instances in terms of the role it played in the speakers' presentations. This latter process involved his subjective interpretation, which he says was not always easy given that *I mean* sometimes appeared to serve more than one function simultaneously.

His analysis generated quite interesting findings. Conference presenters most frequently used *I mean* when they were repairing their language errors or dysfluencies, such as in this example: "normally a district has one or two hospitals and then everything else is either a hospital er i mean a health centre or a dispensary" (from Fernández-Polo, 2014, p. 61). Too many uses of this type of *I mean* in this way, observed Fernández-Polo, could make the speaker appear anxious and unprepared, and thus "might harm the public image speakers project of themselves before their audiences and compromise the success of their presentations" (p. 62). Some uses of *I mean*, however, contributed positively to the speakers' talks. For example, *I mean* sometimes signaled that the speaker was taking a moment to connect with the audience through a minor digression. In the example below, for instance, the presenter says *I mean* to transition to an aside about her frustration with the term "digital divide":

> so let's go to the project now i'm er okay and i wanted to say s-another thing er after i described you the two countries briefly erm with this project we wanted to address three divides first divide *i mean* let me before i say the three divides i wanna say something i'm kind of fed up with the word digital divide because i use it every day you probably use it more than once a day if there's a new concept to bridge the digital divide please let me know i'm happy to you can have the copyright i'm happy to use the word but it should be something more constructive
>
> (Example from Fernández-Polo, 2014, p. 64)

Fernández-Polo's findings were made possible through combining software tools, which identified relevant examples in his corpus, with Fernández-Polo's own human 'brain tools', which interpreted the functions of *I mean* in these examples.

Task 3.2 The function of *So I think* in external business meetings

Handford (2010) also combined manual and corpus-assisted methods in studying N-grams in business meetings. Corpus tools identified *So I think* as a particularly common 3-gram string in the CANBEC business meetings corpus, and then Handford's own analysis of corpus extracts with *So I think* revealed how it is used in actual meetings. Read the following excerpt from a business meeting in Handford's (2010) study and then answer the questions about S1's use of *So I think* at the end of the extract. S1 is a logistics manager of a business and S3 is a representative from an outside supplier. They are discussing how "spot orders" (i.e., those that not planned) should be dealt with.

S1: So there're gonna be a number of spot orders.
S3: Yeah
S1: Now are they gonna be huge quantities? On the whole not.
S3: Yeah.
S1: Sometimes they're gonna be general export packs as well which obviously will help because you might actually say we've got=we've got a stock of this.
S3: Yeah
S1: Someone's cancelled an order. We've got some spare. We can actually deliver in eight weeks as opposed to twelve weeks or something like that.
S3: Yeah
S1 *So I think* we've got to take a lot of this on a case by case.

(Excerpt from Handford, 2010, p. 138)

1   What might be the function(s) of S1's use of the N-gram *So I think* in this business meeting interchange? Why might S1 use it at this juncture?
2   If S1 did not start his last sentence with *So I think* and just began with *we've got to take a lot of this ...* , would his statement seem more or less persuasive or compelling?
3   How might this N-gram have different effects depending on which word is stressed in S1's intonation—*So, I,* or *think*? Try reading the whole sentence three times, each time stressing a different word in the *So I think* cluster.
4   How could you use your observations in 2 and 3 in teaching an ESP lesson on the language of business meetings?

Studying linguistic politeness in genres

The rest of the chapter considers other studies that have combined manual and corpus-assisted analyses of lexicogrammatical features. In the next section, I concentrate in particular on mixed-method investigations of *linguistic politeness* in various genres—a topic of much interest in ESP given that

appropriately polite lexicogrammar is often critical for effective communication within various genres and with various audiences.

Genre-focused politeness studies have typically drawn on Brown and
Levinson's (1987) well-known concepts of *face, face-threatening acts (FTAs)*,
and *linguistic politeness strategies* (see Kádár & Haugh, 2013; Leech, 2014;
van der Bom & Mills, 2015 for further discussions of linguistic politeness).
Regarding face, Brown and Levinson proposed that in our everyday interactions, we attend to two aspects of our hearers' (or readers') identity and
image: their *positive face*, that is, their desire to have their goals be in solidarity with others' goals and to be liked and admired for them, and their
negative face, that is, their desire to have their actions "be unimpeded by
others" (p. 62). In simple terms, you can think of a person's positive face as
their 'please like me' identity desires, and their negative face as their 'please
don't bother me' identity desires. Brown and Levinson also highlight that, in
any person, these two types of face desires are vulnerable to face-threatening
acts (FTAs) from others. If your friend tells you she does not like your new
boyfriend, for example, that criticism is an FTA on your positive face
because it threatens your desire to have you and your goals accepted,
admired, and aligned with your friend's goals. If your friend asks you to
help her move to a new apartment this weekend, on the other hand, that
request is an FTA on your negative face because it threatens to impede other
activities you had planned for the weekend.

Because speakers and writers are aware of their listeners' and readers'
face desires, they often use what Brown and Levinson call linguistic politeness strategies to mitigate the force of their FTAs. Specifically, they may try
to soften their FTAs though *positive politeness* language that attends to
their audience's positive face, and/or *negative politeness* language that
attends to their audience's negative face. Before criticizing your boyfriend,
for example, your friend might first give you a compliment (a positive
politeness strategy), such as *You normally make wise life choices*, in order
to build up your positive face (desire to be liked) and thus soften the blow of
her criticism coming a few seconds later. Or, when asking for your help
with her apartment move, your friend is likely to use negative politeness
forms like hedges and questions (e.g., *Do you think you might be able to
help me move this weekend?*), which tone down the directness of her request
and thus acknowledge your negative face need to be unimpeded.

These face-sensitive linguistic politeness strategies are relevant in any
genre with potential to express FTAs. Some obvious candidates are evaluative reviews of various kinds (Belcher, 2007; Hyland, 2004a; Hyon, 2011) or
genres containing requests and directives (Koester, 2010). Positive and
negative politeness, however, can even be found in genres where we would
not necessarily expect them, such as in RAs and air traffic communications
(Moder, 2013; Myers, 1989; Hyland, 1996). Below I describe a few studies of
lexicogrammatical politeness strategies in two genres—RAs and workplace

interactions. These may give you ideas for studying linguistic politeness in a genre you are interested in.

Hedges as politeness strategies in research articles

You might not think of RAs as being personal, emotional, or threatening enough to require politeness. However, as Myers (1989) observed in his analysis of 60 molecular biology journal articles, when RA authors make claims about their research, they threaten their readers' negative face, that is, their desire to be unimpeded, by implicitly asking them to accept the RA's claims, give the authors credit for the claims, and/or potentially alter or restrict their (the readers') own future scholarship on this research topic. To mitigate these potential FTAs, RA authors use lexicogrammatical devices "to make [their claims] more polite," and, in fact, the very presence of these politeness strategies demonstrates "that the authors are aware of the FTAs" (Myers, 1989, p. 6).

One such negative politeness device Myers noticed in the molecular biology RAs was *hedges*. These are words and phrases that tone down the speaker's or writer's certainty about an idea or claim (Hyland, 2005), and include modal auxiliaries like *may, might, should,* and *could*; adjectives and adverbs like *possible, possibly, probably,* and *perhaps*; verbs expressing some uncertainty, such as *seem, appear,* and *suggest*; and certain sentence constructions like *I + believe/think that* ... Examples of hedges from Myers' study are shown below:

These findings *suggest* a common origin of some nuclear mitochondrial introns and common elements in the mechanism of their splicing.

Thus, a common short sequence of RNA *might* be attached to several mRNAs.

The three short segments ... are *probably* spliced to the body of this mRNA.

(Examples from Myers, 1989, p. 13, italics added)

Because such hedges express the author's claim as a possibility rather than as a fact, they reduce the imposition (i.e., threat to negative face) on the author's colleagues. That is, they suggest that the claim need not be accepted. As Myers noted, "hedging is a politeness strategy when it marks a claim, or any statement, as being provisional, pending acceptance in the literature, acceptance by the community" (p. 12).

Hyland (1996), in his study of 26 articles in molecular biology, also found that besides attending to readers' needs, RA hedges serve "writer-oriented" functions that provide researchers a face-buffer in case their claims are later shown to be wrong. That is, hedges, by making claim statements provisional and less than 100 percent certain, "allow authors to seek acceptance for the highest-level claim they can for their results while protecting them from the full effects of its eventual overthrow" (Hyland, 1996, p. 445). In this way, hedges offer RA authors a strategy of "self-politeness" (Chen, 2001), protecting (at least partially) their own positive and negative face from future threats.

Politeness in spoken workplace genres

Linguistic politeness can also be studied in spoken genres. A number of ESP investigations, for example, have examined politeness devices as a means of promoting harmonious relationships in workplace interactions. In her analysis of 66 office conversations in the American and British Office Talk (ABOT) corpus, Koester (2010) identified several lexicogrammatical politeness forms, outlined below, for reducing the negative FTAs of directives and requests in these conversations. These included:

- *Just* as a hedge in front of an imperative, as in:

  Just email me the names

- Indirect modals (e.g., *can, would, want to, wanna*), as in:

  You *can* go ahead an' put it back in here
  We *wanna* keep the two cover sheets
  I *would* have a quick word with Paul an' just say look this is what
      Zenith are after

- The use of *Let's*, which carries the feeling of a suggestion rather than of a strong directive, as in:

  Let's have a look at that one then
  (Examples from Koester, 2010, pp. 79–80)

Koester (2010) points out that through these "indirect forms" employees achieve "negative politeness, … mitigat[ing] the threat to the addressee's negative face" when trying to direct the addressee's actions (p. 81). It is also interesting to observe in Koester's examples above that the *We, I,* and *Let's* show further deference to the hearer's negative face by not saying to the hearer that *you* have to do something (even though that is what is understood), and suggesting rather that the speaker will help the hearer do the action (even though that probably will not happen).

The relationship between speakers in interactive workplace genres is also important to consider in examining the use (or non-use) of lexicogrammatical politeness devices. Koester (2010), for example, observed that the polite, indirect linguistic forms listed above occurred *less* frequently in collaborative "decision-making" conversations among colleagues, where "the more equal roles of the participants seems to reduce the risk of performing face-threatening acts, thereby lessening the need for mitigation" (p. 84). Handford (2010) as well found that speaker relationships influenced the presence or absence of certain linguistic items known as *backchannels* during business meetings. In Task 3.3 you get to explore his findings about these backchannels and politeness.

Task 3.3 Backchannels, politeness, and business meetings

Backchannels are verbalizations like *mm, hmm, okay*, and *right* that speakers utter when listening to someone talk. In his study of business meetings in the CANBEC corpus, Handford (2010) discovered that the backchannels *hmm* and *sure* relate in interesting ways to speaker–listener relationships, power, and face, as illustrated in the following two excerpts from his study. Excerpt 1 is from an internal (i.e., within the company) meeting between a manager and subordinate on the topic of customer contract renewals. Read it and then consider the following questions.

Excerpt 1
S1: So if they're only taking out for the quarter like till the end of the year.
S2: *Hmm*
S1: and then they're taking out a full year's contract. You would look it would look in your database … your
S2: Yeah
S1: database … that … they should be up for renewal in [1 second] I dunno October some time next year …
S2: *Hmm*
S1: and they wouldn't. They'd then be up for renewal in January two thousand and five.
S2: Oh okay.

(Excerpt from Handford, 2010, pp. 160–161)

1   In Excerpt 1, do you think S2 is the manager or the subordinate? Why?
2   In conducting a frequency analysis of *hmm* in his corpus, Handford found that *hmm* "is over twice as frequent in internal meetings, and is approximately three times more common in manager-subordinate meetings than peer meetings" (p. 160). Why do you think this would be so? Think about what functions *hmm* serves in these interchanges.

Excerpt 2 comes from an external meeting in which S1, an employee from a company, and S2, an outside client, are in a sales discussion.

Excerpt 2
S1: And then you know we've got a couple of questions to ask you and maybe some …

> S2: *Sure.*
> S1: er you know just a few things to ask you about.
>
> (Excerpts from Handford, 2010, p. 161)

> I Handford (2010) found that *sure* as a backchannel did not occur in internal
>   meetings but was frequent in external meetings, like the one illustrated in
>   Excerpt 2. He suggests that this pattern has to do with the expectation
>   that in external meetings "face will be positively addressed" (p. 162).
>   Explain how S2's *sure* expresses positive politeness.

For further discussion of face and linguistic politeness in other spoken business genres, please see Nickerson and Planken's (2016) helpful review.

Cross-cultural lexicogrammatical comparisons

The sections above illustrate how analyzing a genre's lexicogrammatical features—by hand and/or assisted with corpus tools—illuminates these features' functions, including in some instances, the expression of politeness. As we saw with genre moves in Chapter 2, however, lexicogrammatical patterns, even within a single genre, are often quite variable across different cultural contexts.

To get at this variation, lexicogrammatical analysis, like move analysis, can include cross-cultural comparison—at either or both the large, national culture level or small, community culture level. In a comparison of 20 English and 20 Japanese book reviews, for example, Itakura (2013) investigated how and why book review writers in the two sets of reviews (all published in linguistics journals) used hedges as politeness devices when praising the book they were reviewing. Although praise is not where you would expect to see hedges (since it seems the opposite of face-threatening), Itakura points out that in the context of book reviews, "praise is potentially a face threatening act to 'self' (the review writers)" given that review readers may not agree with the praise and therefore could judge negatively the review and the reviewer (p. 133). Hedges offer some protection against these self-face risks of praise. In her analysis of the 360 praise segments in the 40 book reviews, Itakura found that praise was hedged almost three times as often in the Japanese reviews as in the English reviews (31.7 percent of the time vs. 10.5 percent of the time). She attributes this pattern to overarching differences between English-medium and Japanese cultures, suggesting that while the former celebrates positive politeness and solidarity-building (and thus is comfortable with explicit praise), the latter "tends to emphasize negative politeness and encourages distant social relationships and modesty" (p. 145). As such, Japanese reviewers are more likely to be restrained, and "to present themselves as non-committal, non-imposing, and humble" when offering praise (p. 145). Despite these differences, Itakura did still find that the English and Japanese book reviewers used some of the same praise-hedging devices, including modals and epistemic verbs (e.g., *think, believe*). Japanese reviewers nevertheless, though, also employed non-active-voice constructions that added a further sense of vagueness to the praise, as in *It is thought that this book should be valued highly* ... (p. 140).

In a disciplinary culture comparison, Hyland (2005) studied the presence of linguistic devices through which RA authors—all writing in English, but in different disciplines—conveyed their *stance*, that is, their "textual 'voice'" expressing "their judgements, opinions, and commitments" (p. 176). These stance devices include hedges (e.g., *may, possibly*), boosters, which ramp up rather than tone down certainty (e.g., *clearly, highly*); attitude markers, which convey the writer's reactions and emotional attitudes (e.g., *important, unfortunate, surprisingly*); and *self-mention* (particularly, the first person pronoun *I* and related possessive adjectives). As well, Hyland compared the RAs' *engagement* devices, whereby authors explicitly connect with readers, such as through reader pronouns (e.g., *you*), questions, directives, and personal asides. Through both corpus-assisted and manual analysis, Hyland searched for and compared these stance and engagement features in 240 RAs from eight disciplines: four 'soft' sciences (philosophy, sociology, applied linguistics, and marketing) and four 'hard' sciences (physics, biology, mechanical engineering, electrical engineering). He discovered that these lexicogrammatical elements were much more frequent in RAs in the soft fields than in the hard field RAs, which he attributed to the different knowledge-making practices and goals of these academic cultures. For example, because soft sciences tend to be "more interpretive" with "greater possibilities for diverse outcomes," writers in these fields, says Hyland, "must spell out their evaluations and work harder to establish an understanding with readers" (pp. 187–188).

Connecting moves and lexicogrammatical analysis

This final section of the chapter connects back to Chapter 2 by considering how to integrate lexicogrammatical analysis into moves analysis. Such integration allows you to see which vocabulary and syntactic patterns characterize individual genre moves. For example, in RA introductions, a linguistic examination of Move 1, Step a. (Establishing a Territory, Claiming Centrality) reveals that it often features present perfect tense, recency expressions, and words emphasizing importance and currency (Swales & Feak, 2012), as in *In recent years, there has been increasing interest in* ... . Partington's (2014) study of TED Talks (see Chapter 2 for more on this genre) also illustrates how to examine lexicogrammar within the context of moves. Although not using the term moves per se, Partington studied various segments of TED Talks where speakers emphasize the importance of what they are saying and the lexicogrammatical devices that help them to do so (p. 148). One such importance marker was the *Wh-cleft*, a syntactic construction that begins with *What* and includes a copular *be* followed by a complement phrase with the important information. In the following Wh-cleft examples from Partington's TED Talk corpus, the entire Wh-cleft is in bold and the complement is in italics.

What was very surprising to me was *Tom's critique* ...

Does an election produce an accountable and legitimate government? **What an election produces is** *a winner and a loser.*

They don't travel very far. **What they're very good at doing is** *hitchhiking, particularly the eggs.*

What I'm going to do is *to just give a few notes, and this is from a book I'm preparing called 'Letters to a Young Scientist'.*

> (Examples from Partington, 2014, pp. 156–157,
> underlining and bold added)

Notice that in these examples, the Wh-cleft gives extra importance to the complement by pushing it to the end of the sentence, a typical placement for new, emphasized information. As Partington (2014) says, Wh-clefts draw attention to the post-copular element "by making the audience wait for the relevant information" (p. 156). To test this idea, try changing the examples above to 'regular' sentences without a Wh-cleft. You will see that the regular sentences do not give the same punch to the focal idea as does the Wh-cleft. Compare, for instance, *What was very surprising to me was Tom's critique* to *Tom's critique was very surprising to me*, and consider which one focuses your attention squarely on Tom's critique. Partington observed that one sort of place (move) in which these importance-marking Wh-clefts occurred were TED speakers' announcements of the next theme they would discuss, as illustrated in the last example above about the 'Letters to a Young Scientist'.

In a related genre, Deroey (2012) similarly observed that Wh-clefts are found at certain "turning points" in university lectures, such as the introduction, the beginning of an explanation, or a wrapping-up conclusion, where the lecturer is highlighting a particular point (pp. 118, 122). It is worth noting that Partington and Deroey used both corpus tools and manual analysis to identify the Wh-clefts and their functions in their corpora. Partington said he found particularly "fruitful" the "alliance of close reading and concordancing." His initial reading led him to notice "items and pheonomena of interest," which he then looked for more examples of through the concordancing tool and could "judge whether *patterns* of use and behavior might be discerned" (p. 146, italics original). And, using both methods, he and Deroey were each able to discover some move locations of the Wh-cleft structure in the TED Talk/lecture genres.

Stance features in fundraising letter moves

Also combining manual and corpus-assisted approaches, Biber, Connor, and Upton (2007b) examined lexicogrammar within moves of "direct mail letters," a genre used by non-profit philanthropic organizations to solicit money from readers. As the authors point out, fundraising texts like these are similar to other promotional genres like sales letters and job applications where "the purpose is to sell something" (p. 44). Given these letters' "overtly persuasive" nature (p. 62), the researchers were particularly interested in the letters' linguistic stance expressions (i.e., personal judgments, evaluations, and opinions; see earlier discussion on stance), and in the distribution of stance devices across the seven moves (see below). To this end, they analyzed 242 direct mail letters from the Indiana Center for Intercultural Communication (ICIC) Fundraising corpus. A seven-move structure for this genre was identified (see below), and two raters hand-coded all of the moves in each letter. Then, the researchers employed a corpus tool known as a "grammatical tagger," to mark every stance feature, drawing on Biber et al.'s (1999) stance taxonomy, in each move of every letter (p. 62).

Move structure of non-profit direct mail fundraising letters

Move 1: Get attention
Move 2: Introduce the cause and/or establish credentials of org[anization]
Move 3: Solicit response
Move 4: Offer incentives
Move 5: Reference insert
Move 6: Express gratitude
Move 7: Conclude with pleasantries
            (From Biber, Connor, & Upton, 2007b, p. 52. Note: This moves
                        framework also contained steps within the moves,
                                    which I have not included here).

The moves-specific lexicogrammatical analysis revealed several interesting findings, one being that several of the moves used modal auxiliaries but differed in the *types* of modals and the meanings they expressed. For example, in Move 3 (Solicit response), where the letter writers most directly asked for the readers' support, the ability modal *can* was the most common. In the example below, it conveys the judgment that the readers are capable of giving money.

You *can* help people reach their dreams of reading and learning by making a contribution to Indy Reads.

In Move 4 (Offer incentives), on the other hand, prediction modals like *will* were more salient, as letter writers used them to describe future tangible or intangible benefits that readers would experience if they donated to the cause.

Corporate contributors *will* be acknowledged in our newsletter, the annual report and on the Indy Reads webpage.
I am sure you *will* feel good about giving.

And in Move 5, where the writers "reference an insert" (e.g., a form or envelope with the letter), modals of necessity and obligation like *should* were used to direct the reader to do something with the insert:

For your convenience, I am enclosing a copy of Form CC-40, which *should* be filed with your Indiana State Income Tax.

Another common grammatical structure in some of the moves, including Move 3 (Solicit response), were "to-complement clauses," which began with a verb describing the hoped-for stance (e.g., *agree, choose*) of the reader and, in the infinitive complement, made "clear what it is the organization wants to reader to do in response to the letter" (p. 65).

We are hopeful that you *will agree to help.*
When you are contacted by your Campus Campaign volunteer, we hope you'll *choose to become one of the many partners in the community of IUPUI.*
(Examples from Biber, Connor, & Upton, 2007b, pp. 65–66)

By analyzing the distribution of stance items in the letters, Biber, Connor, and Upton were thus able to describe which items were used in what moves. For teaching purposes, such a moves-specific description of a genre's lexicogrammar would be more helpful than, say, simply telling ESP marketing students that they need to use modals in direct mail letters. See if you can try combining moves and lexicogrammatical analysis in Task 3.4.

Task 3.4 Connecting lexicogrammar and moves

1   Select a genre that you have already analyzed in terms of its moves. This could be one of the genres mentioned earlier—for example, wedding announcements, restaurant reviews, legal opinions, RA introductions or discussion sections, lectures, TED Talks. Or it could be another genre that you are interested in. You should gather at least two textual examples of this genre.

2   Carefully examine one of the moves in your sample texts and note the lexicogrammatical features that seem to occur in this move. These features might include particular words or phrases or specific grammatical elements such as modal auxiliaries, active or passive voice, certain tense-aspect forms, or other syntactic constructions. If you have access to corpus tools

that will help you identify these features, feel free to use them. In any case, though, you should also carefully study the features manually and take notes on why they may be used in this move.

3   Explain how these lexicogrammatical features help to achieve the move's purposes and the purposes of the genre as a whole.

In this chapter, we have considered the value of both manual and corpus-assisted approaches to examining lexicogrammatical features of genres, including politeness devices and other stance features. As well, the chapter has illustrated ways of studying these features across cultural contexts and within individual genre moves. In the next chapter, we turn to complementing these structural and linguistic investigations of genres with analyses of their contexts.

Chapter 4

Analyzing genre contexts

As noted in Chapter 1, ESP has been characterized as 'linguistic' and text-focused in its orientation to genre (Flowerdew, 2011). And this reputation is not without basis, as ESP scholarship has focused much on describing genres' structural moves and lexicogrammatical features. Some strands of ESP scholarship and teaching, however, also reflect considerable interest in understanding (and helping students to understand) the social and personal contexts that shape and are shaped by genres. Indeed, even at the advent of ESP genre work, Swales (1985b) urged researchers to turn their sights more toward the settings of students' target genres. He argued that the field had "given text too great a place in nature" and that we need also to understand "the roles texts have in their environments" (p. 219). These environments might include concrete settings such as classrooms, workplaces, and community centers, or more abstract contexts like academic disciplines and whole national cultures. And in each of these contexts, genre-interacting factors may be multiple, including the context's physical conditions; its human members and their varied values, histories, goals, and practices; and the relationships among genres that operate within the context.

This chapter aims to attend to Swales' early advocacy for studying genre environments by exploring 1) what can be learned through context investigations and 2) how to do them. To these ends, the first half of the chapter considers ways that genre context study illuminates several things, including reasons for genres' textual conventions, individuals' experiences using genres, relationships among genres in the same context, and ways that genres impact their settings. The second half of the chapter turns to ethnographic and 'textographic' approaches to studying genre contexts, and gives you opportunities to practice using techniques of these approaches in your own genre context studies.

The value of analyzing genre contexts

The 'why' behind genre conventions

A potential concern about linguistically oriented genre analyses is that their structural descriptions may be treated by ESP students, or even their teachers, as formulas to be strictly followed without sensitivity to the purposes, rationales, or potential variability of these formal patterns. Analyzing genre contexts helps to counter formulaic (and often overly simplistic) treatments of genre by uncovering why genres look, sound, and feel the way they do in relation to their settings, and how they change as their settings change. As Hyland (2006) points out, examining genres (and genre use) in their contexts "can help learners to demystify forms and patterns which might otherwise be seen as arbitrary and conventional" (p. 274).

Swales and Rogers' (1995) study of corporate *mission statements* illustrates ways that such 'demystifying' context investigation might be done. As the authors suggest, mission statements make declarations about a company's goals and principles, and, as such, frequently occupy a revered place in company life, being often prominently displayed "on desks and walls and doors," and invoked at special events or "in times of crisis" (Swales & Rogers, 1995, pp. 225–226). Given their explicit role "as carriers of ideologies and institutional cultures" (p. 225), these statements are also well suited for investigating text–context relationships. Before getting to the specific approach and findings of Swales and Rogers' study, let's take a look at two company mission statements—one from a specialty grocery store and another from an outdoor clothing company—and consider how such text–context relationships might be operating in them.

> Mission statement of Trader Joe's (a grocery store chain):
>
> The mission of Trader Joe's is to give our customers the best food and beverage values that they can find anywhere and to provide them with the information required to make informed buying decisions. We provide these with a dedication to the highest quality of customer satisfaction delivered with a sense of warmth, friendliness, fun, individual pride, and company spirit.
>
> > (Statement publically posted at local Trader Joe's stores)

> Mission statement of Patagonia (an outdoor-clothing company):
>
> Build the best product, cause no unnecessary harm, use business to inspire and implement solutions to the environmental crisis.
>
> > (Statement posted at www.patagonia.com/company-info.html)

These two statements clearly share some common purposes, moves, and language, all focused on promoting their companies' positive goals and identities. Yet their differences also demonstrate that the mission statement genre does not follow a single formula. The Trader Joe's statement, for example, foregrounds its good product values and friendly shopping experience. The Patagonia statement, on the other hand, (although also alluding to its product quality) is loftier and more global in its vision, extending it to solving "the environmental crisis." The texts also differ lexicogrammatically. While the Trader Joe's statement is written more conventionally as two regular (albeit long) sentences, the Patagonia statement, with its series of short verb phrases, has an edgier style.

A study analyzing the cultural environments of Trader Joe's and Patagonia might illuminate why they realize their mission statement moves and language the ways they do. Swales and Rogers (1995) offer such a culturally oriented investigation of the mission statements of two other major U.S. companies: Dana Corporation, an automotive parts supplier, and Honeywell, a producer of temperature control systems. To understand various elements of the companies' respective cultures, Swales and Rogers interviewed the corporate executives, conducted several site visits, and reviewed documents on the companies' histories. Through this contextual digging, they found that the "rationales" for the mission statements "were enmeshed within the context of corporate history, culture and legend," which in turn influenced the specific ways that the two companies expressed the textual features of this genre (p. 237). In this next task, you get to inhabit Swales and Rogers' analytical shoes by considering how what they discovered about the culture of one of the companies—Dana Corporation—could illuminate its mission statement's formal qualities.

Task 4.1 How corporate context shapes mission statement features

Below are excerpts from the Dana mission statement, *Philosophy and Policies of Dana*, that Swales and Rogers (1995) studied. I have included excerpts only from the portion on "People," the longest section of the statement. Read through these excerpts and then answer the question that follows.

People
   We are dedicated to the belief that our people are our most important asset. Whenever possible, we encourage all Dana people within the entire world organization to become shareholders, or by some other means, own a part of their company.
   We believe people respond to recognition, freedom to participate, and the opportunity to develop.
   We believe that people should be involved in setting their own goals and judging their own performance. The people who know best how the job should be done are the ones doing it.
   We believe Dana people should accept only total quality in all tasks they perform.
   We endorse productivity plans which allow people to share in the rewards of productivity gains.

We believe that all Dana people should identify with the company. This identity should carry on after they have left active employment.

[...]

We believe in promoting from within. Dana people interested in other positions are encouraged to discuss job opportunities with their supervisor ...

(Excerpts from Swales & Rogers, 1995, Figure 1, p. 229)

1   What themes and lexicogrammatical patterns stand out to you in these excerpts from the Dana mission statement?

Swales and Rogers (1995), as noted above, gathered various data on the Dana culture. Below are some pieces of these data, each of which I have prefaced (in italics) with the source that Swales and Rogers obtained it from. Think about these data and answer the questions below.

From a site visit to the Dana headquarters: "[W]e were struck by the fact that there were almost no papers visible anywhere (except in the Accounts Department). Rather, the emphasis was on talking to people, their *own* people, the Dana people ..." (pp. 233–234, italics original).

From a statement about Dana in a 1986 issue of the business magazine Industry Week: "As retired President Gerald B. Mitchell tells it, 'We worked to develop communication as an art. There is little, if anything written down; it's all done orally'" (p. 233).

From an interview with Dana's Executive Vice President, who said the following about the Mission statement: "What we have here is a belief system ... It's a bit like when you pledge a commitment, as in church" (p. 234).

From investigating company history: The mission statement had not changed for 20 years.

Observation from an interview with executives on the Dana Policy Committee regarding the Mission Statement: "[T]hey see themselves as but disciples of the company's great leaders" (p. 234).

2   What sense do you get of the Dana company culture from Swales' and Rogers' context data above?
3   Do these data shed light on the mission statement's textual features that you noticed in Question 1? How so, or how not? Are there additional context data that you would collect to better understand the features in the mission statement?

In 2004, Dana published a new version of their mission statement. Rogers, Gunesekera, and Yang (2007) compared the old and new mission statements and found that while they shared some features, they also exhibited notable differences. Among the differences was a greater emphasis, in the new version, on using the company name within the sentence subject (e.g., *Dana* or *The Dana Corporation*) rather than *we*. This change, they suggested, indicated a sense of more centralized control in the company. Also interesting (and perhaps reflecting again a more management-controlled culture) is the mention in the new version of documenting in writing employee performance, and quantifying employee achievement. Excerpts from the "People" section of the 2004 Dana mission statement below illustrate these patterns.

> Dana is dedicated to the belief that our people are our most important asset. We believe people respond to recognition and trust, the freedom to participate, and the opportunity to develop.
> [...]
> Dana is committed to 40 hours of education per person per year.
> [...]
> We encourage professional and personal development of all Dana people. All Dana supervisors must review the job performance of their people in writing at least once a year and work with their people to formulate development plans that will increase proficiency in their given disciplines.
> [...]
> Dana people are expected to generate at least two ideas per person per month with a goal of 80 percent implementation.
>
> (Excerpts from Appendix B: 2004 Statement, in Rogers,
> Gunesekera, & Yang, 2007, p. 28)

Although Rogers, Gunesekera, and Yang did not have access to study the Dana corporate culture as Swales and Rogers had, the authors still received indication that the 2004 statement was influenced by present company life. Specifically, a contact at Dana told the authors the following: "[The company's] leadership team had changed dramatically, starting with a new chairman and CEO. New leaders have brought different values and goals, and our culture is changing" (in Rogers, Gunesekera, & Yang, 2007, p. 22). For ESP teachers and students, one takeaway from these two studies of the Dana mission statements is that formal conventions of genres are not static but rather are shaped by evolving factors in the genre's contexts.

Individual experiences of genre users

In addition to shedding light on reasons behind genre forms, studying contexts also offers glimpses into speakers' and writers' experiences with using genres and what they find helpful, motivating, or challenging about doing so. Human genre users constitute part of any genre's contexts, and 'hearing' about their genre use practices can be useful for those, such as ESP students, learning similar genres and wondering how and why to engage with them.

One context study foregrounding individual genre experiences is that of Seloni (2014), who investigated a Columbian graduate student (Jacob) writing within the difficult academic genre of a master's thesis. Through interviews and email correspondence with Jacob, as well as analysis of his thesis notes, outlines, and drafts, Seloni learned of Jacob's personal composing processes. These processes helped Jacob meet the expectations of his U.S. master's program in visual culture, in part through allowing him to draw on linguistic and other resources from his Columbian background. One of these processes was a 'conceptual map' that Jacob created to organize his thesis content. Written on a large white poster, this map included Jacob's notes for his thesis chapters and incorporated both Spanish (his native language) and English. In an email message to Seloni, Jacob described his map's color-coded system for marking scholars' work and his own ideas for his thesis:

> Green is the theory I will be incorporating. These are the ideas and quotes I am borrowing from books and articles, and how they relate to one another [mainly in English]. Blue and black text is the ideas I'm going to put in my thesis [only in Spanish]. Ideas I have gathered and generated. Basically, these are my main arguments. And, red represents the relationships between texts, and how I am navigating the theory [both Spanish and English].
>
> (Seloni, 2014, p. 89; for a photograph of Jacob's map, see Seloni, p. 89)

As Seloni suggests, Jacob's genre use experiences are informative for both ESP teachers and their students. Specifically, they highlight benefits for ESP students of using "translingual" literacy practices (Seloni, p. 93), which draw on their multiple linguistic skills—including those of their first language—in order to guide their thinking and composing within complex, challenging genres.

Studying individual writers and speakers can also shed light on *why* they choose to participate in certain genres in the first place—particularly when they are not compelled to do so for an academic program or for a job. In such cases, the contextual forces guiding genre use may be more internal to the individual people and their personalities and passions. Swales (1998) considered such personal genre motivations in his study of professionals on the different floors of his building at the University of Michigan. In interviewing and observing the second floor University Herbarium researchers, Swales came to appreciate the fit of each researcher for particular genres. Tony, the Herbarium curator, for instance, had the "bonhomie," "infectious enthusiasm," and "resonant voice" that made him a natural for the public lectures he gave to various organizations (p. 95). A passion for plant names, on the other hand, motivated Ed, another of the Herbarium botanists, to work on an extensive plant nomenclature code book and to write letters to newspapers correcting their "[plant] misidentifications and/or nomenclatural errors" (p. 123).

On the third floor, which housed the English Language Institute, Swales found that his colleague Joan Morley's genre choices were similarly shaped by personal conviction. In an interview with Swales, Joan suggested that her professional writing, which had tended not to include critically evaluative genres, reflected her non-antagonistic nature. As she told Swales, "[I]t isn't worth my time to trash something ... the thing is I'm *not* is a criticizer, and that's probably part of the reason I don't like to do [book] reviews" (Swales, 1998, p. 148, italics original). Instead, her primary body of work included ESL pronunciation and listening textbooks as well as literature reviews and plenary addresses. Joan's professional values also influenced her style of writing in these texts. Swales observed this style to be quite technical and ordered, characterized by lists, charts, and clear explanations, and "keyed to [Joan's] long-standing concerns about the slow development of professional standards in her field and her concern to establish a professional rhetoric" (Swales, 1998, p. 158).

Other genres in the context

Beyond its institutional setting and human users, a genre's context also involves the other genres with which it interfaces, or what Bazerman (1994) refers to as its *system of genres*: "interrelated genres that interact with each other in specific settings" (p. 97). When these systems involve a sequenced set of genres, they have also been called *genre chains*, whereby "one genre is a necessary antecedent for another" (Swales, 2004, p. 18). Most genres you can think of are part of a chained system: A hotel email confirmation follows a phone reservation, which was triggered by a promotional flyer; a safety inspector's report precedes a building permit application that is then submitted with a loan application; a conference's call for papers generates paper abstracts, which then lead to acceptance and rejection notices. Understanding a genre's context, therefore, includes awareness of other texts in the system and the roles the genre plays in relation to them.

One study illuminating a genre system context is that of Tardy (2003), who studied the chain of genres surrounding research grant proposals. In the research funding system, the grant proposal itself is the "core" genre; however, Tardy points out that "grant writers do not and cannot just write a grant" but rather must engage with other texts in the system that "respond to, incorporate, and necessitate one another" (p. 25). From studying these texts and interviewing two experienced science grant writers (a.k.a. Principal Investigators, or PIs), Tardy identified a sequenced genre system for grant funding, which I have summarized in the list below. As you will see, some genres in this chain precede and others follow the core grant proposal genre (italicized).

Genre system of grant funding

- Principal Investigator's (PI) networking conversations with colleagues
- Funding agency's mission statement
- PI's conversation(s) with Program Officer (PO) of funding agency
- Grant-writing support services at the PI's university:

  - Grant-writing workshops
  - Guidelines and tips for writing grants

- PI's application to use human subjects, submitted to Institutional Review Board
- *PI's grant proposal to the funding agency*
- PO's selection of referees to review PI's grant to the funding agency
- Referees' reviews of PI's grant and notification of funding decision
                                (Summary based on Tardy's 2003 analysis)

Particularly interesting in this system is the fact that the written grant proposal depends on several key spoken genres in the context. For example, before completing the proposal, the PI has networking conversations with colleagues who may help him/her find grant funding. One such crucial conversation is with the Program Officer (PO) of a potential funding agency; here, the PI explains the research project to the PO, which may then lead the PO to promote the proposal to the agency. Skipping this spoken genre can stop the chain in its tracks. As one of the two grant writers that Tardy interviewed said: "Everyone says talk to a program officer before even thinking about writing a proposal ... In two of the three [grants] that were not funded, I failed in [this step]. I should have spoken to a program officer, and did not" (interview comment in Tardy, 2003, p. 18).

One sign that a genre like a grant proposal is embedded in a genre system is that it includes concrete "intertextual links" to other texts in the context (Tardy, 2003, p. 23). As Berkenkotter (2001) puts it, these links demonstrate that "texts we see in a genre system are responsive to, refer to, index, or anticipate other texts" (p. 330). Berkenkotter observed such intertextual referencing in the genre system of psychotherapy paperwork. One psychotherapist's notes on a client interview, for example, were shaped by diagnostic concepts in the *DSM IV*, the standard professional manual on mental health disorders (p. 337). As well, details from the psychotherapist's notes could show up in later genres in the client's file like the treatment plan and the termination summary. Participating in a genre, therefore, whether it be like these professional ones or others for different settings, requires not only learning that particular genre as a stand-alone entity but also developing awareness of how it relates intertextually with other genres in its context.

Task 4.2 asks you to think about a genre in terms of the genre system in which it participates.

Task 4.2 Outlining a genre system

1   Select one of the genres below and draw a box around it in the middle a piece of paper.

   a   Course syllabus
   b   Phone call to customer service hotline
   c   Letter of recommendation for graduate school
   d   Marriage announcement
   e   Newspaper editorial
   f   Work visa application
   g   (Another genre you are interested in)

2   Next, outline the genre chain (or a partial one) in which your selected genre participates. Do this by using arrows to connect the names of genres that precede and feed into your selected genre (and into each other), and those that follow your genre.

3   What intertextual links exist between genres in the system you have outlined? That is, how do the different genres in your system reference each other. Give concrete examples.

Impact of genres on their contexts

Although genre context studies often focus on how genres are shaped *by* their contexts, they can also illuminate an inverse relationship: how genres influence their contexts. This latter orientation has been central to Rhetorical Genre Studies (RGS), with its emphasis on the social actions that genres produce in their settings (Bawarshi & Reiff, 2010; Miller, 1984; see also Chapter 1). A social-action focus should also be important in ESP. For it highlights for researchers, teachers, and students that genres are not merely forms you need to master to 'get through' a course or work project, but are indeed mechanisms for *doing* things with consequences in the world. These actions that genres produce may impact large contexts such as whole industries, disciplines, and even countries; or their reach may be narrower, though still powerful, affecting smaller communities or individual genre users or recipients. The consequences of these actions for their contexts may be positive, negative, or both—potentially benefiting some and not others.

To take one example genre with far-reaching social effects, consider political speeches. These texts have incited and ended wars, inspired political movements, changed public perceptions, and created leaders. Barack Obama's electrifying keynote address at the 2004 Democratic National Convention is one instance of a world-changing speech. It changed him from a relatively unknown senator from Illinois into an overnight national star and paved the way for his first presidential run and election as U.S. president. (To watch an excerpt from and commentary on this pivotal speech, see www.youtube. com/watch?v=OFPwDe22CoY&t=112s.) Genres can also impact more localized political structures, as Winsor (2000) found in her study of a "work order" genre at an agricultural equipment company. These orders were produced by the company's engineers and led to the company's technicians performing work. However, the orders did not include a means to recognize the technicians' creative problem-solving in implementing the engineers' directives. As Winsor noted through her field observations and interviews with company employees, "much of the knowledge-generating work that is unique to the technicians vanishes, and only the engineer's planning seems to remain" (p. 176). In this way, this genre did the "political work" of maintaining power hierarchies at the company and of influencing perceptions of company activity (p. 180).

Other context investigations reveal personal effects genres have on individual users. Collin (2014) observed such effects in his study of a U.S. secondary school's Amnesty International club, where members spent part of their weekly club meetings writing texts known as "Urgent Action Letters" (UAL). Composing within this genre, Collin discovered, led the students to internalize the concerns and passions of human rights activists. This identity reshaping came about in part as students borrowed language from another Amnesty International genre, Urgent Action Calls, which served as prompts for the letters. The students adapted this language into their own first-person voice. In the following excerpt, for example, we see how one student, Danielle, incorporates phrases from a UAC regarding the safety of a Bangladeshi social activist within her letter to the Bangladesh State Minister for Women and Children's Affairs. The italicized portions indicate the language Danielle borrowed from the UAC.

> Dr. Shirin Sharmin Chaudhury [Bangladesh State Minister for Women and Children's Affairs]
>
> Although I am pleased with your response regarding the protection of Shampa Goswami, I am imploring you to take all possible measures to insure her safety. I am also urging *you to ensure that a thorough, independent and impartial investigation into the harassment of Shampa Goswami is launched immediately and those found responsible are brought to justice in proceedings which meet international fair trial standards* ...
>
> (From Collin, 2014, p. 29)

Collin points out that the passion for human rights seen in Danielle's and other students' letters were not necessarily what led them to the club. Several students, for example, had joined the club for "strategic reasons" such as to build their résumés or to socialize with friends (p. 26). The fact that they later became committed to social activism through their UAL writing suggests that using a genre (and its language) has the power to change one's personal identity and sense of purpose. Indeed, from his observations of these students and their letters, Collin concluded that "emotional investment in social justice," in fact, "may be a *product* of engaging in activist literacy" (p. 26, italics original)—and in activist genres like the UAL.

As this study suggests, genres can have profound personal effects on their participants. And, as Schryer et al. (2012) discovered, these effects can even occur at the end of life. They examined *dignity interviews*, a therapeutic genre in which clinicians prompt dying patients to recount their most important life events and accomplishments, and to share messages to their loved ones. Questions from the dignity interview protocol include the following:

Are there specific things that you would want your family to know about you, and are there particular things you would want them to remember?

What are the most important roles (e.g., family, vocational, community service) that you have played in life?

Why were they so important to you, and what do you think you accomplished in those roles?

What are your hopes and dreams for your loved ones?

What have you learned about life that you would want to pass along to others?

(For complete dignity interview protocol,
see Schryer et al., 2012, p. 136)

The interviews are transcribed and read to the patients, who can request revisions before the transcript is finalized into another genre, a "legacy document," that is given back to the patient (p. 112). Studying 12 such legacy documents, Schryer et al. found that the dignity interviews had allowed patients "to create a sense of discursive order out of their life events" (p. 132), as reflected in excerpts from legacy documents below.

I think I've lived a really full life. I've had a lot of, probably difficult experiences, in that I was a caregiver at a very early age to a sick mother... I've got three great kids and they're just so supportive in this. They're knocking themselves out to be here for me.

I actually feel pretty alive now, ironically, but I think that's just wisdom ... Your perspective changes when you're facing death, so I think you do see things differently and time is of essence and you appreciate things more ...

(Excerpts from examples in Schryer et al., 2012, pp. 128, 130)

In sum then, studying the actions of genres reminds us (and our students) of their power to transform their contexts and the people in them.

How to study genre contexts

Thus far, we have considered the value of studying genre contexts. The second half of this chapter focuses on how to actually do a context study. It begins with a brief conceptual overview of ethnographic and textographic approaches to investigating contexts, followed by specific guidance on how to collect and analyze data in these approaches. The chapter concludes by considering 'critical ethnography' as an approach for studying power dynamics in genre contexts.

Ethnography and textography

Ethnography encompasses a number of research processes for examining social contexts. Although ethnography's origins are in cultural anthropology, its methods have been used in various fields, including ESP genre studies (Dressen-Hammouda, 2013; Hyland, 2006; Lillis, 2008; Paltridge & Starfield, 2016; Paltridge, Starfield & Tardy, 2016; Smart, 2012). One of the defining features of ethnography is its attention to *emic*, i.e., insider, perspectives, of those who live or work in the context being studied. To elicit these perspectives, ethnographic studies employ *qualitative* methods of data collection, such as interviewing and observing context-insiders and examining texts and other artifacts from and about the community. The analysis of these data is also qualitative in that it seeks to understand "the nature of phenomena" (DeWalt & DeWalt, 2011, p. 2) through close reading of the data for themes. Another characteristic of ethnographies is that they are carried out over extended time periods so that the researcher can gain the context-insiders' trust, elicit their viewpoints, and develop deep insights into the context.

Truth be told, there are few ESP genre context studies that are ethnographies in the strict sense. A major reason for this is that an ethnography is extremely comprehensive and time-consuming, involving not only multiple qualitative data sources but also long-term investigation of the context with multiple, repeated data collection points along the way. To give you an idea of the scope of an ethnography, consider Lillis and Curry's (2010) study of 50 researchers in Slovakia, Hungary, Spain, and Portugal. Over a period of eight years(!), Lillis and Curry collected 50 literacy history interviews with the scholars, 208 other interviews, 1,192 of the scholars' texts, approximately 2,000 email exchanges, 500 pieces of written correspondence between the scholars, colleagues, reviewers, and editors; observations and field notes from 60 site visits, and various institutional and national policy documents.

This tremendous amount of data formed the basis of Lillis and Curry's ethnography of the scholars' research writing contexts. Many ESP scholars, however, may not have the time or desire to complete genre context studies of that scale. Thus, rather than full-fledged ethnography, they may engage in what Swales (1998) has called *textography*, an approach that incorporates ethnographic methods to study a genre's context but with a restricted scope and time frame. As Swales (1998) describes it, textography is "something more than a disembodied textual or discoursal analysis, but something less than a full ethnographic account" (p. 1). Also, the *text* in textography signifies a continued strong emphasis on analyzing textual patterns (as is characteristic of ESP), with the context analysis illuminating forces shaping and being shaped by these textual features (see Paltridge, 2008; Starfield, Paltridge & Ravelli, 2014, for further discussion of textography).

Swales' examination of the three floors of his office building, described earlier in this chapter, was a textography. For it, he drew on a site study of the building (both its past history and current practices), interviews with seven of the building's inhabitants, analyses of their publications, and consideration of their feedback on Swales' emerging interpretations. Thus, as in ethnographies, emic perspectives were gathered via observations, interviews, and historical research, yet ESP-style textual analysis of the participants' genres still remained important. In addition, the scope of Swales' study, while not small, was modest, focusing on the textual lives of seven key members of the building. The next section describes several ethnographic-textographic methods for studying genre contexts and guidance on how to apply them.

Collecting qualitative data

Interviews

Interviews are among the most common means of collecting qualitative data. They work well for ethnographies or textographies because they directly elicit perspectives on the text or context being studied. They can also be adjusted for how controlled or flexible they are, depending on your study's design. There are, for example, *structured interviews*, where the researcher asks the exact same questions to all of his/her interviewees, making it possible to systematically compare each answer across the participants. *Unstructured interviews*, on the other hand, are like open-ended conversations guided only by a loose plan that the interviewer may or may not follow (DeWalt & DeWalt, 2011; Tracy, 2013). This low-control-type interview may work if you are not concerned with response comparability or if you have an opportunity to interview your participant(s) more than once. In many qualitative studies, including those of genre contexts, interviews are often *semi-structured*, having a set of prepared questions to guide the interview and ensure some consistency, but with room for the researcher to spontaneously go off-script in order to explore something of interest that emerges during the interview.

To help ensure that your interviews generate useful information for your context study, it is critical that you spend time carefully planning your questions. The following are some tips for designing effective interview questions, synthesized from advice from DeWalt and DeWalt (2011), Tracy (2013), and others.

1   Think about what you want to find out from your interviewees. If you are studying the context of newspaper editorials, for instance, you might be interested in how the opinion page staff decides on its editorial topics; the processes their writers use to compose the editorials; the kinds of responses they receive from readers; and any impact the editorials have on public policy. Once you have an idea of what you would like to find out, focus your interview questions on these aspects, using the tips below to make sure they elicit the desired content.

2   As a general rule, keep the bulk of your interview questions *open-ended*. Unlike close-ended yes-no questions, open-ended queries, such as *How does your staff decide on the focuses of your editorials on any given day?*, invite extended answers that may even take the interview in unexpected (though fruitful) directions. If you do ask a close-ended question, plan to follow it up immediately with an open-ended tag question like *Why? How? In what ways? Can you tell me more about that?*

3   Avoid *leading questions* that assume particular answers, such as *Your company newsletter probably improves employee morale, doesn't it?*, *What are the biggest problems the hourly workers at this company have with the management?*, or *Which of these factors most shape the content of your lectures—current events, upcoming exams, or your own mood?* These leading questions pigeonhole your interviewees into answering a certain way and thus may not elicit their emic insights into the phenomena at hand. To be more neutral and open, these bad-example questions could be reworded along the lines of *To what extent has your company newsletter affected employee morale?*, *How would you describe the relationship between management and hourly employees?*, *What determines the content you select for your lectures?*

4   Avoid *double-barreled questions*. These are questions that actually contain two or more questions posing as one and ask interviewees to respond to both at once, such as this question: *To what extent is this grant proposal thoroughly developed and appealing to the grant funding agency?* Faced with a multi-faceted question, your interviewee may only answer one part of it. So it is better to split such questions into separate ones.

5   Use clear, simple language and avoid scholarly jargon. If you ask questions like *What rhetorical moves are obligatory in your sermons?*, *How do these lexicogrammatical features reflect your discourse community's values?*, or *Tell me about your translingual literacy practices?*, your interviewee (who is not likely a genre analyst, applied linguist, or anthropologist) will be confused, intimidated, or annoyed by your high-flown language. More accessible versions of these questions would be *What sorts of things do you usually include in your sermons?*, *I notice*

that the phrase "global solutions" occurs a lot in your company's mission statement. Can you speculate on why this might be?, and *You said that you use both English and Korean when you take notes in your graduate classes. Tell me more about why you do that.*

6   Start off your interview with an easy, inviting question to establish a comfortable rapport with your interviewee. For example, *Why did you decide to study nursing? How long have you been reviewing abstracts for this conference? When was your company founded?* Please note that even before this opening question, you may need to explain your study and get your participants' consent to be interviewed. (See more on this in the section below on getting permission to conduct your research.)

7   Special question types. For your interview, you can consider asking some of the following question types described by Tracy (2013), which are particularly useful for eliciting interesting responses from your interviewees.

   a   Tour questions. Ask your interviewee to give you a "tour" of an event or setting. For example, *Can you describe a typical work day for you?* or *Tell me about the steps you go through when writing a legal brief.*

   b   Posing the ideal. Your participants here can describe their vision of a perfect activity, genre, or situation. For example, *What does a perfect conference abstract contain?*, *Describe to me an ideal meeting between you and a client*, and *What are the best types of reader responses to your editorials?*

   c   Motives questions. You may be interested in finding out your participants' reasons for their or others' choices or preferences, for example, *You said earlier that you like giving public lectures; why is that?*

   d   Elicitation questions. One good way to get at your participants' impressions is to present them with an example of something you are interested in (e.g., a genre sample, a video, or an object of some kind, and have them comment on it). For example, *Here is your company's mission statement, which is posted online. What do you think is most important to notice about it?* or *I have here a short article describing your company's culture. Can you read it and tell me how accurate you think it is?*

8   Wrap up your interview with a 'catch-all' question like *Is there anything else you would like to say about X that we haven't covered?* or *Is there a question I should have asked but didn't?* This allows your participant a final chance to share information that may be useful to your study.

9   Close your interview by thanking your interviewee and, if applicable, letting him/her know when findings of your research will be available.

Task 4.3 Creating good interview questions

1   Based on what you have learned above about designing good interview questions, rewrite the following not-so-good questions.

   a   Are sales letters used in this business?
   b   What problems do you have with writing sales letters?
   c   How are sales letters and calls useful for generating new customers?
   d   Describe syntactic characteristics, including tense-aspect constructions, of the prototypical sales letter genre.

2   Select a written or spoken genre whose context you are interested in studying. Think of a type of person who regularly uses or evaluates that genre. Then write 5–10 interview questions you could ask this person about their experiences with that genre and/or the settings in which it is used. Keep in mind the tips for designing good questions discussed above, and try to use at least three of the special kinds of questions (e.g., tour question, posing the ideal, etc.).

3   Write a short reflection on what it was like writing these interview questions, including how easy or difficult it was and what you learned from doing it.

Observations

Another key qualitative method for studying contexts is the researcher's first-hand observations. By watching, listening to, and noticing key aspects of the setting, researchers familiarize themselves with the context. This kind of close observation helps generate what is known in ethnography as *thick description*, that is, "building up a detailed picture of places, people, and resources" that are significant in the context (Lillis, 2008, p. 367). In a genre-focused context study, researchers may observe such things as the physical sites where the genre is used and/or the behaviors of people participating in the genre. While investigating the publishing experiences of international scholars, for example, Lillis (2008) wrote the following thickly described observation of a research department in Eastern Europe:

It is a drab 1960s building with locked doors at ground floor entrance and second floor where the department is. Scrawled on the locked entrance door to the department in black felt pen is a large A (we heard the story later—how the department had battled to secure an A rather than a B grading for their research and the head of department had defiantly and delightedly scrawled the letter on the door). The corridor was dark—little natural light and no electric lights switched on (again later we heard they were saving on electricity bills given [the] small annual budget they had to work within). (Notes, July 2, 2001)

(From Lillis, 2008, p. 369)

Noticing these details of this site helped Lillis to establish "the impact of the relative scarcity of economic resources on scholarly writing in this eastern European institution" (p. 371).

Flowerdew and Wan (2010) also used observation to illuminate factors shaping tax audit reports in Hong Kong. Indeed, observations and interviews complemented their structural moves analysis and "proved invaluable in highlighting the true pedagogical needs of the aspirants to the [tax auditing] profession" (p. 90). Task 4.4 asks you to consider how Flowerdew and Wan's context observations shed light on skills required of writing audit reports.

Task 4.4 Observations of a genre context

During their study, Flowerdew and Wan (2010) observed an auditing team at work at a client site in Hong Kong. Read the following excerpts from their written observations and then answer the questions that follow:

> They seemed to be a relaxed, albeit tired group, but they immediately changed into business mode once the client's accountant came in at 10:15 am. The accountant and the auditors started off discussing the company at hand; who was who, the size of the business, profits and losses of the past few years, and the nature of the business. When the accountant left, the audit senior introduced a discussion of the assignment of tasks ... Each auditor took on a different section of the audit, i.e. the trainee and the audit senior took on the banking section, while the audit assistant worked on sales and expenses and the supervisor worked on fixed assets and debtors.
>
> The group then started to comb meticulously through stacks of invoices and company files, double-checking their investigation with the company's financial statements. Even though Chinese was being spoken, the documents were all in English. The auditors each had their own notebook computer; they moved from combing through a file or invoice (with pencil and ruler), to checking the company's financial statements, to inputting data into their own computers. Through this entire work process there was spoken communication between the auditors ... The auditors even left their seats at one time or another to ask the client's in-house accountant questions regarding a particular invoice or file. Spoken communication was in the form of asking and giving information, explaining, problem-solving and socializing.
>
> Throughout the visit to the company and observation of the audit, the observer was surprised by the number of technical English terms used by

the auditors. The following spoken English terms, mixed in with the Mandarin or Cantonese were noted down throughout the observation: open market value, external valuer, controlled entities, equity methods, assets, depreciate, and material misstatement ...

(Flowerdew & Wan, 2010, pp. 82–83)

1   What can be learned about writing an audit report from Flowerdew and Wan's contextual observations that could not be gleaned from a text analysis alone?
2   How could this information be useful for ESP teachers developing an English for Accountants class? For example, given Flowerdew and Wan's observations, what types of activities might teachers include when covering the audit report genre?

Participant observation

One category of observation that is a hallmark of ethnography is *participant observation*. Here "a researcher takes part in the daily activities, rituals, interactions, and events of a group of people" in order to develop a deep sense of the cultural context (DeWalt & DeWalt, 2011, p. 1). The famous Polish anthropologist Bronisław Malinowski, in his 1922 ethnography of the Trobriand people in Melanesia, argued the following about how participant observation facilitated contextual understanding:

> [I]t is good for the Ethnographer sometimes to put aside camera, note book and pencil, and to join in himself in what is going on. He can take part in the natives' games, he can follow them on their visits and walks, sit down and listen and share in their conversations ... Out of such plunges into the life of the natives—and I made them frequently not only for study's sake but because everyone needs human company—I have carried away a distinct feeling that their behaviour, their manner of being, in all sorts of tribal transactions, became more transparent and easily understandable than it had been before.
>
> (Malinowski 1922, pp. 21–22)

Sometimes it is not possible to immerse oneself in a community's activities, including their genre-oriented ones. In the case of the auditor report study, for example, it appears that Flowerdew and Wan were only able to participate peripherally by being in the same room as the auditors but not by actually doing the audits with them. In other situations, however, you might be able to take part more fully in the context's happenings. Van Willigen (1989), for instance, while studying aging adults in rural Kentucky, "spent time working on church renovation projects, visiting shut-ins and the sick, and attending Bible class," among other activities (p. 58). Starfield (2011) also, when observing South African undergraduates writing essays for a sociology course, immersed herself part-way in their academic activities by attending their weekly class lectures and tutorials.

Taking field notes on observations

In making context observations, of either the non-participant or participant variety, it is a good idea to take detailed notes that you can refer back to later. In ethnography, these are called *field notes*, taken while you are out observing 'in the field', and used not only to record things you literally see and hear, but also your interpretations of what is interesting or meaningful about them. While you are observing, you may only have time to make quick scratch notes or *jottings* about what you have noticed about the context (Emerson, Fretz, & Shaw, 2011). However, these should then be turned into complete sentences and paragraphs as soon as possible because "[t]he notes get 'cold' and detail is lost the longer the interval between jotting and writing" (DeWalt & DeWalt, 2011, p. 165). In these fuller field notes, it is important to include as many particulars about the context as you can remember, as well as your initial thoughts about them. These notes will help you greatly in your data analysis and writing phases, and you will be able to pull examples from them to illustrate patterns in your data.

In turning a jotting into a full description, you have a chance to reflect on and interpret context details that you might otherwise not notice. Field note composing also encourages a creative writing style that is sometimes missed in scholarly texts. Recall, for example, Lillis' vivid description of the "drab 1960s building" of the Eastern European research department. Indeed, interesting excerpts from 'thick' field notes can make an article or chapter fun to read (and to write). Task 4.5 gives you practice with writing your own notes.

Task 4.5 Writing field notes

1   Select a context you are interested in observing. This could be an everyday context like a city bus, a local park, or a restaurant; a workplace context such as a business meeting; or an academic context like a graduate seminar you are taking.

2   Select a time when you can observe an activity in that context, such as a conversation, ritual, game, or other occurrence, for at least 15 minutes. This could be an activity related to a genre you are interested in within that context.

3   While or soon after you observe the activity, write jottings of key details and words from the scene.

4   Within four hours, expand your jottings into a detailed field note of at least 300 words with complete sentences and paragraphs. Feel free to use a creative style in your notes.

5   Be ready to share what this field note experience was like for you.

Historical investigation

To understand a genre's context, it is also useful to study the context's history. Historical investigation may involve gathering documents from or about the context during a particular period of time as well as interviewing people familiar with the setting at different points in its history. In studying the mission statements of Dana Corporation and Honeywell, for example, Swales and Rogers (1995) researched the companies' leadership and visions over several decades, in part through past news articles and interviews with company leaders, and connected the companies' periods of stability or change to their mission statements' discourse. Starfield (2011) too, in her investigation of students' academic writing experiences at a South African university, examined archival texts on the student body demographics. She also collected data on "the university's response to apartheid and segregated education," as well as student newspapers and political pamphlets on campus during the year of her study (p. 180).

Gaining access to a context

If you are planning to study a genre context, you will need to gain access to it and get permission to study it. The most readily accessible contexts are probably ones that you already participate in and have the trust of the members. If you are interested in studying religious sermons' functions in your own church, for instance, you will likely be able to observe the weekly church sermons, interview your minister about them, and mine your church's archives for previous sermons. If you are not a member of the context, another option is to contact a friend or colleague who is. Flowerdew and Wan (2006), for example, report that one of them knew the senior account manager at the Hong Kong accounting firm where they were able to study tax computation letters. Alternatively, you could volunteer at the site in order to get your foot in the door for your research project. Mendoza-Denton (2008), for instance, was a volunteer tutor in a California secondary school where she studied Latina girl gangs and their members' cultural and linguistic practices, including their use of phonological and discoursal forms marking in-group membership.

If you have no such ready 'in' to your desired context, gaining access may still be possible. But you will need to get the permission of a context member who has authority to green-light your research or to connect you with someone who can. DeWalt and DeWalt (2011) recommend contacting the "gatekeepers" of the context (p. 42). In a school setting, these might be program directors or principals; in workplaces, managers or business owners; in non-profit groups, directors and so on. In studying farm worker communities in Mexico, DeWalt and DeWalt spoke with community leaders and then attended meetings of an agrarian reform organization where they presented their research project and asked for the community's consent to do it. In this process of gaining permission, you might also offer to contribute something, such as sharing your research results with the community. Winsor (2000), for instance, presented her findings about work order reports to the agricultural equipment company she had studied.

You may also need to gain official permission from your university or research institution to collect data on your context. Any data involving human participants, such as interviews, observations, or participants' texts (e.g., student essays or employee reports), usually requires *informed consent* given by your participants after they have been informed of your research project and of any risks or benefits of participating in it. Obtaining informed consent helps ensure that individuals in your study will not be harmed or exploited. Many universities have guidelines for what to include in informed consent, as well as an institutional review board or ethics committee that reviews your data collection procedures before you are allowed to carry out your study.

Analyzing qualitative data

Ethnographic data collection methods tend to generate lots of transcripts, notes, and other texts to sort through. Analyzing all of these data in terms of what they suggest about your genre context can be challenging (though also enjoyable). This next section describes several concepts in qualitative data analysis to guide you through this process: triangulation/crystallization of data, reading data for patterns, and integration of emic and etic interpretations.

Triangulation/crystallization of data

In ethnographic or textographic studies, the researcher typically gathers and compares data from several methods so as to gain a fuller sense of the context than would be possible from just a single data source. This analysis of data from multiple sources is what is known as *triangulation*, a process whereby you see whether a pattern is supported by more than one type of data; for example, do your interviews and observations *both* suggest that managers at a company have difficulty writing end-of-year progress reports? A related notion is *crystallization*, the idea that you can look at the same phenomenon from different angles, as through different sides of a crystal (Tracy, 2013). Departing from triangulation's focus on cross-validation across data sources, crystallization involves embracing various data points "even when they do not converge" (Tracy, 2013, p. 236). For example, the documents from a church archive may tell you one thing about the church's history, while interviews from church members may tell you another. Within a crystallization approach, this is okay. Differing data sources, even when contradictory, contribute to a "multi-faceted, more complicated, and therefore more credible picture of the context" (Tracy, 2013, p. 237). Triangulation and crystallization of data also contribute to the 'thick description' valued in ethnography.

An additional way to help triangulate or 'crystallizate' your data analysis is to check your impressions with insiders in the community you are studying—a process that has been called *participant verification* or *participant feedback* (Dressen-Hammouda, 2013; Flowerdew & Wan, 2010). Swales (1998) used such a process in his textography of the University Herbarium, asking Bill, the Herbarium director, for feedback on his (Swales') chapter drafts.

Reading and coding data for patterns

After or even while gathering data from various sources, qualitative researchers read and re-read their data looking for interesting *patterns* or *themes*. And as you did with genre moves (Chapter 2), they *code* their data in terms of these recurring patterns (DeWalt & DeWalt, 2011; Tracy, 2013). This coding can be done in a relatively informal way, such as by using colored pens to mark key themes in the data. If a researcher were studying the genre of nursing care plans in a hospital context, for example, s/he might mark in green everything in her data that addresses how this genre evolved in the hospital setting (code: evolution), blue for how the genre is currently used in the hospital (code: current uses), red for what parts of this genre nurses think are most important (code: important parts), and yellow for how this genre affects patients (code: impact on patients). The researcher could then look across his/her data from all of the sources—interview transcripts, field notes, historical documents, and so on—and find all of the sections s/he coded in yellow, for instance, and notice what triangulated or crystallizated patterns emerge around this theme of impact on patients. Also, as with coding moves, you may revise your initial codes in response to new patterns emerging during your research and writing processes.

Of potentially great help is software specifically designed for coding and analyzing qualitative data. Two such software programs are atlas.ti and NVivo, which allow you to assign codes to different parts of your data files and then easily pull up all parts of your data that you have assigned a particular code. For instance, taking our previous example of the nursing care plans, I could select the code "impact on patients" and all of the sections I marked with this code in field notes, interviews, and other data will appear in a list. This capability can save significant time in finding examples of particular patterns.

Interpreting patterns via emic and etic perspectives

As you identify patterns in your context data, you can draw on both emic (insider) and etic (outsider) perspectives to interpret what is meaningful in these patterns. Although it is emic views that are foregrounded in ethnography, outsider perspectives are also important because they illuminate what may not be noticed by insiders. If you invite a friend to your house for a holiday celebration, for instance, your friend may notice certain ways that your family members talk to each other at dinner (e.g., your brother always interrupts you) that you do not recognize because you are so used to these behaviors.

Smart (2006, 2012) also found in his ethnography of genres in the Bank of Canada that both emic and etic views helped him to interpret interviews he conducted with three senior economists at the Bank. In each of these interviews, the economist interviewed described the Bank as "steering the economy on a course into the future, towards a particular goal" (2012, p. 154). Smart then related this emic view of the bank's economists to an outside (etic) concept of 'activity system', which he was familiar with as a discourse scholar and which emphasizes, in part, the role of collaboration among people and activities in service to common goals. Of particular use was a paper Smart had read on the activity system of ship navigation, whereby crew members work collaboratively gathering information about the ship's bearings in order to steer toward the harbor. This activity system concept and ship example, in tandem with the insider economist interviews, allowed Smart to see more clearly how the Bank of Canada's economists work together in a collabortive activity system, taking 'sightings' of the nation's economy, using genres to interpret those sightings, and, as such, helping to put the Canadian economy on a particular course. In your own studies of genre contexts in which you are not an insider, you may also find that your particular background knowledge and experience offer you etic insights into the situation that complement those of the insider members.

Critical ethnography

For this last section of the chapter, we consider *critical ethnography*, an approach to studying contexts that includes special attention to power dynamics and power inequities. Critical ethnography employs the same qualitative methods described above (interviews, observations, and so on) but does so not only to describe contexts but also to *critique* those aspects of contexts that empower some participants while oppressing others (Madison, 2012; Starfield, 2011). In this way, it brings a social justice orientation to its research focuses. As Madison (2012) writes, critical ethnography "begins with an ethical responsibility to address processes of unfairness or injustice within a particular *lived* domain" (p. 5, italics original).

In ESP, critical ethnographies of genre contexts have not been common, a fact that is consistent with ESP's reputation of being more 'pragmatic' than critical in its orientation to genre analysis and genre-based teaching (see Chapter 5). But there have been a few critically focused ESP context studies. Lillis and Curry (2010), for example, examined working conditions that negatively impact the production of RAs by scholars in non-English-medium countries. These conditions include cultural prejudices the scholars face when trying to publish their articles in international journals. Starfield (2011) as well investigated racial prejudices restricting black undergraduates' chances of success in writing academic essays at a previously all-white South African university. Her various sources of qualitative data revealed that within the dominant discourses at the university, black non-native English-speaking students were assumed to be "non-legitimate 'foreigners'" who were incapable of getting above the minimum 50 percent passing mark on their essays (pp. 182–183). In addition, Starfield found that students' personal life experiences were devalued by the faculty for whom they were writing. In her role as a critical ethnographer, Starfield not only raised awareness of these power dynamics but also made recommendations for changing such dynamics in this and similar settings. She writes that for those students "who feel particularly 'foreign,' we need to find ways to listen to what they bring and enable them to access the knowledges and skills that universities offer while not feeling they need to lose what they bring with them" (pp. 190–191). Thus, in critical ethnographies, including those in these ESP genre contexts, the researcher is not only a descriptive observer of a context's power issues and but also often an advocate for the context's participants.

Task 4.6 Genre context study

This task asks you to draw on some of the chapter's concepts in planning your own context study. Complete either Option A or Option B.

Option A: planning a genre context textography

1   Think of a genre you are interested in studying *and* the context where that genre functions: for example, a university course, a business, a health clinic, a community center, a government office, or some other context.
2   What have you noticed about the textual features (e.g., structural moves and lexicographical elements) of this genre?
3   What would you like to find out about the genre's context (or the context's human members) that could help you understand the genre, its textual features, uses, and/or the impact on its users?
4   What qualitative methods could you use to collect data to help you find this out?

5   Select one of the people from the context whom you might interview. What questions would you ask him or her about the context?

6   What opportunities would you have to engage in participant or non-participant observations of the context?

7   What other data would you like to collect about the genre to give you emic (insider) perspectives on how it operates?

8   How do you imagine that your data might triangulate or crystallizate around certain patterns?

Option B: planning a critical textography

1   Think of a genre you are interested in studying *and* the context where that genre functions: for example, a university course, a business, a health clinic, a community center, a government office, or some other context.

2   Who has power in that context? (It could be more than one type of participant)

3   What genres are influenced by the power relationships in that context? (For example, do the more powerful participants establish standards for a particular genre? Are those with less power able to participate fully and successfully in the genre, or not?)

4   To what extent do the ways that the genre is used and evaluated in that context serve (or not) the interests of those with less power in the context?

5   Whom would you interview or observe in that context to explore its power dynamics and how they have evolved over time?

6   How comfortable or uncomfortable would you be with doing a study where your goals are to critique the context's power dynamics and be an advocate for those affected by them?

This chapter has considered what studying contexts reveals about genres, including reasons behind their textual features, individuals' motivations and strategies for participating in them, their relationships to other genres, their effects on their contexts, and—particularly in critical ethnographies—their connection to power issues in the context. You also learned about several qualitative methods for conducting ethnographies and textographies of contexts.

This chapter wraps up Part II of the book, on ESP genre analysis. Part III now turns to applications of genre analysis for ESP genre-based teaching and genre learning.

Part III

ESP genre-based learning and teaching

Part III of this book explores genre-based teaching and student learning in ESP contexts. As you will see in the next few chapters, much ESP instruction asks students to analyze genre moves, lexicogrammar, and contexts, with the goal of helping them become more conscious and effective genre users. Thus, the genre analysis techniques you learned in the Part II will be important touchstones for the teaching applications in the upcoming chapters. Chapter 5 begins by reviewing research on the usefulness of genre-based teaching. It then addresses considerations involved in designing an ESP genre-based course, including needs and rights analysis, the role of critical pedagogy, and overall course structures. Chapter 6 turns to more micro-aspects of genre-based teaching, focusing on how to select and/or create texts and classroom activities that promote genre learning. Chapter 7, the final chapter, looks to future domains for ESP genre research and teaching, including the study of playful genres and ways this may help students learn to adaptively transfer their genre knowledge to new situations. As in Part II, these next chapters provide you with multiple opportunities to practice implementing the concepts discussed.

Chapter 5

Designing genre-based courses

This chapter focuses on how to design a genre-based course. With the term *genre-based*, I refer to instruction that explicitly attends to genre concepts and genre analysis in order to help students become more effective genre participants in their target contexts. The chapter begins by considering evidence that such instruction facilitates students' genre learning. It then turns to processes of creating a genre-based course, including analysis of students' 'needs' and 'rights' and consideration of how 'wide-angle', 'narrow-angle', and/or 'critical' a course may be. The latter portion of the chapter explores four genre-based course designs (genre-focused, theme-focused, project-focused, and site-focused) and ways that each can address course goals and student interests.

The role of instruction in genre learning

Although studies assessing the impact of genre-based instruction on student learning have been relatively few (Cheng 2006), available research indicates that such teaching can enhance learning. Tardy (2006), in fact, in her extensive review of genre learning scholarship, identified classroom instruction as one of multiple factors that builds students' genre knowledge and skills. Several studies published after Tardy's review also demonstrate that genre-based teaching improves students' performance in specific genres as well as their general rhetorical awareness of how genres work. I outline the findings of several of these investigations below.

Regarding specific genre performance, Pang (2002) found that students wrote better film reviews after receiving direct instruction about this genre. This positive effect was found across two groups of first-year Hong Kong undergraduates, one group receiving "textual analysis" instruction and the other group receiving "contextual awareness building" instruction (pp. 151–152). The textual analysis group analyzed moves, evaluative vocabulary, and verb tenses in sample film reviews, while the contextual awareness-building group examined the film reviews' purposes and audiences. Quality comparisons of the film reviews that students wrote pre- and post-instruction showed that *both* groups improved in their film review writing performance after the instruction, suggesting that linguistic- and context-oriented genre teaching can each be beneficial. Similarly, Yasuda (2011) discovered that in a Japanese college EFL course, genre analysis and production activities on the email genre led students to produce emails that were more appropriate, organized, and linguistically sophisticated than emails they wrote at the beginning of the course. Focusing on listening performance in the lecture genre, Zare and Keivanloo-Shahrestanaki (2017) also found that EFL course instruction regarding 'importance markers' in English-medium lectures improved the listening comprehension abilities of Iranian medical students.

Research also points to genre-based teaching's positive effects on students' overall rhetorical consciousness. Cheng (2007, 2008), for instance, in his study of a Chinese international student (Fengshen), observed that RA analysis tasks (in Cheng's EAP course) helped Fengshen to understand "influences of disciplinary practices on move patterns and the roles of voice, argument, and stance in academic writing" (2008, p. 65). In this way, as Fengshen indicated in his textual annotations and interviews with Cheng, the genre-based course led him to become a more "writerly reader" and "readerly writer," one who was able to reflect on why writers (including himself) make certain rhetorical choices (Cheng, 2008, p. 67; 2007, p. 304). Negretti and Kuteeva (2011) similarly observed that through comparison tasks on RA genre features, Swedish undergraduate ESP students developed "metacognitive awareness" of RA strategies, which they sometimes were able to apply to their own writing (p. 107). And in a Turkish university EFL course, Yayli (2011) found that textual analysis and production activities helped students to develop a conscious rhetorical orientation to various genres, even those not covered in the class. One of the students (Fatih), for example, remarked that the class instruction about purpose, context, and audience in email messages "was like a revolution to me ... I started to do all writings and readings with these new concepts in my mind" (p. 127).

These studies thus indicate that genre-based instruction can help students become skillful and aware genre participants. It is also important to acknowledge, however, that classroom teaching is necessarily only one contributor to students' genre learning. Indeed, 47 out of the 60 studies in Tardy's (2006) review examined ways that students gained genre knowledge in "natural (i.e., non-manipulated) settings," such as job and internship sites, or discipline-specific mentoring environments (p. 82). In these 'practice-based' contexts, as Tardy called them, several factors were crucial to students' genre learning, including intentional or unintentional exposure to genre models, practice using genres, and spoken interactions with expert genre users. In this reality, an ESP course would only be one of many elements that might shape students' genre development.

It is with such a measured, though still positive, outlook on genre-based teaching, that I turn now to how to put together a genre-based course, beginning first with needs analysis. Before going there, I would also like to note that most classroom learning studies have only assessed short-term effects of genre-based instruction on students, leaving their long-term impact largely unexplored (Henry & Roseberry, 1998; Tardy, 2006). This possible future area for ESP genre research is considered in Chapter 7.

Needs and rights analysis

Needs analysis has been a hallmark (and perhaps *the* hallmark) of ESP course design. It refers to the process of determining what English knowledge and skills students need and/or want to develop for their target contexts, and what they require to get there (Belcher, 2006; Brown, 2016; Dudley-Evans & St. John, 1998; Hutchinson & Waters, 1987). As Belcher (2006) writes, "It is probably no exaggeration to say that needs assessment is seen in ESP as the foundation on which all other decisions are, or should be, made" (p. 135). In keeping with this orientation, this next section approaches needs analysis as a first step in designing an ESP genre-based course. It begins by describing three categories of student needs discussed in ESP scholarship (target needs, learning needs, and rights), and then considers different methods for assessing them in terms of genre. This is followed by five examples of previous needs analyses that each illustrate a particular way of approaching this process.

Target needs

Target needs are the knowledge(s) and abilities—including those related to genres—required of students' target situations, such as their academic programs, workplaces, or everyday life contexts (Brown, 2016; Dudley-Evans & St. John, 1998; Hutchinson & Waters, 1987). Sometimes identifying these target needs or deciding which to foreground in an ESP course is challenging because different *stakeholders*—students, teachers, ESP program administrators, future employers, and others—may have divergent views on what genres or genre concepts are most important for students to know. For a group of architecture graduate students, for example, target needs might include an ability to perform within the spoken 'design critique', a genre common to architecture graduate programs (Swales et al., 2001). In a particular English for Architecture class, however, students might rather study, say, architecture research proposals because of a program requirement they need to pass. Or perhaps their ESP teacher prefers to focus on architecture lectures and on teaching students to analyze the moves of this genre because she has seen her students struggle with it. In a situation with such mixed perspectives, the ESP course designer might adopt what Brown (2016) calls a "democratic view of needs," taking into consideration what the "majorities of all stakeholder groups ... want, desire, expect" (p. 13). With this democratic approach, a needs analyst for the English for Architecture course could determine that *several* target genres warrant some attention in the course.

Learning needs

ESP needs analysis also takes into consideration students' *learning needs*, that is, the resources, processes, and activities needed for students to learn the target material (Brown, 2016; Dudley-Evans & St. John, 1998; Hutchinson & Waters, 1987). Among the first to emphasize a 'learning-centered' approach to ESP, Hutchison and Waters (1987) emphasize that "[w]e cannot simply 'assume' that describing and exemplifying what people do with language will enable someone to learn it" (p. 14). Rather, students may require particular conditions to grasp, retain, and apply the content presented in the classroom. To identify what these conditions are involves, as Brown (2016) points out, "examining issues like the selection and ordering of the course content," teaching methods and materials, and "the types of activities students will engage in" (p. 24). In our English for Architecture course, for instance, the ESP course designer might find students' learning needs to include opportunities to analyze the target genres; step-by-step guidance in composing within the target genres; interesting visual and audio materials; practice with presenting spoken design critiques; and activities involving fun and humor. And because each individual student connects with material in his/her own ways, learning needs for any ESP course can be quite diverse.

Things to consider

step-by-step guidance

ways to teach

Student rights

In addition to thinking about target and learning needs, some ESP researchers have emphasized that we ought as well to consider students' *rights*, a concept associated with *critical English for Academic Purposes (EAP)* (Belcher, 2006; Benesch, 2001a, 2001b; Helmer, 2013; Pennycook, 1997; Starfield, 2013). Like critical ethnographic approaches discussed in Chapter 4, critical EAP is concerned with power hierarchies and social justice, and, as such, seeks to help teachers and students not only to understand external target requirements but also to expose and push back against those requirements that hurt students. Within this framework, Benesch (2001a), a critical EAP proponent, has defined *rights* in terms of exploring students' potential to negotiate target expectations and to change those that do not serve their interests. As she states, "rights analysis allows for the possibility of challenging and transforming unreasonable and inequitable arrangements" (p. 108).

Benesch (2001a) describes how she attended to student rights in her own experience teaching an EAP writing course linked to an undergraduate psychology course. She learned from some students in her class that the psychology professor's lecture-heavy teaching approach was not conducive to their learning because they wanted more time to discuss the material. To help them assert these learning preferences, Benesch encouraged them to ask more questions during lectures (i.e., negotiating a right), which the students did, leading the class to become somewhat more participatory. Of course, in some contexts, target needs and expectations may make it difficult for students to assert a right that runs counter to these expectations or to try to meet them in unconventional ways. This tension between needs and rights is something that ESP practitioners wrestle with as they attempt to design courses that serve students' interests. Tardy (2009) acknowledges this tension in her own genre-based teaching, stating, "The biggest challenge that remains for me as a writing instructor has been to balance the need to help my students write in ways that are deemed appropriate and successful within various social groups with the need to help my students manipulate, break, and change genres and the power relationships embedded in them" (p. 282).

The next section describes methods for identifying students' needs and rights, both of which I include under the umbrella of needs analysis.

How to do a needs analysis for a genre-based course

To determine needs, it is important to collect data and not rely solely on your own or others' intuitions of what students need or want, which may be inaccurate (Long, 2005; Jasso-Aguilar, 2005). For a genre-based course, these data should ideally come from various stakeholders interested in the students' genre development, in order to ensure a balanced, triangulated, and/or crystallized (see Chapter 4) profile of students' needs and interests (Long, 2005). Table 5.1 lists a number of data collection methods that a genre-based course designer might use to identify students' target genre needs (i.e., what genres and aspects of these genres students need to or want to know), their learning needs, and their rights. In the section on rights, the focus is on gathering data that illumine the 'room' students have (or not) to resist aspects of the target genres, and the consequences for them and others of doing so. Also included in the table are possible measurements of students' *current knowledge*, which can help course designers decide what material is less relevant to cover (that is, if students already know it). For description of other needs analysis data sources, see Long (2005) and Brown (2016).

As you review the lists in this table, you may recall that you have practiced several of these methods, including text analyses, interviews, and observations, in Chapters 2, 3, and 4. In fact, assessing students' target genre needs, learning needs, and rights draws heavily on genre and context analysis techniques we have already covered.

Table 5.1 Some possible data for assessing students' genre needs and rights

Needs and rights	Data sources
Target genre needs	• Textual analysis of genres students need to know in their target contexts, including the genres' purposes, moves, and lexicogrammatical features • Interviews/surveys with expert informants (e.g., faculty and employers) about the genres in the target context and the functions they serve • Previously published findings on the target genres • Participant or non-participant observation of the target contexts and of uses of genres within these contexts • Interviews/surveys with students about what genres they are interested in learning and why
Current genre knowledge	• Written or spoken diagnostic tests related to the target genres • Role-plays measuring students' ability to perform target genres • Interviews/surveys with students about what they already know about the target or related genres • Interviews/surveys with faculty, employers, and previous instructors of the course about students' current genre knowledge
Classroom learning needs	• Interviews/surveys with students about their learning styles, instructional preferences, and class activities they enjoy • Journals students keep about learning from class tasks and which ones they value most • Observations of how students respond to different class activities and assignments • Interviews with past instructors about methods and activities students find engaging
Genre rights	• Analysis of variation allowed in the target genres across different exemplars and situations • Interviews with expert informants and instructors about openness to students departing from conventions of the target genres • Interviews with students about target genre features they feel comfortable participating in or resisting, and why

Examples of needs analysis

A number of ESP needs analyses illustrate ways of collecting and using data like those described in Table 5.1. I briefly describe five such analyses below, each of which has particular emphases, research methods, and outcomes that could apply to a needs analysis for a genre-based course. These five examples may give you ideas for doing a needs analysis of your own.

*Basturkmen (2010): identifying target and learning needs through
multiple methods*

In designing an English for Police course, Basturkmen (2010) and her colleagues conducted a multi-method, triangulated needs analysis of New Zealand police officers, many of whom were non-native English speakers. The researchers assessed the officers' target needs by interviewing a senior officer about genres the officers had to use, examining samples of those genres, and observing first-hand the officers' language use by doing 'ride-alongs' with them on their patrols. In addition, regarding their learning needs, the course developers gathered feedback from the officers about what language learning and teaching styles they preferred. They also ascertained the officers' current genre and general English knowledge through language proficiency tests and interviews with them. From these data, the course developers identified several facts that guided their priorities for the English for Police course:

- The police officers had to speak English in stressful situations and sometimes had difficulties with English pronunciation when speaking under pressure.
- They had not yet mastered particular features of written police genres. Junior officers, for example, often used vague language in reports that needed to be more precise, especially as these reports were used as evidence in court trials.
- In terms of their learning needs, although they had access to online lessons and individual tutorials, officers "showed a strong desire for a social form of learning" with face-to-face classes and a teacher.

(Basturkmen, 2010, p 77)

**Task 5.1 Analyzing a target police genre:
suspect description**

As noted above, Basturkmen and colleagues identified police officers' target needs in part by analyzing samples of genres the officers frequently used. She and her fellow ESP course designers compiled these samples within a "police language corpus," which they also later used in their English for Police course materials (Basturkmen, 2010, p. 77). This task gives you a chance to analyze one of the genres in the corpus, a *suspect description*, attending to what officers would need in order to perform this sort of text. Read the suspect description below and then answer the following questions.

> Male Caucasian 5 foot 10 inches. About 19 years old. Lean but muscley build. Blonde hair very short, maybe a number two style cut. Bright red

hooded sweatshirt with cut off sleeves with 'Players' across the chest in white writing. Dark blue jeans, scruffy looking torn at the bottom. Wearing black shoes possibly boots. Ethnic design tattoo on right lower arm.

(from Basturkmen, 2010, p. 79; I added
punctuation for ease of reading)

1   Assuming that this text is a good model of a suspect description, what would a police officer need to know about the order of moves for describing a suspect's appearance? For example, what is described first, second, and so on?

2   What kinds of vocabulary would officers need to learn for this genre?

3   What other sources of data would you use to check the accuracy of your answers to 1 and 2 and/or learn more about how suspect descriptions function in actual police work? In other words, how would you triangulate your textual observations with other sorts of data?

4   To what extent do you think police officers would have the 'right' to resist or challenge conventions of this genre? Explain your answer.

Louhiala-Salminen (2002): observing a day in the life of a genre user

Taking a different approach to needs analysis, Louhiala-Salminen (2002) observed one middle manager's discourse activities on a single day, in order to identify target needs of international business employees. Specifically, in this case study approach, she and her research team spent a day 'shadowing' a Finnish business manager ("Timo") in a multinational computer company to see how he and his colleagues used English and other languages in various daily communications (pp. 214, 216). They audio-recorded and took observation notes on Timo's interactions and phone calls, and collected the written texts he read or wrote during the day, all of which were email messages. They then interviewed Timo and other employees the next day to follow up on their observations. The researchers' Timo-tracking revealed that spoken and written genres were "totally intertwined" in Timo's communications. That is, "many of the phone calls were to confirm an issue in an e-mail message, e-mail messages referred to phone calls, and they were constantly discussed in face-to-face communications with colleagues" (p. 217). And amid their many textual interactions, employees frequently code-switched between English and Finnish (and sometimes Swedish). From this snapshot of one businessman's daily discourse behavior, Louhiala-Salminen was able to gain a sense of the multiple, intersecting texts business managers need to negotiate. She also concluded that the pace of daily business communications is rapid, with little time "to do outlining, planning, or drafting" (p. 226).

Downey Bartlett (2005): comparing authentic and inauthentic genre exemplars

Another way to identify target genre needs is by comparing real and false representations of them. Downey Bartlett (2005) offered such a comparison for a particular 'service encounter' genre that many people engage in on a regular basis: ordering coffee. She recorded, transcribed, and analyzed 168 real coffee orders at two cafés and one coffee cart, all in the U.S. She then contrasted these naturally occurring, authentic genre exemplars with fictitious food and beverage service encounters in ESL textbooks. Through this comparison, Downey Bartlett was able to pinpoint genre knowledge needed for performing a coffee order that was not reflected in the made-for-textbook dialogues. The following three service encounter examples from her study—the first from an ESL textbook, and the other two from her café recordings—illustrate several revealing differences between authentic and inauthentic food/drink orders; see if you can notice what they are.

Textbook service encounter (A is the server; B and C are customers)

A   What can I get for you?
B   I'd like a chicken sandwich and a cup of coffee, please.
C   I want a cheeseburger. Let's have some French fries.
B   Good idea
A   Would you like any dessert?
C   Let's have some apple pie.
B   Oh yes!

> (From Denman, 2000, p. 49, cited in Downey
> Bartlett, 2005, p. 333)

Naturally occurring service encounter 1 ((.) signifies a pause; S is the server; C is the customer)

S   Morning. What can I get for you?
C   Yeah good morning (.) yeah, can I get a—? Let's see (.) grande coffee of the day with whipped cream and your little small coffee.
S   The tall?
C   No the small
S   The short?
C   Yeah, the shortie
S   Grande and a short?
C   Exactly

Naturally occurring service encounter 2

S   Out of five. 6 cents is your change. Need your receipt?
C   Can I take one of your tuna salads?

S   Anything else?
C   No that'll do it. Thanks
S   That's gonna be 4.94
                              (Examples from Downey Bartlett, 2005, pp. 317 and 323)

As Downey Bartlett points out, and as the first example demonstrates, textbook food-ordering dialogues are often written in unrealistic language and (overly) complete sentences; real-life coffee orders, by contrast, contain "structural nonfluencies … (e.g., fillers and incomplete sentences)" and elliptical grammar, where the listener is expected to fill in the missing sentence parts (p. 329). In addition, in real orders (unlike in their textbook representations), the server often presents the customer with multiple alternatives to respond to. And it is worth noting in the second extract above that, within these alternatives, some 'everyday' vocabulary like *tall* and *short* have specialized meanings that novice coffee orderers may not know. Through contrasting these authentic text samples with more 'canned' textbook dialogues, therefore, Downey Bartlett is able to reveal a number of things that learners actually need to know in order to navigate their own coffee orders and possibly other food service encounter genres.

Benesch (2001a): assessing students' rights to resist genres

As noted earlier, ESP needs analysis may also include a focus on student rights. With a rights orientation, the researcher explores when and why students might challenge target genre demands, along with the consequences (positive or negative) of doing so. Benesch's (2001a) investigation of her EAP students' rights in the psychology lecture was accomplished through conversations with the professor and students, observations of the psychology class, and written assignments from her students. From these data, Benesch found that although the professor did not reduce his lecture coverage to accommodate more discussion time (as had been requested by the students), he allowed the students to ask questions during his lectures and overall seemed to appreciate their participation, telling Benesch that it created "a totally different atmosphere, in a positive direction" (Benesch, 2001a, p. 120). From a rights analysis perspective, Benesch showed that it was possible for these students, at least in a restricted way, to resist and change their roles in a target genre (academic lecture) in order to address their own interests. The experience of doing so, Benesch said, "may encourage [the students] to challenge other unfavorable situations inside and outside of classrooms" (p. 120). Rights analyses, of course, also have the potential to illuminate situations where resistance to target expectations is not met with openness and may in fact have negative repercussions for students.

Jasso-Aguilar (2005): going beyond a single stakeholder

This last example illustrates how a needs analysis can be designed to check or challenge a single stakeholder's beliefs about students' needs. Jasso-Aguilar (2005) succeeded in such a challenge through her study of maids in a Hawaiian hotel and their English language needs. The hotel's human resources department wanted to offer the maids an English course so that they could make small talk with the guests and show "the company's 'aloha', a strategy geared towards increasing business" (p. 149). Jasso-Aguilar, through triangulated data collection and analysis, found the hotel's perceptions of the maids' needs to be inaccurate. She conducted participant observation as a hotel maid herself and interviewed the maids and other hotel personnel. From these data, she determined that the maids did not in fact need to use English extensively with hotel guests, nor did they have many opportunities to do so. Rather, as she observed, "the job of day-shift housekeepers occurs in solitude ... By the time they go up to clean their rooms, most of the guests have left, and even encounters with the few guests still around do not require more language than short greetings" (p. 138).

Interestingly, the spoken genre where Jasso-Aguilar observed the maids needed English most was one that the hotel task force seems not to have identified: morning group briefings with the head maid. Because these briefings not only covered the maids' daily work assignments but also were a space where maids discussed their feelings about the job, they were "potentially very rich situations for language learning and language socialization" (p. 142). Jasso-Aguilar's multi-method analysis (including her own participant observation) painted a more accurate picture of the maids' English needs within particular genres. As well, it raised a caution against listening solely to an institutional stakeholder paying for the ESP course.

Task 5.2 Designing a needs analysis

This task gives you an opportunity to synthesize what you have learned so far about needs analysis through one of two options:

Option A: evaluating an existing needs/rights analysis

1   Find an ESP course of interest to you, such as a business English class, a speaking or writing class for a specific discipline or multiple disciplines, or other specialized English course at a workplace, university, secondary school, or community center. For ideas, see also Woodrow (2018).

2   Talk to the designers and/or teachers of that course and find out how they went about determining the topics, materials, and activities to include. Pay particular attention to methods they used for collecting information on students' needs and how that information guided their course design.

3   In terms of student rights, ask the course designers about the extent to which their students may question, resist, or change target genre conventions, and what the effects are of such resistance.

4   Write a paper evaluating how well it seems the course designers' analysis methods captured information about students' target genres, current genre knowledge, learning needs, and potential to innovate and resist within the target genres. Make specific recommendations for what other data the course designers could collect to enhance their analysis, and to check their intuitions about what the students need.

Option B: planning your own needs/rights analysis

1   Identify a type of ESP course that you would like to teach (e.g., English for business, writing for engineers, English for flight attendants, English for U.S. citizenship applications, or other specialized English course).

2   Write a paper describing and justifying the methods you would use to assess:

   a   the target genre knowledge required of the students;
   b   the students' current genre knowledge (i.e., what they already know about the target genres or ones similar to them);
   c   students' learning needs (i.e., types of teaching/learning styles and activities that will help them to learn the material);
   d   possible 'spaces' for students to question, resist, or change the target genres.

3   In writing your paper, consider how you might adapt some of the needs analysis methods used in the five example analyses discussed in this chapter. And be specific about how you would apply the methods (for example, which stakeholders you would interview, what questions you would ask, what texts you would collect, how you would analyze them, what situations you would observe, and so on.)

From needs analysis to course design

After gathering information about your students' needs and interests, you can begin to design your genre-based course. This next portion of the chapter turns to this design process, beginning with three questions that ESP teachers should consider in creating their courses: how narrowly or widely to focus the course, whether to promote critique of genres, and how to engage students' learning. The chapter then describes four genre-based course designs that respond to these questions and students' interests in varied ways.

How genre-specific should the course be?

Wide-angle vs. narrow-angle

A long-running question in ESP is how broad or narrow an ESP course should be (Basturkmen, 2010; Belcher, 2006; Bruce, 2005; Hyland, 2002, 2016a; Widdowson, 1983). *Wide-angle* courses focus on fairly general English skills, such as would be covered in a course on academic English, whereas *narrow-angle* courses are geared for students with specialized English language needs. If a needs analysis reveals that all of your students are in a nuclear physics doctoral program, then a narrow-angle course is likely the way to go. If, however, your students' target English goals are more varied or indeterminate, such as with undergraduates from different majors, then a broader focus may be more appropriate. How wide- or narrow-angle a course is will likely influence the teacher's choice of focal genres. An English for Nurses course, for example, might cover quite field-specific genres, such as care plans and medical history interviews, while in an undergraduate writing course for mixed majors, the teacher might focus on critique essays or multimedia research papers (among others) that involve rhetorical strategies common to various fields.

One argument in favor of a wide-angle course is that its content applies to a range of contexts where students may later find themselves. For academic contexts, however, Hyland (2002) strongly cautions that what we think of as common linguistic or discoursal features actually manifest quite differently in particular disciplines. Making the case for keeping the 'S' in ESP, Hyland argues that the notion of academic English "misleads learners into believing that they simply have to master a set of rules which can be transferred across fields" (p. 392). Students, he says, also need to understand how genre 'rules' are closely tied to beliefs, values, and knowledge-making practices of individual communities. But what about the mixed student group with a range of target needs? Here, Hyland suggests that students be assigned to contrast genres across their respective fields. In this way, a course maintains its specificity and relevance to each student's target needs, and at the same time, "[b]y making contact with those outside their field, students may more easily come to see that communication does not entail adherence to a set of universal rules but involves making rational choices based on the ways texts work in specific contexts" (p. 393). (See also discussion in Hyland, 2016a.)

Genre acquisition vs. genre awareness

Whether you adopt a broad or specific focus for your course depends as well on whether the goals for your students are aimed at *genre acquisition* or *genre awareness*, categories distinguished by RGS scholars Russell and Fisher (2009), and also taken up by some in ESP. The narrower of these two categories, genre acquisition, involves learning a specific genre so that you can recognize it and/or reproduce it according to its conventional forms and functions (Johns 2008, 2015b). The English for Police course described earlier (Basturkmen, 2010), for example, might help its students acquire several key police genres, such as the suspect description, and could assess their acquisition by how well they produce such texts in their police work. Genre awareness, on the other hand, involves more global knowledge *about* genres— that is, how they work in general terms, rather than skill in any one particular genre (Clark & Hernandez, 2011; Devitt, 2009, 2014; Johns, 2008, 2011). Task 5.3 below gives you an opportunity to think about what global genre awareness might encompass.

Task 5.3 Exploring genre awareness

Think back on what you have learned about genres and genre analysis in the first four chapters of this book, and do the following:

1   Make a list of general principles that apply to all (or at least most) genres. Think of this as "general facts about genres" list.
2   Discuss with a partner or write a brief reflection on how you could design a course that helps students develop awareness of these genre facts, and speculate on how such awareness would help them to figure out new genres in any field, workplace, or everyday situation.
3   Comment on whether an ESP course with genre awareness as its goal could be narrow-angle, wide-angle, or both.

In an ESP course, attention to genre acquisition or to genre awareness each has its benefits. Regarding acquisition, as students learn more genres, they are more likely to have relevant knowledge to draw upon in various contexts (Devitt, 2004, 2007). As Devitt (2007) points out, "Writers with fuller genre repertoires ... can move among different locations—with their different genres—more easily" (p. 222). In addition, knowing general principles about genres (e.g., that they have moves, vary across communities and individuals, and so on) and genre analysis strategies helps students approach unfamiliar genres in the future (Beaufort, 2007; Johns, 2008; Wardle, 2007). As Johns (2008) asserts, genre awareness offers individuals "rhetorical flexibility" to adapt their knowledge to "ever-evolving contexts" (p. 238). One genre-awareness curriculum aimed at this flexibility is Devitt, Reiff, and Bawarshi's (2004) undergraduate writing textbook, *Scenes of Writing: Strategies for Composing with Genres*. Throughout much of the book, the authors emphasize the following general guidelines (which I have listed below) for figuring out any genre and its relationship to its context.

1   Collect samples of the genre
2   Identify the scene and describe the situation in which the genre is used (e.g., its setting, topic, participants, purposes)
3   Identify and describe patterns in the genre's features (e.g., its content, rhetorical appeals, organization, grammar, words)
4   Analyze what these patterns reveal about the situation and scene (e.g., its values reflected in the features, and what participant roles are encouraged or discouraged)

(Condensed from Devitt, Reiff, & Bawarshi, 2004, pp. 93–94; for specific questions students consider in each of these steps, please see their book.)

Such a genre awareness curriculum is in some ways wide-angle, helping students to develop knowledge and strategies that are applicable across contexts. Yet it can also be narrow-angle in the specific genres selected to teach genre principles. Johns (2015b) and colleagues, for instance, developed a curriculum for secondary school students that focuses on the specific genre of college application essays—a very relevant genre for the students' target needs—yet the course also had broader genre sensitivity goals, including attention to audience and individual writer personas. Thus, in answer to the question we began this section with of *How specific should the course be?*, we might say that a genre-based ESP course can be both narrow and wide, acquisition-oriented and awareness-oriented, although it may lean further toward one end or the other of each of these two continua depending on teacher and student preferences.

How critical should the course be of its genres?

Another running question for at least some ESP practitioners is how critical the course should be of the genres that it teaches. Critical EAP, mentioned earlier in the section on rights, promotes curricula where students question and critique genres that do not serve students' interests academically, economically, politically, or otherwise, and/or that perpetuate unfair power hierarchies in universities or larger societies (Benesch, 1993, 1996, 2001a, 2009; Chun, 2009; Helmer, 2013; Morgan & Ramanathan, 2005; Pennycook, 1997; Starfield, 2013). As Benesch (2001a) writes, "In addition to preparing students for current and future academic assignments, a worthy but insufficient goal, [critical EAP] keeps open the possibility that students might view these assignments as unreasonable, poorly conceptualized, unclear and so on" (p. 61). Without allowing for critical views of academic discourses, argues Benesch (1993), traditional EAP approaches are problematically "accommodationist," endorsing "current power relations in academia and society" that may "limit the participation of nonnative-speaking students in academic culture" (pp. 711, 713). Similarly, Pennycook (1997) has linked traditional

EAP with "vulgar pragmatism" (p. 256, using a term from Cherryholmes, 1988), because it serves an efficiency-driven goal of helping students learn dominant genres without questioning the potentially damaging politics and ethics of this enterprise.

You might wonder what could possibly be harmful about acquiring status quo genres in academic disciplines or professions. Critical EAP scholars have pointed to several areas of concern. Pennycook (1997), for example, has suggested that teaching academic English is not a neutral enterprise, given that English "is deeply bound up with international capitalism and tourism" as well as "the spread of particular forms of culture", which serve the interests of some at the expense of others (p. 258). Or as Belcher (2006) notes, critical pedagogy experts may see conventional EAP "as a form of domination, supporting the spread of English, and thus strengthening, in EFL settings, the hold of the developed world on the less developed" (p. 143). At a more local level, critical EAP scholarship has considered ways that academic genres potentially marginalize students in their degree programs. Casanave (1995), for example, found that in a U.S. sociology graduate program, the research and theory paper assignments, as well as the professors' lectures, alienated the ethnic minority and international students, who felt that these texts did not prepare them to serve their own cultural communities. Outside of academic contexts as well, institutionalized genres have been critiqued for their diminishment of certain perspectives and realities. Devitt, Reiff, and Bawarshi (2004), for instance, observe that the Patient Medical History Form (PMHF), a prominent genre in the U.S. medical world, constructs patients and their illnesses in terms of only their physical symptoms, rather than also their emotional and mental states, and in doing so, "limits the extent to which [patients] can be treated" (p. 151).

Three views of critical pedagogy in genre-based courses

Although critical EAP scholarship has increased in prominence (see Starfield's 2013 review of the "critical turn" in ESP, p. 463), orientations to it have not been uniform. Below I outline three perspectives on critical pedagogy, citing the views of scholars under each. I would also like to emphasize, however, that individual researchers often occupy more than one position at different times or sometimes simultaneously depending on their teaching situation. Indeed, in designing your own genre-based course, you might find yourself interested in several of these stances.

VIEW 1: EMPOWERMENT THROUGH LEARNING (NOT RESISTING) GENRES

The default position of much ESP teaching has been fairly 'non-critical'. That is, ESP courses have focused mainly on helping students acquire target genres rather than on encouraging them to reflect on, be critical of, or resist genres that support oppressive hierarchies or have negative consequences for individuals or communities. Underlying this default view is a belief that, at least in academic and professional contexts, students are best served, and even empowered, through learning the standard genres of their future areas of study and work. In EAP, Santos (2001) has expressed a strong version of this view, writing, "I certainly find nothing ethically disgraceful in helping students accommodate to, or assimilate to, the dominant academic discourses because I regard this as essential for academic success" (p. 183). In supporting her position, Santos says that she has never heard of students wanting to take an "oppositional stance" to academic discourse, and therefore "it seems rather presumptuous to insist [such resistance] would be of much greater benefit to them" (p. 183). Reading through leading ESP journals, one gathers that Santos' perspective is shared, even if not explicitly stated as so, by many ESP researchers, given that their articles focus on explicating and teaching target genres without much critical reflection on the outcomes they enable.

VIEW 2: CRITICAL AWARENESS OF GENRES AND THEIR EFFECTS

Other ESP practitioners advocate raising students' awareness of the political effects (including negative ones) of genres, and at the same time letting students decide what to do with that critical awareness. Harwood and Hadley (2004) embrace such a view within what they call "Critical Pragmatic EAP" (p. 357). One way they enact this approach is through corpus-based lessons showing students the types of linguistic variation and norm-breaking that is possible in academic genres. Students then consider how they feel about either following or flouting genre norms and the consequences of doing so. These reflections may then help them decide on whether and when to assimilate or eschew mainstream discourse practices. Also taking a similar approach, some ESP and RGS practitioners suggest encouraging students to ask critically pointed questions of any genres that they encounter, such as *What types of communications does this genre facilitate or constrain?*, *Whom does this genre include or exclude from participation?*, *What values does it embody?*, *Whose interests does it serve?*, and *What actions does it make possible or make difficult?* (Devitt, Reiff, & Bawarshi, 2004; Devitt, 2014; Johns, 2011). Through such heuristics, students develop habits of mind for exploring the ethical consequences of genres, and can then decide what to do with the information they discover.

VIEW 3: RESISTING AND CHANGING GENRES AND THEIR CONTEXTS

On the most 'critical end' of the critical ESP spectrum are approaches that encourage students to resist and change genres that they perceive are harmful to themselves or to others (Benesch, 2001a, 2001b; Canagarajah, 2006;

Devitt, 2014; Pennycook, 1997; see also review by Starfield, 2013). In her undergraduate writing classes, Devitt (2014), for example, assigns students to write letters requesting revisions to institutionalized genres, including letters "to advertisers asking them to change their form of advertising, to newspapers asking them to allow more variation in wedding announcements, and to university officials asking them to change the depiction of their majors in brochures" (p. 156). While these actions, says Devitt, do not fully address "the complexity or reality of power in our worlds," they give students experience with challenging status quo genres, "creat[ing] an opening for students to realize that what has always been is not what must always be" (p. 156). In a similar vein, Canagarajah (2006) recommends encouraging students to consider how they might change textual conventions "to suit their interests, values, and identities" (p. 603).

Some ESP scholars, however, have cautioned that challenging genre norms is not always feasible for students. Grujicic-Alatriste (2013), for example, asserts that because genres "are supported by powerful interests," students may be limited in how much they can change "established forms" and may face negative consequences or even job loss when they try to exercise such changes (p. 462). RGS scholar Elizabeth Wardle (2009) also recommends that, in encouraging students to critique genres, university writing teachers should be careful that such critique is not itself stressful or confusing for students. She writes, "[T]o the extent [students] have the power and authority to change academic genres to better meet their needs, we should help them understand how to do so ... [But] we must be certain that our analytical genre work will help them succeed, not paralyze them with doubts" (p. 783).

Task 5.4 Defining your own view of critical EAP

1   Which of the three orientations toward critical genre pedagogy described above (and listed again below) resonate with you as a current or future teacher? Why?

- Empowerment through learning (not resisting) genres.
- Critical awareness of genres and their effects.
- Resisting and changing genres and their contexts.

2   Could you see yourself combining these perspectives in designing a genre-based course? Explain.

How can the course facilitate student learning?

Along with how wide or narrow, critical or accommodationist a genre-based course ought to be, a third key question for a course designer is what material will engage students and motivate them to learn. Indeed, the needs analysis process discussed earlier is a first step in addressing this question, helping the designer determine what genres students will find relevant for their goals. It is also important to keep in mind that just because some part of your course meets a target need, it will not necessarily inspire students to learn without also making the learning process engaging. As Hutchison and Waters (1987) put it plainly (p. 48),

> [I]f your students are not fired with burning enthusiasm by the obvious relevance of their ESP materials, remember that they are people not machines. The medicine of relevance may still need to be sweetened with the sugar of enjoyment, fun, creativity and a sense of achievement.

I briefly suggest here two ways to "sweeten" a genre-based course design to promote learning. One is to focus not only on target genres but also on non-target genres that add variety and entertainment while still illustrating important genre principles. In a narrow-angle class for, say, urban planning master's students, a teacher could weave in such genres as TED Talks, apartment advertisements, and online dating profiles to complement and even illuminate the more 'serious' urban planning genres in the course. (See also Johns' (1997, 2015a) recommendations for using 'homely' genres in EAP courses.) A related way to create a motivating course design is to give students a say in its structure (Belcher, 2006; Nation & Macalister, 2010). Yayli (2011), for example, collaborated with her Turkish university EAP undergraduate students to identify five genres of interest for her course: informational essays, argumentative essays, curriculum vitaes, email messages, and recipes. A *negotiated syllabus* (Nation & Macalister, 2010) like this can not only increase students' investment in learning in the course but also provide the teacher with ongoing feedback about students' preferences and learning needs—especially important given that "instructors are not always good judges of what will interest and motivate their own students" (Belcher, 2006, p. 139).

Four genre-based course designs

This next section presents four genre-based course designs and considers how each may address the design issues we have covered regarding students' needs and rights, wide and narrow course focuses, critical pedagogy, and student learning. Rather than strict templates, these four designs—*genre-focused, theme-focused, project-focused*, and *site-focused*—are flexible course-creation strategies that can be readily mixed and matched in a single course.

Genre-focused courses

Although all genre-based courses are in some ways *genre-focused*, I am using this label here for courses organized explicitly around specific genres.

This style of curriculum is seen, for instance, in Feak, Reinhart, and Rohlk's (2009) EAP speaking textbook *Academic Interactions: Communicating on Campus*. A number of their chapters center on and, in fact, are named after interactive academic genres that university students need to engage in— email messages, office hours meetings, classroom discussions, and panel presentations. A similar approach is seen in Gimenez's (2011) English for nursing textbook, *Writing for Nursing and Midwifery Students*, which has sections focused on such genres as care critiques, reflection papers, action plans, and research proposals. Shulman's (2006) *In Focus: Strategies for Business Writers* also has units with genre-centric titles like "The Concise Memorandum," "The Strategic Business Plan," and "The Professional Presentation."

In terms of specificity, a genre-focused course is, by definition, aimed at helping students acquire knowledge of and skill in specific genres. In this way it serves narrow-angle goals. At the same time, though, while teaching these specific genres, such a course can be wide-angle in building students' overall awareness of genres as means for achieving social actions. As Devitt (2014) points out, "Analyzing the contexts and features of a new genre provides an inroad to understanding all genres" (p. 152). Varied stances regarding critical pedagogy are also possible within a genre-focused course. An instructor, for example, may teach students to accommodate to particular target genre conventions, or s/he can take a more critical approach, raising ethical consciousness about certain genres and their effects. Or as illustrated in Feak, Reinhart, and Rohlk's (2009) *Academic Interactions* textbook, accommodationist and critical approaches can be combined. This book—pragmatically—familiarizes students with conventions of spoken academic genres, but at the same time it offers students strategies for asserting their interests within potentially marginalizing genres. In the unit on classroom discussions, for example, students learn verbal and non-verbal means of taking the floor even when it means interrupting the current speaker. As the authors advise students,

> You may need to be persistent in order to get a turn. If you always wait until there is a long pause, until someone takes a breath, or until you think someone has completely finished a sentence, you may never get a chance to speak.
>
> (Feak, Reinhart, & Rohlk, 2009, p. 160, underlining in original)

Task 5.5 Sequencing in a genre-focused course

In organizing a genre-focused course like those described above, the course designer must determine how to order the specific genres in the course. Hyland (2007) suggests several factors to consider in creating a course's genre sequence: 1) the urgency of the genres in terms of addressing students' needs, 2) the level of difficulty of the genres, and 3) the natural order in which the genres occur and interact in the real world.

This task gives you practice applying these considerations in ordering a set of genres for an ESP course. The course is for graduate students and focuses on the "supporting genres" of academic writing, as described in Swales and Feak's (2011) EAP writing textbook *Navigating Academia*. These supporting genres are often "occluded" (Swales, 1996). That is, they are "rarely part of the public record" and thus without available models, but are nonetheless important for academic careers (Swales, 1996, p. 46). Below is a list of a number of such genres that Swales and Feak cover in their book, but presented here in scrambled order.

- Responses to reviewers and editors
- Statements of purpose
- Email requests, reminders, and apologies to peers, advisors, and colleagues in the field
- Acknowledgements in journal articles, theses, or dissertations
- Article manuscript submissions to journals
- Curriculum vitae (CVs)
- Author biostatements in journal articles
- Job applications
- Personal statements (e.g., like those required for PhD program applications in the U.S.)
- Letters of recommendation (that one is asked to write for students or colleagues)
- Statements of teaching philosophy
- Small grant applications

1   Without looking at Swales and Feak's table of contents, list these genres in an order that would make sense in a course for graduate ESP students. Relate your order to one or more of Hyland's (2007) criteria for genre sequencing a) most-to-least urgently needed, b) least-to-most difficult, and c) natural ordering they occur with respect to each other. Justify why your sequence would work well for the course.

2   In their textbook, Swales and Feak group the genres above into several categories. How would you group these genres and what headings would you use for these categories?

3   If possible, after completing steps 1 and 2, look at the table of contents of Swales and Feak's book, and compare these authors' ordering and grouping with yours. Which do you like better and why?

4   Now think of another ESP course you would be interested in teaching. List the genres you could center the course around, and explain the order you would put them in and why.

Theme-focused courses

Another way to organize a genre-based course is around themes (Hyland, 2004b). In such a design, each course unit revolves around a particular topic, with genres, as well as other elements related to the topic, embedded along the way. One example of a theme-organized curriculum is Shawcross' (2011) *Flightpath*, an aviation English textbook for pilots and air traffic control officers. As reflected in a number of the chapter titles below, most of the book is structured around aviation-situation topics:

Ground movements
Runway incursions
Environmental threats
Decision making
Approach and landing incidents
Handling a technical malfunction

Within each of these, Shawcross' materials address topical issues the aviation specialist must deal with, along with "communicative functions" (p. 4) (including specific genres) needed in particular situations and language features linked with those functions. The chapter on the theme of environmental threats, for example, includes an exercise on aviation weather reports transmitted through the Automatic Terminal Information Service (ATIS). For this exercise, students have to listen to two examples of this genre, identify what information seems to be mandatory and optional (e.g., visibility, precipitation, temperature, dew point, wind velocity), and what order these informational moves occur in (although Shawcross does not explicitly refer to them as moves).

One benefit of such a theme-based design is that it readily accommodates multiple elements, including but not limited to genres. Shawcross' text, for instance, weaves in aviation genres amid information on aircraft-threatening conditions (e.g., windshear, icing, volcanic ash), aviation-related vocabulary exercises, and listening practice with air traffic control radio transmissions. Thus, for student groups who need coverage of topical content, language skills practice, and genres for a particular field or profession, a theme-based design offers a useful umbrella for all of these. Another advantage of this course type is its potential to motivate students with engaging themes. In my own undergraduate writing course for multilingual students, for example, I select topics that students find interesting and fun—such as romantic love—and in assignments on these topics, students gain experience with reading and composing in various genres. In one unit, for example, on the theme of biological perspectives on romance, students read popular and scholarly articles, watch a film portraying an arranged marriage (*The Namesake*, based on the novel by Jhumpa Lahiri), and listen to a radio broadcast on neurological love chemicals. They also write a "chemical love story" (a hybrid playful genre, which I describe more fully in Chapter 7) and an empirical-style research report on a love-related topic of their choice.

Besides allowing teachers the freedom to choose interesting topics and texts, a theme-based approach is flexible enough to promote narrow-angle genre acquisition, through practice with producing specific text types related to the theme, and/or wide-angle genre awareness. Indeed, a course's theme may even *be* genre awareness, as is reflected in some undergraduate writing textbooks like Wardle and Downs' (2017) *Writing about Writing* and Devitt, Reiff, and Bawarshi's (2014) *Scenes of Writing: Strategies for Composing with Genres*.

Project-focused courses

A project-focused design is one in which all elements, including genres and themes, cohere around a unifying project that students in the course complete individually, in small groups, or as a whole class. Possibilities for such projects are many. A course might be centered around students developing, for example, an online magazine, a marketing campaign, an employee safety workshop, a documentary film, a health education fair, or another project. This design is not mutually exclusive with genre-focused or theme-focused approaches. The difference is that in a project-focused course, the genre work and thematic content are always in service to the overarching project. This synthetic quality of project-focused courses is something that makes them appealing to both students and teachers. Because the individual assignments in the course are tied to something larger, they can be more meaningful than a series of discrete tasks with different purposes. Also, when a class project involves producing something of value for a real-world audience, students are often motivated to give it their all and can achieve much personal satisfaction in seeing it through to completion.

Project-focused designs have substantial precedent in second language teaching (Beckett & Miller, 2006; Herbolich, 1979; Stoller, 2002). One of the earlier documented ESP project-based curricula was Herbolich's (1979) engineering English course at the University of Kuwait, where students completed a "box kite" project, which involved making their own box kites, writing manuals for how to build one, and launching their kites together one windy day! Commenting on Herbolich's work, Swales (1985a) writes that "it demonstrates that a successful project can generate an educationally valuable sense of personal satisfaction for all parties involved—something that is not so easy to achieve in any other way" (p. 131).

More recently, some EAP and L1 English writing courses have incorporated *multimodal* projects, integrating print, visual, auditory, and digital material in a variety of genres (Alexander & Rhodes, 2014; Bowen & Whithaus, 2013; Hafner, 2014; Molle & Prior, 2008). Hafner (2014) describes one delightful example of such a project in an English for Science course he over-saw at City University of Hong Kong. In this course, undergraduate science and math majors worked in small groups to create documentary videos posted to YouTube explaining a scientific investigation they had conducted. Particularly challenging about their project was that they had to explain their scientific phenomenon in a way that would appeal to a non-specialist online audience. To this end, one group designed their video in the form of a TV program reporting on their experiment of how smell affects taste (see "Taste Me if You Can!" posted by user en2251 at www.youtube.com/watch?v= 8-1FAV1_VTg). This project was genre instructive in that it engaged students in thinking about, selecting, and mixing features of several genres. In parts of their video, for example, students integrated television show conventions, such as a logo for their fictitious "Scientific Channel," opening credits accompanied by rock guitar music, and even an end-of-show blooper. Other sections of the video, on the other hand, incorporated the organizational structure of scientific RAs, with segments entitled "introduction," "experi-mental material and procedure," "result," "discussion," and "conclusion." Within these sections, the students also mixed genres and styles. In reporting on their group's experimental method, for example, the narrator (dressed as a scientist in a white lab coat; see Figure 5.1) explained his group's experiment on whether smell affected ability to identify jelly bean flavors, mentioning—like an RA author would—the researchers' hypothesis and the number and sex of the experiment's participants. Departing from RA conventions, however, the video also showed actual participants blindfolded, holding their noses, and chewing on jelly beans—a display of 'on the ground' research processes not captured in written academic reports (see Figure 5.2).

Figure 5.1 "Taste me if you can!" (screenshot A)
Source: en2251, YouTube (15 Oct. 2009). Available at www.youtube.com/watch?v= 8-1FAV1_VTg.

Figure 5.2 "Taste me if you can!" (screenshot B)
Source: en2251, YouTube (15 Oct. 2009). Available at www.youtube.com/watch?v=8-1FAVI_VTg.

In engaging students in such synthetic, multi-genre work, project-based courses serve both narrow-angle genre acquisition and wide-angle genre awareness goals. In Hafner's curriculum, for example, students gained experience composing in specific genres (e.g., TV documentary and research reports) and media, while at the same time they may have become more generally conscious of how texts work in contexts. Regarding this broader rhetorical sensitivity, Hafner writes that students had to think about how to best construct creative documentaries for their viewers. Specifically, they drew on "the multimodal affordances of digital video and ... craft[ed] narratives which they hoped would compel their audience" (p. 679). This process of crafting multimodal projects with their recipients in mind could also serve critical pedagogy purposes, leading students to reflect on how particular media and genres afford or limit the possibilities for communication and persuasion. A possible extension activity to further these genre awareness and critical pedagogy goals might ask students to change their documentary into a formal essay, a blog post, a newspaper editorial and/or a text message, and discuss how each genre allows or constrains the impact on different audiences.

Although exciting and motivating for students, a project-focused course like Hafner's requires substantial advance work on the part of the instructor. Hafner (2014) reports that his students were provided with several workshops, as well as online technical resources, to assist with different phases of the documentary project (reading, scripting and storyboarding, performing and filming, and editing). Other project-focused designs, however, may be somewhat simpler to implement. My colleague Nancy Best, for example, has integrated a multimodal project in her first-year writing course using Weebly™, a user-friendly website design program (see www.weebly.com). Through this platform, Best's students create websites about their individual academic majors (e.g., biology, theatre arts, criminal justice, and so on) aimed at audiences of other students who are in their major or who are considering it. In the process of building their websites, students compose in (and build several webpages around) a range of genres, including interviews with faculty in their major fields, informational summaries on career and graduate school opportunities, frequently-asked-questions lists, and analyses of journal articles in their major fields. Best reports that her students not only learn about various genres but also are highly motivated by the website project, finding it meaningful to research their own fields and to integrate images, video, and audio creatively in their websites (Best, personal communication, July 2016).

Site-focused courses

Genre-based courses can also be *site-focused*, that is, built around 'real-world' sites outside of the course itself, such as another course, a workplace, or a community organization. A key advantage of these courses is that the 'realness' and immediacy of the outside site and audience can motivate students to learn the genres needed for this site. Some site-focused courses overlap with project-focused designs, as they often require students to produce projects (e.g., a presentation, a manual, and so on) for their sites. Below, I give an overview of three site-focused designs that have been discussed in relation to genre-based teaching: *linked courses, service learning*, and *site simulations.*

Linked courses

Linked course designs involve an ESP course connected to another course that the students are concurrently enrolled in. In such a configuration, the other course serves as a site motivating much of the work in the ESP course. Earlier in this chapter, I discussed Benesch's (2001a) use of critical pedagogy in EAP courses linked with a psychology course. At San Diego State University, Johns (1997) has also taught in linked arrangements for first-year undergraduates enrolled simultaneously in a "literacy" (EAP) course and a general education (GE) course in a field such as history, geography, or literature (p. 83). Johns' literacy course helps the students gain a fuller understanding of the site genres by asking them to analyze the GE course's readings, lectures, and exam and assignment prompts, and to interview the GE course faculty and upper-level students about the course. In some linked courses, the EAP and GE faculty may collaborate on their course designs, as did Johns and a history professor, who drew on each other's course goals to "co-construct" syllabuses and develop complementary paper and presentation assignments (Johns,

1997, p. 143). By giving students practice investigating and using the outside course's genres, these linked arrangements can promote both acquisition of specific genres as well as awareness of how genres are related to the values and practices of their contexts. Linked configurations can also motivate students to do well on their ESP assignments, as these are connected to their success in the site course as well.

Service learning

The focal sites for ESP courses may also be 'off-campus'. In *service learning* designs, for example, students in an ESP or other course contribute service to an outside-of-school site, such as a business, government agency or community organization, and reflect on how their service experience relates to the course. The students' service work may promote their genre learning as it engages students in producing texts of various kinds for their sites. Jolliffe (2001), for example, discusses several service learning courses that did just that, including a civil engineering course at the University of Utah, where students write technical traffic-related reports for "governmental bodies and local organizations that are petitioning for new roadways and traffic patterns" (p. 100). Jolliffe also describes a service-learning course he teaches in which undergraduates tutored secondary school students at a public high school and, from this experience, write texts that address "a real problem involving urban education that the students have uncovered in their work as a tutor" (p. 101). These student-produced texts have included a parent manual for how to start a high school summer reading program, a guide for instructors with hearing-impaired students, and a website for parents of children with eating disorders.

Like other site-focused designs, service learning can be highly motivating to students because of the realness of the contexts for which they are completing their class assignments. In addition, it allows students to see that genres (and their own texts within those genres) perform actual work in their sites, an important wide-angle and critical lesson that they can transfer to future situations. A civil engineering student who wrote one of those traffic reports, for example, might discover that it had influenced a city's transportation policy, or another who created the eating disorder website might later receive words of gratitude from a struggling parent. Such feedback from the site can make the course's genre work particularly meaningful to students, as they see that it serves real people outside of their ESP course.

Site simulation

Service learning, while potentially very enriching for students, can be a challenge to set up, particularly if there are limited local sites available and/ or if students lack transportation to off-campus locations. An alternative that avoids these logistical challenges is *site simulation* through a computerized Virtual Learning Environment (VLE). Russell and Fisher (2009) describe one such VLE that simulated a workplace (and its genres) in a technical communication course for agricultural and bio-systems engineering undergraduates. Through software called MyCase, the authors designed a virtual, fictitious bio-technology company called Omega Molecular, for which the students served as consultants. For their consulting work, the students read, wrote, and listened to a variety of genres, including company email messages, a state-of-the-company report, an investor bulletin for a venture capitalist, and a speech by the Omega Molecular CEO. What made their work different from that within a 'regular' genre-based course was that the VLE simulated for the students how genres would flow and interact in a dynamic workplace context, rather than just presenting the genres one at a time as one might do in a genre-focused design. For example, when students logged in and "[went] to work" at Omega Molecular, they read recent emails from fictitious Omega employees and watched videos of meetings and other events that simulated current goings-on at the company (p. 171). Moreover, like at a real workplace, the writing assignments were called "deliverables" (p. 183), and their deadlines were fluid, posted on a company calendar that changed in response to situations unfolding in the company's virtual time and space (Russell & Fisher, 2009). And by having to draw on these texts at Omega Molecular to produce their own texts, students again learned how genres interacted with other genres in the company's "genre system or ecology" (p. 188).

With respect to critical pedagogy goals, working with genres in a simulated or actual site exposes students to power dynamics in real-world contexts and ways genres may respond to (or even change) those dynamics. Russell and Fisher (2009), for instance, note that in the Omega Molecular simulation, when students wrote an "investor's bulletin", they had to "do so in a communicative environment where there [were] contradictory interests and complex power structures operating in different 'areas' of the environment" (p. 173). Peck, Flower, and Higgins (1995) also report on a dynamics-changing project in which inner-city Pittsburgh high school students created a "Whassup with Suspension" newsletter in response to their frustrations with authoritarian school suspension policies (p. 200). The fact that this newsletter became "required reading for teachers and students" at a real high school (p. 200) illustrates how a student genre project can make a critical intervention for social change in its target site.

Combining course designs

The four course designs described above can be freely combined depending on students' needs and interests. A business English course, for instance, might start out as genre-focused, covering individual texts like memoranda, strategic business plans, and spoken presentations. It then, though, could also include a project where students produce these texts for a real or hypothetical business site with particular contextual demands. As another example of design mixing, my theme-focused undergraduate writing class could, in addition to exploring romantic love topics, spend time on the conference presentation genre, leading to a final project whereby students present their romantic-love research papers at a 'mini-conference' attended by faculty, family, and peers. Task 5.6 gives you a chance to consider what course designs (or combinations thereof) you would be interested in using in your own ESP class.

Task 5.6 Designing your own genre-based ESP course

Select an ESP student population whose needs and interests you know something about. Then do the following:

1 Develop a weekly outline for a 15-week (three hours per week) course you would teach with these students. In your outline, for each week, list the themes, genres, and assignments you would include.
2 Write a brief paper explaining:

- how your course reflects one or more of the four genre-based course designs discussed in this chapter (genre-focused, theme-focused, project-focused, site-focused)
- how narrow-angle or wide-angle your course is in its focuses; here you may wish to bring in the concepts of genre acquisition and genre awareness
- whether there is room for student input into your course structure and content and, if so, how the course syllabus would be negotiated
- the orientation your course might take regarding critical pedagogy
- how your course would motivate student learning.

This chapter has covered issues that ESP teachers may consider as they design a genre-based course that speaks to students' needs and interests, and that motivates them to learn. The next chapter continues this exploration of genre-based teaching, focusing on how to design specific lesson materials for a course and how to assess the impact of those materials on students' genre learning.

Chapter 6

Creating and assessing genre-based teaching materials

Developing a genre-based ESP course involves not only planning its overall structure and focus(es) but also selecting and/or constructing lesson materials that implement your course vision. The importance of these materials cannot be underestimated. They are a key, if not *the* key, conduit between your course goals and student learning. In a genre-based course, materials provide students with memorable genre examples as well as opportunities to analyze, critique, and use genres in ways that promote genre acquisition and genre awareness within and beyond the course. Given their importance, it is not surprising that designing effective teaching materials takes "considerable time, resources, and expertise," especially given that "experienced designers constantly question and problematize what they are doing" (Harwood, 2010, pp. 17, 13).

This chapter offers you guidance on how to create and assess genre-based materials. I will focus on two components that make up such materials: 1) tasks (also known as activities) and 2) texts. The chapter begins with an overview of several task types—rhetorical consciousness-raising, text production, and process—and discusses why each may facilitate students' genre learning within different course designs. I will then consider how to sequence such tasks within a curricular unit, as well as how to select or create texts for your tasks, and to evaluate the effects of these materials on students' learning. Throughout the chapter, you will have opportunities to practice designing your own genre-based materials and assessments, and as you do, to draw on the genre and context analysis techniques you learned in Chapters 2, 3 and 4. If, in your future teaching, you use pre-existing materials (such as from other teachers or from published textbooks), this chapter can still inform how to adapt these materials to fit the focuses of your particular courses.

Genre-based tasks

This section discusses three categories of tasks in genre-based ESP courses: *rhetorical consciousness-raising, production,* and *process.*

Rhetorical consciousness-raising

Rhetorical consciousness-raising tasks are perhaps the hallmark of ESP genre-based teaching. As their name suggests, they are designed to heighten students' awareness of genre features and of how they function in their contexts (Hyland, 2006, 2016b; Paltridge, 2001; Swales, 2011/1981, 1990). The rationale behind these tasks is that the more conscious a person is of how a genre works, the better prepared s/he is to participate in it, as a speaker, listener, writer, or reader.

This idea, as Hyland (2007) points out, also parallels a belief in *noticing* in ESP's 'sister' field of second language acquisition: that in order for learners to acquire a new feature of a second language (e.g., a grammatical construction, a phoneme, a pragmatic usage pattern), they must first *notice* the feature in the language input around them (Bergsleithner, Frota, & Yoshioka, 2013; Schmidt, 1990, 1993). Applying this notion to classroom materials, second language teachers have used grammatical consciousness-raising activities to draw learners' attention to target language syntactic forms and meanings (Ellis, 2002; Rutherford & Sharwood Smith, 1988). Such tasks reflect a *cognitive* approach to learning and teaching, which emphasizes students as "thinking beings" who notice features in the linguistic data around them and "apply their mental powers in order to distil a workable generative rule from the mass of data presented" (Hutchinson & Waters, 1987, p. 43). As such, grammatical consciousness-raising tasks are often *inductive* in nature; that is, they present students with examples (e.g., a list of sentences in present perfect) and ask them to notice general patterns in how the grammatical form(s) is/are used.

Similarly, rhetorical consciousness-raising tasks promote active, inductive thinking by asking students to do their own analyses of genre moves, lexicogrammar, purposes, and/or contexts, in order to *notice*, and therefore learn, how the genre works, including how its features vary across situations (Hyland, 2006; Paltridge, 2001; Swales, 2011/1981, 1990). Essentially, then, rhetorical consciousness-raising activities put students in the role of a genre analyst, doing the kinds of investigations that you did in Chapters 2–4.

With their attention to noticing, these tasks address students' *learning needs*, and align well with either narrow-angle genre acquisition or wide-angle genre awareness goals. They are also compatible with any of the course designs discussed in Chapter 5, as they lead students to analyze genres relevant to particular class themes, projects, or outside sites. In the following section, I offer several examples of rhetorical consciousness-raising tasks that can be adapted for various spoken and written texts and classroom contexts.

Same topic, different genres

For a basic level of genre-consciousness, one must recognize that different genres exist. To cultivate this fundamental awareness, students can be asked to contrast how two texts of different genres present the same subject matter. In my undergraduate writing course on romantic love, for example, I present students with two writings by anthropologist and love researcher Helen Fisher, and together we identify genre-influenced differences between her two texts. Both texts, excerpts of which are shown below, are on an experiment that Fisher and her colleagues conducted on brain activity of people in love.

Text 1

"Have you just fallen madly in love?" We used this line again when we placed a new advertisement on the psychology bulletin board on the SUNY Stony Brook campus. But this time we called for men and women who were willing to recline in a long, dark, cramped, noisy machine while we scanned their brains. Once again, we sought only those who had fallen crazily in love within the last few weeks or months, people whose romantic feelings were fresh, vivid, uncontrollable, and passionate.

(Fisher, 2004, p. 61)

Text 2

Briefly, 10 women and seven men were recruited by word of mouth with flyers seeking individuals who were currently in love. The age range was 18–26 years (M=20.6; median=21), and the reported duration of 'being in love' was 1–17 months (M=7.4; median=7). Each participant was orally interviewed in a semistructured format to establish the duration, intensity, and range of his or her feelings of romantic love.

(Fisher, Aron, & Brown, 2005, p. 59)

As you can see, and as my students also notice, Fisher's two texts have quite different ways of describing the same experiment. In Text 1, Fisher uses conversational, engaging language to relay how she and colleagues recruited people who were "crazily in love" and "willing to recline" in their "noisy machine"; while Fisher, Aron, and Brown's Text 2 is much more formal and detached, curtly reporting on the numbers and ages of the participants and using academic-style nominalizations like "duration" and "intensity" to describe participants' romantic feelings. Notice also that while the active voice in Text 1 (e.g., "we placed a new advertisement ...") reminds us of the researchers' own human presence, Text 2's passive voice (e.g., "Each participant was orally interviewed ...") emphasizes the experimental processes and occludes the experimenters. In class, we discuss how these textual differences are shaped by Fisher's source genres and contexts: Text 1 is from one of Fisher's popular-audience books, and thus its language is meant to entertain—not just to inform—its non-specialist readership. The second text, on the other hand, from Fisher, Aron, and Brown's article in the *Journal of Comparative Neurology*, follows formal RA conventions expected by its scholarly audience. The takeaway for students from this comparison is that different genres exist and, equally importantly, that people use them to tell the same 'story' in different ways, highlighting, embellishing, or hiding particular details depending on their particular purposes and contexts.

This task can also be used to compare spoken genres. As a follow-up activity, for example, my class watches videos of Fisher describing her research in a TED Talk and on a day-time talk show, as seen at the following links, respectively: www.youtube.com/watch?v=OYfoGTIG7pY and www.youtube.com/watch?v=nUTdLJxDr-E.

Here again we see that different genres and situations shape Fisher's discourse and persona, even in such details as her lecture-style delivery, black turtleneck, and eyeglasses in the TED Talk and conversational manner and softer appearance on the talk show.

Text reassembly

Rhetorical consciousness-raising tasks can also get students to think about genre moves. A particularly effective and fun moves-noticing activity is text reassembly. Here students put back in order the pieces of a 'jumbled' text, which requires them to observe what each piece of the text is doing (i.e., its move(s)), and the piece's appropriate place in the text organization (Swales, 2011/1981; see also Paltridge, 2001). In Task 6.1 you get to try this type of activity as you reconstruct the pieces of a book review, a frequent critique-type genre assigned in university courses (Nesi & Gardner, 2012; Swales & Feak, 2012).

Task 6.1 Reassembling moves in a book review

The following text pieces were excerpted from a book review written by law student, Rebecca Curtiss, for an Immigration Law course at City University of New York (CUNY). Each segment is labeled with a letter for ease of reference during class discussion, although the letters do not give any clues about the correct order of the pieces. Read through these segments, and with one or two classmates do the following:

1   Reassemble the segments in what you think was their original order relative to each other.
2   Label the move(s) in each segment; in doing so, remember that a move describes the segment's *function* in the text (see Chapter 2).

3   Discuss with your classmates the moves you identified and why you think your proposed sequencing works well for this book review.

4   Explain whether you think such a text reassembly task and a follow-up class discussion would be effective for teaching students about genre moves. For example, to what extent would this activity engage students intellectually and emotionally? How might you adapt such a task for an ESP course and genre you are interested in teaching?

A couple of notes about this activity: The task is more fun if you cut the text into pieces, put these in an envelope, and give each small group an envelope. Then, after each group has collaboratively reassembled the pieces, they write up their order of the piece letters on the board. The original text may need to be shortened in order to make the task manageable for an in-class activity. For example, I omitted portions of Curtiss' book review, although the segments shown below still give a sense of key moves in her text.

F   Dow chooses to use story as the primary device to guide the reader through dense immigration laws and history. Detainees and detention center workers and wardens provide personal accounts of their experiences with the immigration detention system. Dow supplements the stories with historical, legal and cultural background. The combination of first person histories and background context provides the reader with a clear connection between immigration policy and its practical effects.

C   The very first line of Dow's prologue is "She can tell it better than I can." This quote was taken from a conference Dow attended where an immigrant woman told her story of immigration detention. The use of the first person voice to narrate the detention experience is powerful. First, this technique humanizes a system dedicated to dehumanizing those confined within it. Second, the stories are captivating and moving. Third, stories of detained people allow the person a moment of empowerment in an otherwise disempowering environment.

R   The 2004 publication, *American Gulag: Inside U.S. Immigration Prisons* by Mark Dow, is an exposé of the modern immigration detention system pre- and post-September 11. In this book, Dow exposes the horrific conditions experienced by immigration detainees in detention centers scattered around the country as if an archipelago that is essentially hidden in plain sight.

A   The legal reader can use and adopt the story telling technique in litigation as well as legislative reform. In collecting narratives, the practitioner can look to Dow's journalistic technique and sources. He is tenacious in his collection of stories from different individuals involved with the immigration system and researching immigration policy. His endnotes and bibliography provide a wealth of source information to supplement any litigation or policy campaign.

E   *American Gulag* is an extremely valuable work for the legal audience not only for its substance but also for the technique and style of the book. The stories are revelatory and provide much needed information about the secretive system of immigration detention. Dow's journalistic style and technique also offers insights to the legal advocate on how to investigate and present a compelling and complete narrative.

P   The vast majority of detainee stories were from men ... The index lists "women detainees" and contains references to abuse of women, menstruation, miscarriage, shackling while giving birth, rape and sexual abuse. All of these topics are mentioned in the book but given surprisingly little attention. The stories of women in the larger culture are so often ignored. Unfortunately, Dow continues that familiar practice. In order to truly address the conditions of all detainees in the immigration system he needs to give adequate voice to detained women.

Z   Dow initiates his examination of the immigration system by discussing 9/11 and the immigration policy and practice that directly [followed] from the 9/11 attacks precisely because most people will consider current immigration practice from the post 9/11 perspective. From there he takes the reader to Miami where he claims the contemporary era of immigration detention begins with Cubans and Haitians in the 1980s. Dow then moves into a multi-chapter discussion of immigration detainees housed in criminal facilities, the effect of corporate run criminal facilities and the 1996 laws.

Source: Excerpted segments from a book review written by Rebecca Curtiss for an Immigration Law class. Curtiss' entire review can be found on the following page of the CUNY School of Law Legal Writing Center website: www.law.cuny.edu/legal-writing/forum/book-reviews.html.

Examining move variation

In a reassembly task like the one above, student discoveries may naturally lead to a list of moves for the genre at hand, such as, based on Curtiss' text, book review moves like: introduction of the book, content summary, positive evaluation, negative evaluation, description of the book's readership, and concluding evaluation. Such lists are helpful for introducing students to some of a genre's possible parts. It is also important, however, for students to recognize that not all instances of a genre have the same moves or express them in the same way. 'Within-genre' comparisons are thus helpful for building awareness of this variation. In an EAP course with students from different disciplines, Swales (1990) suggests assigning students to collect samples of the same genre across their fields, to collaborate with classmates (in related and distant disciplines) in identifying similarities and differences across their texts, and to present their findings in a class plenary session. As Swales suggests, such comparison activities are also a way to deal with the "*managerial* problem" of teaching a heterogeneous class (1990, p. 216, italics original).

It may be interesting as well for students to examine genre move variation within the *same* field, noticing the freedom genres allow for individual speakers and writers, as illustrated in the following task.

Task 6.2 Comparing texts of the same genre

The short excerpts below show how Rebecca Curtiss and Bronyn Heubach, two law students at the City University of New York (CUNY), express negative evaluation moves in their book reviews written for an Immigration Law course. Although the two students are evaluating different books, they both offer some degree of criticism of their respective books—but in different ways. Read these excerpts and answer the following questions.

Excerpt from Rebecca Curtiss' review:

> The vast majority of detainee stories were from men ... The index lists "women detainees" and contains references to abuse of women, menstruation, miscarriage, shackling while giving birth, rape and sexual abuse. All of these topics are mentioned in the book but given surprisingly little attention. The stories of women in the larger culture are so often ignored. Unfortunately, Dow continues that familiar practice. In order to truly address the conditions of all detainees in the immigration system he needs to give adequate voice to detained women.

Excerpt from Bronyn Heubach's review:

> [W]hile I agree with the author, the strength of his arguments is less than I would have hoped for. For instance, the entire book rests on the premise that we are actually living in an age of global apartheid. While I am a progressive thinker this is the first time I have encountered the idea of global apartheid, so it is even more doubtful the average reader will have encountered this idea, either.
>
> (Curtiss' and Heubach's reviews can be found in their entirety on the CUNY School of Law Legal Writing Center Website: www.law.cuny.edu/legal-writing/forum/book-reviews.html)

1   How do Curtiss and Heubach differ in their ways of expressing negative evaluation of their focal book?
2   Which of these students' styles could you see yourself using if you were writing a book review? Why?

A task like this showing differences within the same move (negative evaluation), within the same genre (book review), and within the same context (an Immigration Law course) compellingly illustrates for students that within genre move boundaries, students still have 'space' to express their unique voices and styles.

Noticing lexicogrammatical features   *Assignment*

In addition to global move structure, consciousness-raising activities may attend to word- and sentence-level linguistic features of genres. The next activity, for example, asks students to notice evaluative words in book reviews. Such language indeed provides a great 'in' for discussing relationships between a genre's lexicogrammar and context, given that, as Thompson and Hunston (2000) point out, "[e]very act of evaluation expresses a communal value-system" (p. 6). Hyland (2004a), in fact, has identified values-shaped evaluative vocabulary in published book reviews across disciplines, finding, for instance, that while reviewers from marketing and applied linguistics frequently use the words *significant* and *insightful* to express appreciation for a book, engineering reviewers are particularly drawn to *comprehensive* and *practical* to convey their praise (p. 51).

In the activity below, students observe positive evaluative words and phrases in the two law students' book reviews and hypothesize the connections between these words and their disciplinary context. A teacher could pre-identify Curtiss' and Heubach's evaluative sentences and put them on a handout for students to analyze, or, for a more challenging option, ask students to find the evaluative expressions themselves within Curtiss' and Heubach's whole reviews. To illustrate the handout version of the task, I have listed below several sentences from Curtiss' and Heubach's reviews. Students must find, circle, and label the part of speech of the evaluative vocabulary in these sentences. Try doing this yourself.

American Gulag effectively exposes and explains how this occurs.

The stories are captivating and moving.

Nevins' research is thorough and comprehensive, as evidenced by the broad range of resources he draws from.

Nevins convincingly shows that no other answer to the question of who bears responsibility for immigrant deaths at the border quite resolves the entire issue.

The positive words and phrases that students notice are then listed in a chart on the board. In the partially completed chart shown below (based on more sentences than the four above), the words are categorized by their parts of speech to show the range of word types that express evaluation. In parentheses the evaluative word's neighboring word(s) are included; these are sometimes evaluative themselves, intensifying the reviewers' praise.

Nouns	Verbs	Adjectives	Adverbs
a wealth (of source information) (valuable) contribution	(effectively) exposes provides (very valuable information) (effectively) demonstrates	substantive (lessons) practical (lessons) valuable (information) comprehensive (framework) captivating (stories) moving (stories) tenacious (in his collection) thorough (in his research) persuasive (elements)	effectively (explains) effectively (uses) convincingly (shows)

Viewing this chart, the class discusses patterns in the writers' word choices and what they suggest about the values of law as a discipline. For example, expressions such as *convincingly shows, effectively exposes*, and *moving* and *captivating* indicate that persuasion, not unexpectedly, is central to the field of law. As well, phrases like *wealth of source information* and *thorough and comprehensive* (research) point to the field's emphasis on building an argument.

Of course, one cannot draw definitive conclusions about a genre or a discipline from just two texts in a single university course. Nevertheless, through analyzing even a small number of texts, students may begin to develop a genre awareness habit of mind, whereby they attend to textual features and potential connections of these features to their cultural contexts.

When lexicogrammatical analysis tasks involve a larger number of texts, corpus tools (see Chapter 3) are useful for generating samples of features and sentence-contexts where the features occur. In her ESP course for Italian undergraduates, Gavioli (2005) drew on such tools to develop consciousness-raising activities for word and sentence patterns in English-medium business genres. For example, in a task around *bid*—a word that had puzzled Gavioli's students when reading and listening to business news—the class examined a software-generated concordance of 249 *bid* occurrences in English-language news articles. In viewing the modifiers to the left of *bid*, students noticed that the word often occurred in the phrase *a takeover bid*, such as in the concordance lines below:

- keen to mount a takeover bid but would encounter fierce …
- signed to ward off a takeover bid. If Pearl decided to …
- said AMP's takeover bid 'is unacceptable and …

(From Gavioli, 2005, p.161)

To explore the usage of *bid* in this phrase, students examined the 'extended contexts' (i.e., the surrounding sentences) of the 20 occurrences of *a takeover bid* in the corpus, a few excerpts of which are shown below. See if you can notice patterns in these contexts of *a takeover bid*:

> followed by a spate of bid rumours, the most sensational of which was that Adia, the big Swiss-based recruitment consultant, was about to launch a takeover bid.
>
> GEC, Ferranti's main British rival in radar, is also keen to mount a takeover bid but would encounter fierce Ministry of Defence opposition on the grounds that it would damage competition ...
>
> Mr. Louis-Dreyfus will have to work hard to recover the company's standing. He may also have to fight off a takeover bid.
>
> (Excerpted from Gavioli, 2005, pp. 95–96)

From their analysis of these corpus examples, Gavioli's students (and maybe you too) observed that *bid*, and in particular *a takeover bid*, in business discourse is often used for transactions involving big companies, forthcoming possibilities rather than done-deals, and conflict. The corpus tools greatly enhanced the possibilities for such consciousness-raising around this phrase, giving students rapid access to multiple samples of it in a genre of interest to them.

Exploring genre contexts

Tasks can also be designed to raise students' consciousness of genre contexts. As suggested by Chapter 4, such context exploration is important for understanding the rationale for a genre's textual features, as well as processes for comprehending or composing in the genre and the genre's impact on its participants. In her own undergraduate EAP courses, Johns (1997) heightens the context-consciousness of first-year students in part by having them talk with professors about their disciplinary research practices. Working with more established scholar-students, Curry and Lillis (2010) have developed context-focused tasks for international academics seeking to present or publish their research in English-medium conferences or journals. Their materials in particular focus on "the social practices of professional text production" (p. 325), one of which is professional networking, which they find contributes greatly to international scholars' success navigating academic genres. To introduce international researchers to networking's importance, Curry and Lillis present them with real cases of scholars whose "text histories" (p. 328) involve significant collaboration with others. The following is an excerpt from their case example of 'Istvan', a psychology professor at a central European university:

> Istvan's prolific publishing record in his L1 and English (some 25 books and 15 book chapters and articles in his L1, plus some 15 articles and

book chapters in English) has enabled him to establish two laboratories ... Istvan's chief and longest-lasting research network began in 1997, when two U.S. researchers read an article on cognition Istvan had published and invited him to visit them. Istvan has since co-authored seven articles with them, working by e-mail and occasional visits ...

This description is followed by a concrete illustration of how Istvan collaborated with his student and U.S. colleagues to revise a previously rejected article manuscript:

> Istvan secured funding for TU [his student] to reconduct the experiments ... Then Istvan drew on TU's new findings to craft a quite different version of the article. He sent this draft to WK [his colleague] in the United States, who suggested detailed word- and sentence-level changes and pointed to confusing areas such as explanations of the research methodology. Istvan submitted the next revision to a new English-medium international journal, which accepted the article pending specified changes.

Later in Curry and Lillis' activity, the international scholars reflect upon what can be learned from Istvan's networking practices, through questions such as:

> What different roles do these members of [Istvan's] networks have? What do they contribute in terms of methodology, data collection and analysis, writing, reviewing drafts, making revisions to text?
>
> Are you involved in research networks that extend beyond your local context? If so, how? If not, do you know of any international networks that you might want to join?
>
> What do you (or could you) offer to and receive from others in the network, particularly in relation to writing an academic journal article?
>
> (Excerpts above are from Curry and Lillis, 2010, pp. 333–335)

Like other consciousness-raising tasks, Curry and Lillis' activities are meant to demystify genres that are important to students. What makes their activities unique in the heavily text-analytic world of ESP is their focus on contextual factors that make production in genres possible (see Paltridge (2017) for further suggestions on classroom applications for exploring genre and context).

Consciousness-raising for genre critique

For ESP courses with a critical pedagogy orientation (see Chapter 5), activities can also lead students to notice what actions or power relationships a genre makes possible (or not), and which users they advantage or disadvantage. In their undergraduate writing textbook, Devitt, Reiff, and Bawarshi (2004) offer a set of critical consciousness-raising questions, a few of which are shown below, that engage students in these kinds of observations:

- Whose needs are most served by the genre? Whose needs are least served?
- Does the genre enable its users to represent themselves fully?
- Does the genre effectively accomplish what its users intend it to do?
- Does the genre limit the way in which its users can do their work?

(From Devitt, Reiff, & Bawarshi, 2004, p. 161)

Reflected in these questions is the recognition that genres can effect both benefit and harm in the world, sometimes simultaneously. With such awareness, students might also analyze how to make particular genres more ethical in their capabilities. In one illustration of this possibility, Devitt, Reiff, and Bawarshi (2004) describe an assignment in which two of their undergraduates examined a U.S. school genre known as an individual education plan (IEP). Required by law for learning-disabled students, IEPs describe annual learning goals based on a beginning-of-the-year meeting with teachers, principals, specialists, and parents. What the two undergraduates observed is that these plans do not include any input from the learning-disabled students themselves, "who have the most to gain or lose" from their IEP (p. 180). To integrate these students' participation in their learning plans, the undergraduates proposed changing this genre to include an additional form, one which would have a friendly appearance and be entitled "This Year I Would Like To," with "space for the learning-disabled student to list five personal goals" (p. 180).

Critique activities can also evaluate positive aspects of genres for individuals and communities, as seen in Auerbach and Wallerstein's (2004) *Problem-posing at Work: English for Action,* a critical pedagogy English language textbook for immigrant workers. Along with readings and discussions on various workplace issues, the authors include genres that can empower disempowered workers. One such spoken genre is refusal of unsafe work, illustrated in the following exercise, where students must notice the moves that an employee, Manny, uses to perform this genre.

Read the following dialogue: Find the place where Manny 1) reports the problem, 2) makes a suggestion, 3) offers to do another job, and 4) refuses to work.

Remember that you can only refuse if death or serious injury might result and if the other conditions for refusing apply.

Manny:	I don't think we should work on the scaffolding.
Foreman:	What's the problem?
Manny:	The rope is loose and it's not safe.
Foreman:	There's plenty of support. Don't worry.
Manny:	Could you get someone to fix it before we go up?
Foreman:	We need to get the job done today. Just get to work.
Manny:	Could we work on the ground floor instead?
Foreman:	No, I told you we need to get this done.
Manny:	I'm sorry, but I'm not going up there until it's fixed. We could get killed.

(From Auerbach & Wallerstein, 2004, p. 184,
slightly reformated).

To complement this moves analysis task, students could also explore contexts when using this refusal genre actually kept immigrant workers from unsafe work or helped them gain other rights. Auerbach and Wallerstein indeed offer an encouraging example of two workers who, after refusing a treacherous job assignment, were disciplined by their company but then subsequently won their case with the U.S. Occupational Health and Safety Administration (OSHA).

For a critical consciousness-raising activity that asks students to evaluate a genre's ethical potential on their own, you might assign something like the following prompt, which I have synthesized from several tasks in Devitt, Reiff, and Bawarshi (2004, pp. 161, 180).

Choose a genre that you are interested in evaluating. Analyze the effects—positive and/or negative—that this genre has on its users by answering and taking notes on the "Questions for Critiquing Genres" above, as they apply to your chosen genre. Then explain either or both of the following: 1) how this genre should be changed to maximize the good it is able to do for those it impacts; 2) how you could use this genre, in its current or changed form, to make a positive difference in your own life or in the lives of others.

Thus far, we have looked at several possible rhetorical consciousness-raising tasks, including:

- comparing two genres for how they present the same subject matter
- reassembling genre moves
- identifying lexicogrammatical features, manually and through corpus tools
- noticing genre variation by comparing texts across fields or across individual writers and speakers
- reflecting on case studies of genre contexts
- exploring the work that a genre does and to whose advantage or disadvantage.

Other possible consciousness-raising tasks include the following (synthesized from Hyland, 2006; Paltridge, 2001; Swales, 2011/1981):

- color-coding moves in texts
- coming up with labels for moves according to what they are doing in a text
- surveying published advice about a genre feature and comparing this advice to examples of the genre feature that students find
- examining similarities and differences between a genre in English and in students' home languages
- discussing how English-medium genre features relate to or conflict with students' sense of identity and culture
- and others! For examples of various rhetorical consciousness-raising tasks, see also Swales and Feak's (2012) book *Academic Writing for Graduate Students: Essential Tasks and Skills.*

You may now be interested in designing consciousness-raising activities of your own. The next section offers you some guidance for how to do so.

How to create rhetorical consciousness-raising tasks

Given that consciousness-raising activities are strongly based in the genre analysis techniques you learned in Chapters 2–4, you already have a great foundation for creating them. Below I suggest several general steps for designing these activities.

1   Select a genre that is relevant to your students' needs and to your course design, including your course themes, projects, or target sites.
2   Decide on an aspect of this genre that you would like your students to become more aware of, such as the genre's moves, lexicogrammatical features, purposes, or contexts. Although you may want the class to focus on all of these aspects, start with one and then develop additional activities later for the other aspects.
3   Do your own analysis of your selected aspect by collecting sample texts that illustrate that aspect and applying the genre analysis skills you have learned earlier in this book.
4   Now, for the activity itself, select one or two example texts, or create one of your own, that will illustrate clearly for students the specific textual or contextual features you would like them to notice about the text(s). (See also the section later in this chapter, "Text selection")
5   Design a task for students to do with the selected text(s) that will lead them to notice the focal feature(s). A few things to keep in mind as you create the activity:

a   Give students a specific focus in the task, such as identifying a particular move (or a small number of moves) in a text; circling all instances of a specific grammatical pattern, or discussing the power relationship between two people using the genre. Having a narrow focus will keep students on track, make the task more interesting, and allow it to be accomplished within a reasonable time frame. A broad directive like "Analyze this text" could be overwhelming (or boring) to students and not achieve the desired consciousness about a specific feature.

b   Whenever possible, include a focus on both form and function of the genre feature or its contexts, to give students a sense of how formal features serve particular purposes for the people who use the genre.

c   Let students do the noticing. You may be tempted to explain to students how the genre or context feature works. But your 'lectures' are not likely to stick in students' minds as effectively as will students' own discoveries during the task. As Tomlinson (2010) points out, "If learners notice for themselves how a particular language item or feature is used ... they are more likely to develop their language awareness ... [and] are also more likely to achieve readiness for acquisition" (p. 93).

d   Encourage collaboration in the task so that students learn from each other and have more fun along the way. In other words, the "notice for themselves" that Tomlinson refers to can be done in pairs or small groups, and then followed up with whole-class discussion.

e   Make the activity enjoyable. Students will be more motivated to have their consciousness raised if they enjoy the process. So select interesting texts to analyze; design the task so that there is more than one possible answer to debate during the whole-class discussion; make the task into a kind of puzzle, such as reconstructing the original move order, guessing the gender of the text author, speculating on the meaning of a phrase and then checking it against the corpus data, assigning students to research a genre feature for homework and giving a prize for the most unusual example found; and so on.

Text production activities

An important complement to rhetorical consciousness-raising is text production. In their study of an engineering communications course, Artemeva and Fox (2010) discovered that even if students were aware of a genre, they were not able to perform it effectively without prior production experience. Specifically, most students at the beginning of the communications course could identify a technical report and its characteristic features; however, only 11 percent of them could actually write such a report. In fact, when asked to do so, many wrote secondary-school type essays with "descriptive narratives containing emotional language and rhetorical questions" (p. 494). Those few students who did produce a technical report had written one previously, leading Artemeva and Fox to conclude that "situated performance" in a genre—and not just genre exposure or recognition—is "a primary vehicle for genre acquisition" (p. 497). In her study of four multilingual graduate students, Tardy (2009) similarly found that the students' repeated practice composing in their disciplinary genres was key to building their writing ability and confidence.

With this importance of text production in mind, I offer below several examples of production tasks. These activities vary in how 'controlled' they are. The *controlled practice* tasks lead students to imitate specific genre features and thus may be particularly suitable for newcomers to these features. The *scaffolded production* and *interpretive production* activities, on the other hand, require more independent decision-making, with the scaffolded tasks providing students with guided preparation for those decisions and the interpretive ones less so.

Controlled practice of a genre feature

Some production tasks tightly control student output, such as this activity from Feak and Swales' (2010) RA writing course for postdoctoral fellows in perinatology. Here the fellows practice using "pre-fronted prepositional phrases," which Feak and Swales observe are "usefully 'snappy'" structures for describing what data are omitted from a study, as in "Of the remaining 874 infants, 68 were excluded because of missing information on ..." (p. 292). Try doing this exercise (see below)—which Feak and Swales report was done aloud and "suitably enjoyed" by the postdoctoral fellows (p. 292)—remembering to front the prepositional phrase but retain the original sentence meaning.

Rephrase the following so that they conform to [the sentence pattern] above:

1   Michael Jordan is the most famous of all recent basketball players.
2   65 percent of those who failed to respond to treatment had some form of diabetes.
3   Only two of the six variables investigated produced statistically significant results.
4   1,509 women were excluded if there was missing information of leisure activities out of a total sample of 48,145.
5   2% (N=36) of the total cohort were lost to follow-up (i.e., moved, delivered elsewhere, records not found) and were excluded from the analysis.

(From Feak & Swales, 2010, p. 292)

In this controlled practice, students need only to transform the order of the sentence parts, without composing any new content. Such a narrow focus on form can be useful when trying out a genre feature for the first time. In subsequent, less controlled activities like writing a research method section, students could then try using this feature within their own sentences. Also worth noting is the way the task's five sentences are sequenced according to complexity. The first one, about Michael Jordan, is short and 'everyday'; the next two are longer and more 'research-y'; and the last two are longer still and, in fact, the only ones that illustrate data-exclusion statements in method sections—the original point of Feak and Swales' lesson. This activity thus illustrates how even a controlled task can start with something students can easily do and then gradually build up to greater challenges.

Bosher (2010) offers another example of a controlled sentence-revision activity, this time focused on the nursing genre of narrative notes. Used within patients' charts to record their physical conditions and symptoms, these notes are interesting lexicogrammatically in their "telegraphic" language (i.e., abbreviated sentence grammar) to express only essential "thought units" (p. 357). In the task below, Bosher gives her multilingual prenursing students practice with this feature by transforming complete-sentence descriptions of patients into nursing note style. Try doing this yourself—it is an interesting challenge!

> For each of the situations below, write a narrative nursing note for the patient's medical record. Change the full sentences to thought units, using telegraphic language. Refer to previous exercises for the specialized terminology, concise wording, precise wording, and common abbreviations that you need to complete this activity. The first one has been done for you.
>
> Example:
>
> On January 6, 2005, at 9 a.m., Mr. A tells you that he took a long time to void and that he had pain while voiding. He stated that he flushed about half a cup of urine down the toilet.
>
> Narrative nursing note:
>
> 1/6/2005 0900 States that he voided with difficulty. Approx 125 ml amber urine discarded by self.
>
> 1   On January 7, 2005, at 3 p.m., Mrs. B said that she had a bad pain just under her breastbone that went toward her left shoulder. The pain lasted 10 minutes. During that time, she had trouble catching her breath. She was sweating.
>
> (From Bosher, 2010, pp. 365–366; four more items to transform are also included in the exercise)

Like Feak and Swales' prepositional fronting activity, Bosher's task provides students with the topical content, leaving them to alter only the sentence structures. As you may have noticed, though, her task is less controlled than prepositional fronting and thus more challenging. Although the directions say students can refer to prior exercises on note phrasing, they must still figure out their own way to boil down the description into note form. Also, there are likely multiple acceptable note 'answers' to each item (as opposed to the single-answer style of the prepositional fronting task), illustrating the fact that even certain controlled practice tasks allow for some originality.

Scaffolded text production

Some production activities are substantially less structured, requiring students to generate much of the ideational content and language of their texts. These 'freer' activities nevertheless can still offer students substantial direction on how to use the target genre. Such guidance is sometimes described as *scaffolding*, that is, support or assistance given to novices acquiring new skills or knowledge. Feak, Reinhart, and Rohlck's (2009) *Academic Interactions* textbook illustrates well some possibilities for scaffolded production tasks. In their chapter "Communicating by Email," for example, students are assigned to write three hypothetical apology email messages to professors, but this task only occurs after the chapter has described typical email message moves (e.g., *greeting; the apology; a brief explanation or excuse; your action plan*) (p. 76); asked students to analyze five sample email apologies for their effectiveness in achieving these moves; and engaged them in controlled practice with *be sorry* constructions (e.g., *I'm sorry about/for/that*). Given all of the preceding preparation, by the time students encounter the following prompt, they have been substantially scaffolded with strategies for producing various parts of the apology email genre:

> Compose three email messages, each of which includes an apology and an explanation. You may choose from the situations given or choose situations of your own. Be sure to include the subject heading and an appropriate opening and closing [...]

> 1 You missed a meeting with your advisor to go over courses for the upcoming semester.
> 2 You couldn't finish the assigned paper in time to turn it in on the due date.
> 3 You are always late to English class because the class you have before it is quite far away from campus.
> (From Feak, Reinhart, & Rohlck, 2009, p. 82)

Interpretive text production

In other tasks, students must work more independently, interpreting (and sometimes researching) what genre moves and linguistic elements are fitting for the context at hand and then using these in their own texts. I offer here two examples of such interpretive production tasks, both of which require students to assess a new context and determine how to express themselves within the genre and situation.

The first example involves a university French course designed around a simulated site, a fictitious Paris apartment building for which the students take on the identities of the building's residents (Dupuy, 2006; Michelson & Dupuy, 2014). Within these identities, students engage in a range of genres, including answering-machine messages, conversational interactions with fellow residents, advertisements, invitations, postcards, and Facebook profiles and posts. For the Facebook texts, students must interpret their characters' personas and select linguistic forms that capture what their characters would say and how they would say it, given their characters' ages, professions, personalities, and so on. One student, Trevor, in the voice of 'Pascal LeBlanc'—"an 81 year-old retired philosophy professor" (p. 35)—posted in French the following Facebook comment about the job interview performances of two of the other characters (Jean Paul LeClerc and Thierry Pinot).

> *Apparement Jean Paul LeClerc a fait une bonne impression avec la représentante de Disney—il savait tout de l'organisation en Europe et aux États-Unis. Thierry Pinot, en revanche, n'a pas réussi dans son entretien.*
>
> (Apparently Jean-Paul Le Clerc made a great impression on the representative from Disney—he knew everything about the organization in Europe and in the U.S. Thierry Pinot, on the other hand, was not successful in his interview.)
>
> (From Michelson & Dupuy, 2014, p. 35)

Michelson and Dupuy note that, in the post above, Trevor used the formal academic French expression *en revanche* for 'on the other hand', which "indexes his character's age and profession" better than would a similar expression like *par contre* (p. 35). Trevor, they said, also later commented that he was conscious of the fact that formal speech would be one of the markers of his character's identity.

Bosher's (2010) university prenursing course also engages students in interpretive production, this time in the spoken genre of workplace confrontations between nurses and their patients or hospital personnel. In one confrontation exercise, the students role-play the nurse and are reminded to follow an 'assertiveness' move structure known by the acronym DESC or

DISC, which signifies "Describe the situation; Express your feelings *or* Indicate the problem the behavior is causing; Specify the change you want; and Consequences: identify the results that will occur" (Bosher, 2010, p. 358, drawing on Davis, 2006). Beyond these general guidelines, students are on their own to interpret what is called for in challenging situations like the following (and to come up with an appropriate response). Think about what you would say as the nurse in this situation (with only the DESC structure to guide you) and why you would produce the utterances that you did.

> You are a nurse providing care for a patient who states that he does not understand you because of your accent. He also states that he has never had to work with a foreign nurse before. He wants another nurse. It is your responsibility to interview the patient to find out how he is feeling and determine how much pain he is experiencing. The patient is recovering from an appendectomy, but there seem to be complications. You need to interview the patient right away and get the information to the doctor. How do you respond to the patient's concerns about working with you? How do you get the information you need?
>
> (From Bosher, 2010, pp. 367–368)

Interpretive production activities like these may be most effectively introduced after students have developed relevant genre knowledge and/or substantial linguistic proficiency to draw upon. In Michelson and Dupuy's Paris apartment simulation class, for example, the students were intermediate-level (in a fourth-semester French course). And in a nursing English class like Bosher's, one imagines that students might first engage in controlled and scaffolded tasks to equip them with linguistic and cultural strategies needed to navigate the interpretive role plays.

I would also like to point out that all of the production tasks we have discussed in this section—controlled, scaffolded, and interpretive—can be integrated into the various course designs (genre-focused, theme-focused, project-focused, and site-focused) described in Chapter 5. Moreover, these production tasks serve, to different degrees, both genre-acquisition and genre-awareness goals. Regarding this latter point, all three categories of production activities can help students acquire facility in using specific genres or genre features. The less controlled (i.e., scaffolded or interpretive) tasks also build awareness of genre–context relationships by compelling students to consider what genre elements they might employ (or not) in particular situations.

Process activities

In addition to consciousness-raising and production experience, classroom tasks can focus on *processes* for producing or 'receiving' texts in particular genres. Below, I consider some examples of process activities around source-based research writing and university lectures.

Revising a literature review

Whether as a stand-alone entity or a section within a scholarly paper, the research genre known as a literature review is challenging to write in, requiring synthesis of others' research and strategic framing of this synthesis to serve one's own purposes. Newcomers to this genre may thus appreciate learning processes for how to write an effective literature review. One such process is revision, and, in fact, a literature review may require multiple revisions before it becomes effective. In the chapter "Drafting, Redrafting, and Redrafting Again," Feak and Swales (2009) offer an engaging set of activities illustrating possibilities for revising a literature review in response to expert feedback. Their students/readers are presented with three drafts of a literature review, each written by a doctoral student, "Joyce," who is studying dissertations in education. They are to evaluate these drafts and to consider Joyce's advisor's suggestions for revision. Below is an excerpt from Joyce's first draft reflecting her initial attempt at a literature review.

> It seems that six pieces of research have examined the structure of PhD theses or dissertations. Dong (1998) surveyed graduate students and faculty in science and engineering departments at two universities in the southeast of the United States, and found on average that 38 percent of the students were using the article compilation or "anthology" format. In another study, Stålhammer (1998) found that the compilation format was common in the psychology department of a Swedish University ...
>
> (From Feak & Swales, 2009, p. 64)

The advisor, say Feak and Swales, communicated to Joyce that her literature review was "flat and boring" (p. 65). In response, Joyce wrote a second draft, a portion of which is shown below.

> There is, in fact, a small, growing and fascinating collection of recent studies that have examined the structure of the dissertation. Given their limited number, their geographical distribution is amazingly wide. There are two studies from the United States (Dong 1998; Swales 2004) and single studies from Sweden (Stålhammer 1998), Hong Kong (Bunton 1998), the United Kingdom (Thompson 1999), and Australia (Paltridge 2002). We thus have a global snapshot of what has been going on in recent years in terms of dissertation structure. Overall, the findings indicate that the alternative anthology format is alive and well,

especially in science, technology, and engineering ... Clearly, it is time for the traditional PhD dissertation to be given a decent burial.

(From Feak & Swales, 2009, p. 66)

On this draft, the advisor made the following comments, among others:

- OK, Joyce, don't you think this is a bit overly enthusiastic? Do you really think the previous work is fascinating? And what's this about a global snapshot? Can you tone it down a bit?
- I don't think it's your place to decide whether the traditional dissertation should be abandoned. I think you may be losing sight of your purpose.
- You haven't discussed any of the studies. You've grouped them together according to country, but is that the most meaningful way to approach these studies?

(From Feak & Swales, 2009, p. 66)

On the third draft, Joyce significantly reconfigured the organization and tone of her literature review, illustrated in its opening sentences below.

The previous section has shown that there is growing debate about the role and value of the doctoral dissertation as a "capstone" educational achievement. This in turn has led to a growing acceptance of alternatives to the traditional expanded IMRD format for the dissertation by many university authorities (such as Dissertation Handbook, University of Michigan, p. 20). Perhaps because of these developments, a small, but widely distributed, body of research has recently emerged that attempts to investigate the actual structure of dissertations in a number of contexts. According to these studies, the main departure from the "traditional" structure would seem to be that of an "article compilation," sometimes known as an "anthology" type (such as Dong, 1998) ...

(From Feak & Swales, 2009, p. 67)

Feak and Swales' Joyce series demonstrates for novice researchers that revision is key in literature review writing, often involving substantial re-thinking and reframing in response to feedback, and not just surface editing. As well, their follow-up discussion questions (not shown above) on each of Joyce's drafts serve consciousness-raising purposes, leading students to notice what textual features make each of her drafts effective or not.

Synthesizing sources for a literature-based report

Beyond recognizing that revision is an important process, students may also need help with *how* to revise (and before that, how to plan and draft) literature reviews and other texts. Advocating greater attention to such processes in genre teaching, Dovey (2010) observes that students particularly struggle in source-based writing with how to connect and integrate sources effectively. Indeed, it took Joyce several tries before she grouped her sources according to types of alternative dissertations the source authors examined. To help her graduate EAP students synthesize their sources within the genre of "literature-based reports"—texts that inform "non-technical readers" about research on a topic (p. 58)—Dovey gives them several tasks to guide them through steps in the synthesis process. In an early activity, students construct a "tree diagram" for each of their sources that outlines, in pictorial form, key ideas and sub-ideas discussed in the source (p. 55). Students then map common ideas found across their sources onto a "concept matrix," (p. 56), an example of which is shown below for a student's literature-based report on "E-health" (Table 6.1). As you can see, creating this matrix would compel students to identify which of their sources address the same topics and sub-topics, thus helping them to organize their reports and integrate relevant sources within particular topic sections of the reports. Also useful is the fact that the matrix requires students to note the page numbers where each source addresses certain topics, a process step that students will be grateful they did when they begin to compose their reports.

Dovey points out that before she implemented these activities for her students, "exposure to expert product [i.e., genre models] was not an adequate means of facilitating writing from sources" (p. 58). Process tasks like the tree diagram and concept matrix, however, she says "have resulted in an improvement in the organisation, coherence and cohesion of the final document" (p. 58).

Listening to a university lecture

In addition to aiding students with their text productions, process activities can assist students in genre *reception*. Examples of such activities are found in Salehzadeh's (2006) *Academic Listening Strategies* textbook, which aims to equip students with strategies for listening effectively to university lectures, a genre that poses particular difficulties for non-native English speaking students due to its "messy" spoken language features (p. 34). To help students with the process of dealing with these features, Salehzadeh asks them to listen to or read the transcript of an authentic lecture and identify such elements as fillers (e.g., *okay, all right, um, well, uh*), informal terms and slang, reductions (e.g., *gonna*), contractions (e.g., *should've*), and incomplete or ungrammatical phrases and sentences (p. 29). In one activity, for instance, students observe examples of these features in an authentic introductory biology lecture, a portion of which is included in the transcript below. See if you can find some of the spoken language elements listed above in this segment.

Table 6.1 Concept matrix in the process of writing a literature-based report

E-health: an investigation of its implementation in developing countries

Author and year of publication	Introduction		Benefits of E-health in developing countries			Barriers to E-health in developing countries				Potential solutions to barriers in developing countries			
	Background on E-health	*Health in developing countries*	*For patients*	*For health experts*	*For public health-care and hospitals*	*Financial*	*Technological*	*Law and policy*	*Cultural and social*	*To financial barriers*	*To technological barriers*	*To law and policy barriers*	*To cultural and social barriers*
Anderson 2006						481		481					
Buys-schaert 2009							7	7–8	8	21	18		19
Chen & Xia 2009						219	219	219	219	220	220	220	220
Gupta 2009	8	8–9											
Hjelm 2005			61	60	65								
Kaur & Gupta 2006			24	27	27–8		28	30					
Nykanen 2006			284	286	286								

(Continued)

Table 6.1 (continued)

E-health: an investigation of its implementation in developing countries

Author and year of publication	Introduction		Benefits of E-health in developing countries			Barriers to E-health in developing countries				Potential solutions to barriers in developing countries			
	Background on E-health	*Health in developing countries*	*For patients*	*For health experts*	*For public health-care and hospitals*	*Financial*	*Technological*	*Law and policy*	*Cultural and social*	*To financial barriers*	*To technological barriers*	*To law and policy barriers*	*To cultural and social barriers*
Oak 2007							22						
Ouma & Herselman 2008	561	561								564	563	564	563
PHRMA 2002	2–3	3											
Srivastava 2007	11					12	12	12	12				
Yellowlees 2005											334		

Source: From Dovey, 2010, p. 56.

Professor:	um, I'll move on. All right? ...um, biology, simple definition here, is just the study of life. So, that, begs the question ... what is alive?... okay who's gonna give me a definition of what's alive?
Student 1:	things that, react and reproduce
Professor:	react, and reproduce. Do you have a grandmother?
Student 1:	Yeah
Professor:	Is she reproducing?
Student 1:	Not lately
Professor:	Is she alive?
Student 1:	Yeah
Professor:	So your definition doesn't work. So she's dead she's you you're happy to redefine her as dead?
Student 1:	uh ... maybe I should've said the possibility of reproducing
Professor:	Capable of reproducing? At some point in her life cycle?
Student 1:	Right

(From Salehzadeh, 2006, p. 29, slightly reformatted)

Through such tasks, students can become more comfortable with spoken language features and learn not to let these distract them from important lecture content during the process of listening.

Reception activities may as well help students with the process of paying attention to particular information. Salehzadeh, for instance, assigns students to listen in lectures for stressed words, which are "louder and longer and spoken at a slightly higher pitch," as these often covey the lecturer's key points (p. 42). Even without Salehzadeh's audio samples, experiment with how this would work: Practice reading aloud the biology lecture segment above, imagining the voices and styles of the professor and the student, and underline what words you stressed. What types of words are they? If students went through this process of paying attention to these stressed words (and filtering out the rest), would they be better able to understand important points from this lecture excerpt?

Sequencing genre-based activities

As you develop tasks for your ESP course, you will need to consider how to sequence them within a lesson or multi-lesson unit. Below I offer some guidelines for doing so.

1   Consider what activities your students need now and later within your overall course plan. In the French apartment-building simulation, for example, because students initially had to decide the building location and the identities of their characters, their first tasks included researching Paris neighborhoods and Parisian lifestyles and reading such texts as

maps and surveys about the French work week (Dupuy, 2006). In your course you can consider which genres and aspects of those genres and their contexts students will need to understand first, and then later and then later still, and order your activities accordingly.

2   Sequence activities so that they build upon one another. Related to the 'as needed' ordering principle in point 1 is what Dudley-Evans and St. John (1998) call the "building block" criterion for sequencing (p. 163), similar to 'scaffolding', discussed earlier. If you want to cover verb tenses in conference abstract moves, for example, you can first include a task on abstract moves, which will serve as a foundation for a subsequent class discussion on tense shifts across these moves.

3   Address one element of a genre at a time (at least at first). Genres, as you know by now, are multidimensional, characterized by organizational and linguistic elements, actions they accomplish, communities and individuals that use them, and much internal variability. Your students, however, do not need to apprehend all this at once. As Tardy (2009) points out, a multidimensional understanding of genre is "built up gradually through time, experience, and practice," and thus "[i]t may be somewhat overwhelming for novices … to dive head-on into an investigation of generic complexity" (p. 285). In your activity sequence, therefore, it is okay to begin with an exercise that deals with one genre dimension and then gradually include other tasks that address additional dimensions.

4   Vary the task types in your activity sequence. Given that different activities build different types of genre knowledge and skills, it is useful to include a range of tasks in each of your course units. Variety also helps prevent boredom, as one type of activity (e.g., moves analysis), no matter how engaging at first, could become tedious.

5   Include an interesting "hook" activity at the beginning of the sequence. Try to begin each unit with an enjoyable task that captures student interest. In my own lesson sequence on the book review genre, for example, I start by showing the class two YouTube videos of The Hustle dance (see Chapter 2) followed by discussion of the dancers' moves and ways that dance genres are similar to written genres. This activity energizes the students and gets them in a good mood for the next activity on analyzing book review moves.

Text selection

Genre-based tasks are usually based around one or more texts. In rhetorical consciousness-raising activities, for example, texts illustrate particular features of a genre or its context; in production tasks, they serve as models to follow or modify, or as content sources to incorporate; in process activities they can be used in various phases of text construction or reception. Equally important, a good text can add interest to a lesson. Below I discuss several types of texts—authentic, teacher-created, and student-generated—that you might select for your genre-based tasks and particular advantages of each text type.

Authentic texts

The prevailing view in ESP regarding classroom materials is that texts should be 'authentic', that is, taken from the real world rather than created exclusively for teaching (Basturkmen, 2010). The argument for using authentic texts is straightforward: To prepare students for the world outside of our classrooms, we should expose them to realistic examples of genres they will encounter 'out there'. Johns (1997), for example, asserts that "[t]he texts we choose should be full and unabridged, preserved just as they have been written, with letterheads, headings, spacing, fonts, visual detail, errors, and, if possible, even the quality and color of the paper" (p. 118). The same can also be said of spoken genre exemplars—that is, that they should retain all of their naturally occurring elements, including "ums" and "ahs," errors and repairs, and overlaps and interruptions across speakers.

An ESP materials designer can obtain authentic texts from existing corpora, some of which are freely available (see Chapter 3). Both Salehzadeh (2006) and Feak, Reinhart, and Rohlk (2009), for instance, have incorporated MICASE texts into their EAP listening and speaking materials. And Angouri (2010) drew on a collection of 21 audio-recorded business meetings to develop materials on meeting turn-taking, which is often livelier and messier than how it is represented in business English textbooks. You might also choose to collect your own text samples for genres you are researching or teaching, as Basturkmen (2010) did for police genres, Downey Bartlett (2005) for coffee service encounters, and Feak and Swales (2010) for perinatology RAs.

Teacher-created texts

Although authentic texts are important for representing genres accurately, so-called non-authentic materials, i.e., those created by teachers, curriculum developers, or textbook authors, may still have benefits in a genre-based course. For one, they can be composed with the language level and learning needs of the students in mind, often making them more accessible than authentic texts. In addition, teacher-created materials may at times be superior for illustrating certain target genre features. This is especially true when ESP practitioners are faced with what Swales (2009a) calls the "no perfect text" problem (p. 6); that is, the impossibility of finding a suitable genre exemplar despite long hours of "leafing through textbooks, manuals, journal articles or websites" (p. 5). When faced with such a dilemma, Swales has composed his own genre models. In fact, here's a surprise for you: The three "Joyce" literature review drafts discussed above were written by

Swales himself(!), who also constructed the fictional Joyce character. Reflecting on his reasons for doing so, Swales (2009a) notes that it would have been nearly impossible to find real-world samples with the journalistic style of Joyce's second draft and the integrative synthesis of her third draft, especially by one student. In cases like these, "when no amount of searching or sleuthing" will produce the desired genre exemplars, Swales encourages teachers to exercise their "textual creativity" (p. 12).

Student-generated texts

Students can also be a source of texts for your course. Johns (1999), for example, asks her undergraduates to bring to class samples of genres from their everyday lives, such as laundromat flyers or their favorite magazines, and to analyze them for their purposes, visual designs, linguistic elements, and their impact on communities. These 'homely genres' (Johns, 1997; Miller, 1984) provide students with an accessible inroad to examining how genres shape and are shaped by their social contexts, thus priming them "to view academic discourses as socially constructed as well" (Johns, 1997, p. 39). In other courses, students may be asked to collect multiple samples of a particular genre for use during and after their ESP course. Both Charles (2014) and Lee and Swales (2006), for example, have taught students to build their own computerized corpora of RAs in their disciplines and to analyze them using corpus software.

Having students collect their own texts has several benefits. The texts are usually relevant to students' personal, academic, or professional interests, so students may be more motivated to study them. Student-collected texts are also another source of authentic materials, and a whole class of student sleuths can generate a larger and better pool of genre exemplars for class discussion than the solo teacher searching for the elusive awesome text.

Task 6.3 Finding, creating, and asking for texts

1 Select one spoken or written genre. Pick a genre that you have not yet chosen for other tasks in this book. Here are a few options to get you going:

   a a brief news summary on the radio
   b a letter of complaint to an airline
   c a job application letter
   d another genre of your choice.

2 Do all of the following:

   a Find an authentic (i.e., real world) text illustrating this genre
   b Create your own text illustrating this genre.

c   Ask your students (or if you are not presently teaching, a peer) to find
    a text illustrating this genre.

3   Looking at your three or more texts generated in step 2, discuss which of
    these texts would work well for developing activities around the genre, and
    why? If more than one of these texts would be useful in their own ways,
    explain that also.

Assessing the impact of course materials

After selecting your texts, designing accompanying tasks, and figuring out a
reasonable activity sequence, you may want to find out if your genre-based
materials actually work. Do your tasks, for example, help students to become
more skillful at using a particular genre, or to develop genre awareness, or to
become more confident speakers and writers? Are the materials interesting
and motivating to students? This final section turns to how you might address
such questions through various assessment measures, including portfolios,
text annotations, pre- and post-tests, and student interviews.

Portfolio assessment

One way of assessing the impact of your materials on student learning is
through *portfolios*. These are collections of texts that students compile to
represent their work and development throughout a course (Hyland, 2007,
2016b; Johns, 1997). Portfolios typically contain both *primary texts*—that is,
those that students have produced for class assignments—and one or more
reflective texts in which students comment on their primary texts and their
experiences creating them. The primary and reflective texts in tandem offer
teachers insight into students' learning, as they demonstrate genre skills
students have acquired, their awareness of factors shaping their texts, and
their intellectual and rhetorical development over the trajectory of the
course. Although portfolios typically showcase students' written work, they
may also include recordings of students' spoken texts or multimodal texts
combining print, video, and audio media.

Portfolios can be used in various course designs. Johns (1997), for example,
has assigned portfolios in linked courses (see Chapter 5). In one of her EAP
courses linked to an undergraduate history class, students included within
their portfolios the following entries:

- a source-driven paper based on one of their history course assignments
- a reflection on their paper and what they learned from doing it
- a summary and critique of a spoken presentation they gave in the history
  class

- a reflection on how this summary/critique was similar to or different from other summaries they had written
- a first-person account of an event in which they were "an actor in history" (p. 147)
- the first page of one of the readings required in the history class
- a reflection on why that reading was important, difficult, and/or interesting to them; and what they had learned from it
- a timed essay they had written in the EAP class (based on prompts from their history class), and reflection on how it was similar to or different from other genres in their EAP and history class.

Varied entries like these offer teachers interesting data on what students have learned through their courses.

Textual annotations

Another way to assess students' genre learning is through textual annotations. Here students make notes in the margins of a text (or orally aloud) to articulate what they are noticing about the writer's or speaker's genre choices. Cheng (2008) has used such annotations to evaluate his students' developing awareness of these choices within the RA genre. He has focused, for example, on the annotations of an engineering doctoral student, Fengshen, whose comments on part of an RA introduction are shown below; the article excerpt

Table 6.2 Graduate student's annotation of an RA introduction

Excerpt from research article introduction	*Fengshen's annotation*
This article describes a network architecture and protocol that supports both of these dimensions of service portability: *device portability* and *location independence*. These portable services bring with them many challenges, but even more opportunities.	This is the end of introduction in this article. After giving the objective of this article, the author continues to evaluate the new method. He does not give a road map for the next part. The last sentence is very interesting to me. The author acknowledges that this new way would bring many challenges but he is very optimistic because he is confident that the opportunities it brings us are predominant. My guess is in the discussion part, some of the challenges will be brought up, so the author already paves his way for it in the beginning of the article. This tells us that echo in the whole article and pave your way for later parts are very helpful for your readers to understand your paper.

(From Cheng, 2008, p. 61, reformatted)

is on the left and Fengshen's annotation on the right. Cheng suggests that annotations like this one reflect Fengshen's "deepened understanding of how writer, reader, and purpose interact in a piece of text" (p. 65).

Pre- and post-tests

To evaluate students' acquisition of specific genre skills, teachers may also compare students' performances on production tests prior to and after the genre-based instruction. Yasuda (2011) employed such pre- and post-tests to ascertain if her EFL course activities on the email message genre improved her Japanese undergraduates' own writing of email messages. Below are the pre- and post-prompts that Yasuda asked her students to respond to: Prompt 1 at the beginning of the 15-week course and Prompt 2 at the end of the course. To ensure that the data were comparable between these two time periods, the prompts were similar, both requiring students to make requests of an "improvement committee" in response to "perceived shortcomings in a particular area" (p. 119).

> Pre-test, Prompt 1: Welcome to ABC University ...! You might want us to improve several things about the school, for example, school facilities, cafeteria, and bookstore, etc. Please write an email and tell us your requests. You must make at least two requests.
> Post-test, Prompt 2: Welcome to Atsugi City! You might want us to improve several things about the city, for example, the city's environment, entertainment, and public transportation, etc. Please write an email and tell us your requests. You must make at least two requests.
>
> (From Yasuda, 2011, p. 119)

In comparing students' email responses to these prompts, Yasuda found that after the instruction (i.e., on Prompt 2), students' messages had improved in organization, linguistic sophistication and appropriateness.

Interviewing students

It can also be illuminating to ask students directly how useful they found the course materials. Yasuda (2011), for example, supplemented her email-writing tests by interviewing students in part about "how successful the genre-based writing class was in helping them develop their genre awareness, language use, and writing ability" (p. 119). Similarly, in my own study of a genre-based EAP reading course, students were interviewed about whether their reading abilities or habits had changed or not since the course began and about how useful they found the class activities (Hyon, 2002).

Combining measures

It is possible, and often very fruitful, to combine assessment measures in order to achieve a multi-angle, triangulated perspective on your course materials. Cheng, for instance, used both student interviews and annotations, and, in our respective studies, Yasuda and I combined pre- and post-tests with interviews and written surveys. Portfolios as well could have complemented these other measures. Tardy (2009) also collected a variety of data to evaluate four multilingual graduate students' development of genre knowledge. These included texts that the students produced for their EAP writing course and their disciplinary courses; interviews with the students and their writing course teacher, and observations of the writing class and teacher–student conferences. Through these, Tardy was able to piece together a rich picture of influences inside and outside of EAP writing course materials that contributed to the students' genre learning.

You may now have some ideas for developing and evaluating ESP genre-based teaching materials of your own. The next chapter offers you further ideas for doing so, as it explores future directions for genre research and teaching.

Chapter 7

Exploring future issues
Genre play, learning, and transfer

This final chapter looks to possibilities for future ESP genre work in two emergent and interrelated areas: 1) *genre play* and 2) *genre learning transfer*. Taking each of the two topics in turn, the chapter considers why they are worth studying, current observations about each, and possibilities for future research on them and their intersections. The chapter concludes by considering how teaching that includes genre play may build students' adaptability as genre learners and users.

What is genre play and why study it?

Genre play as a phenomenon is most certainly not new, but ESP's interest in it has recently grown and promises to continue to do so for some time. As conceived of in some current scholarship on the subject, genre play involves a speaker's or writer's purposeful movement away from prototypical forms or functions of the genre s/he is using. A person who intentionally writes an RA without punctuation, or mentions their favorite ice cream on a mortgage application, or designs a funeral announcement as a crossword puzzle is engaging in genre play. These sorts of departures from genre norms have been variously described as genre innovation (Tardy, 2016), creativity (Bhatia, 2008, 2014), improvisation (Schryer, 2011), inventiveness (Hyon, 2008), resistance (Bawarshi, 2003), and play (Devitt, 2011; Tardy, 2016). In this chapter I stay with the term *play*, as it captures key senses of the other descriptors, including novelty, intentionality, and fun.

In her recent book *Beyond Convention: Genre Innovation in Academic Writing*, Tardy (2016) presents a number of reasons for studying genre play, or innovation, as she primarily calls it. I integrate several of her reasons here along with a few additional thoughts.

1   Genre play extends our concept of what a genre is and does. Although we may typically think of genres as fairly strict textual frames constraining how we speak and write, genre play reminds us of the creative forms, functions, and messages that are possible within these frames.

2   Related to 1, studying genre play offers us insight into our own human nature. For example, the existence of genre play in nearly all of life's domains, including serious, convention-dominant ones, suggests ways that humans are drawn to pushing boundaries and transgressing norms.

3   Genre play seems to be increasingly prevalent in spoken and written texts of various sorts and in various spheres. Tardy (2016) observes that in the world of research writing, for example, "more attempts at and opportunities for innovation within genres seem likely" given the great "diversity" and "mobility" of scholars collaborating on and distributing their work around the world (p. 18). Bhatia (2014) has similarly suggested that genres now are more likely to be complex than "pure" given the "the complex communicative realities of the present-day professional and academic world" (p. 92). One such reality is the advent of various online and social media technologies that encourage the blending of and playing with modalities and genres, and that showcase (for a wide audience) various cultural and individual approaches to doing so.

4   In such a genre-innovative world, it can be confusing for our students to know when it is okay for them to play with genres. Therefore, as Tardy (2015) emphasizes, investigating how genre play is *received* in different situations is important for illuminating—for both us and our students—when genre innovations are "allowable and rewarded" and, alternately, "when adhering to convention is a wiser option than breaking from it" (p. 360).

5   Finally, as will be discussed at the end of this chapter, research on genre play can illuminate its usefulness in genre-based teaching, particularly as a means for building students' flexibility as genre participants in a genre-innovative world (Hyon, 2015).

Forms of genre play

ESP scholars and others have explored several varieties of genre play, including *genre stretching, genre mixing*, and *genre parody*. This next section considers what can be observed about these different play types, or strategies, and reasons why individuals may choose to engage in them.

Genre stretching

As its name implies, *genre stretching* involves departing from or pushing against a genre's conventions, but in a way that stops short of 'breaking' the text's genre. A company that writes a car maintenance manual with jokes, for example, is genre stretching, as is also a professor who delivers a lecture via song or a restaurant owner who includes scratch-and-sniff pictures in her menu. In each of these cases, the 'stretchers' are creating unusual members of their genres (manual, lecture, menu) but they would be genre members nonetheless, albeit playful ones. Some scholars have used the similar term 'genre bending' (e.g., Bhatia, 2014) to refer to genre norm-deviations, although bending has sometimes entailed more radical genre transformation than stretching.

In terms of why people stretch genres, as Bhatia (2014) points out, in some instances it may be to fulfill their own "private intentions" (p. 99). Dunn (2005), for example, has found that in Japanese wedding speeches, speakers may defy genre norms to compensate personally for their lack of ability to follow these norms in the usual way. Typically in this genre, says Dunn, speech-givers share personal anecdotes about the bride and groom. Certain guests, however, choose to speak at length about things seemingly unrelated to either member of the wedding couple because they do not have enough personal knowledge of the couple to offer in their speech. Dunn observed that a groom's colleague at an electronics company, for instance, included in his speech "a detailed description of the production process for color filters for liquid crystal television screens" (p. 224). Alternatively, guests may use these departures to promote themselves or their company, as did one guest who, "[a]pologizing for sounding 'a bit like an advertisement,'" continued on to mention that his company "would be featured in an upcoming television news program" that he "invited everyone to watch" (p. 224).

Self-promotion may, in fact, be a driving force behind much genre stretching, as illustrated well in an innovative lease-renewal letter Tardy received from her apartment building's rental company (Tardy, 2016). The letter, which began with a standard salutation and notification that Tardy's lease was expiring, included this humorous twist on the closing move:

> We truly, truly, truly hope you decide to stay with us but we also understand that residents eventually have to move. Should you decide not to renew, we will be very sad and require extensive psychological therapy, so please renew.
>
> (Tardy, 2016, p. 13)

Tardy suggests that this instance of genre stretching helped to further the company's "playful, off-beat" brand identity—an image that the company readily cultivated in other ways as well, such as giving tenants move-in gifts and front-door doughnut deliveries (p. 42).

Also related to private intention, genre stretching can be a means for speakers and writers to resist dominant discourses and assert alternative individual or cultural identities and ideologies (Tardy, 2016). Canagarajah (2006) has observed this phenomenon with Tamil scholars publishing in international contexts, including one scholar, Sivatamby, who, when writing an RA for an international English-medium journal, left out typical introductory moves such as literature review, creating a niche, and article preview, omissions that are characteristic of some Tamil research publications. Cana-garajah (2006) suggests that such opting out of certain genre norms is one way that multilingual writers like Sivatamby locate "spaces within the dominant conventions to insert [their] own voice and preferred conventions" (p. 600).

While genre stretching serves these individualized purposes for its users, it can also (sometimes simultaneously) fulfill the conventional functions of the genre. The lease letter Tardy received, for example, although idiosyncratic in its promotion of the company's fun image, did encourage her to renew her lease—and its playful style achieved this in an effective, memorable way. Ashmore's innovative doctoral thesis (1985) and later book, *The Reflexive Thesis: Wrighting Sociology of Scientific Knowledge* (1989) is another inter-esting example of norm-stretching to achieve official genre purposes. His text— which focuses on the topic of reflexivity in his discipline, the sociology of scientific knowledge (SSK)—pushes the boundaries of all major parts of a doctoral thesis. His opening abstract, for instance, ends abruptly in the middle of a sentence about word length. The first chapter takes the form of a faux university lecture in which a "Plump Bald-headed Old Geezer" in the back of the room challenges the lecturer/author, who, disturbed, says to himself: 'How did he get in here? ... I was supposed to be this week's Expert, expected to expound on an important and interesting topic for their edification and instruction ..." (Ashmore, 1989, p. 15). And there are many more inventive elements throughout the book, including the final Notes section, which addresses the reader in the following unusual 'voice':

> Welcome to the Notes. I hope you will visit this section of the text regularly. Quite a lot will be going on here and it would be a shame to miss it all. But to get to the business of this particular note. May I ask you by which route you have arrived at Chapter One, note 1?
>
> (Ashmore, 1989, p. 227)

With all of these innovations, one might wonder whether Ashmore's text is a real thesis, or just a parody of one. But interestingly, these playful, parodic features serve his thesis' scholarly argument, which in this case is about reflexivity in SSK, a discipline that studies the status of knowledge claims in other fields but, as Ashmore highlights, is not always reflexive about its own claims. Through playing with thesis conventions, Ashmore puts a con-sciously reflexive spotlight on his thesis and, more broadly, on the need for reflexivity in SSK.

Genre mixing

Another form of genre play is *genre mixing*, that is, the blending of features from multiple genres within a single text (Bhatia, 2014). Examples of hybrid-genre texts are indeed many and varied, from a marriage proposal on a fortune cookie strip to a graphic-novel cookbook (e.g., Capps, 2013). One sphere where Bhatia (2014) has observed genre mixing to be common is advertising, where marketers are "always on the lookout for novel strategies to promote their products and services" (p. 154). In such texts as "advertorials" (p. 101, 154), for example, elements of the news editorial genre are mixed into an advertisement to help persuade consumers to buy the product. One thinks here of advertorials for medical treatments, where journalistic formatting and language are meant to lend credibility to the advertiser's potentially questionable claims.

In academic settings, as well, students have been observed to playfully mix genres for various purposes—some also self-promotional—even in response to not intentionally playful assignments. Tardy (2016), for instance, reports that in her first-year undergraduate writing course, an Argentinian international student majoring in art, Juan Tauber, submitted a highly innovative set of hybrid texts for the final portfolio project. For the portfolio's required reflective cover letter, Juan wrote something that read like "a prologue to an art history book," and—even more creatively—told in the voice of a fictional art historian discovering Juan's writing posthumously (Tardy, 2016, p. 157). The excerpts below give a sense of Juan's mixed cover letter/ prologue.

> Continuing my research on the life and work of the acclaimed underground artist Juan Tauber (1978–2015) I recently discovered a series of essays, presumably written by him in the winter of 2008, that provide solid examples of the artist as a young person and his early ideas on art ...
>
> As the records show, Juan Tauber was born in 1978 in a small city named Rio Cuarto in the province of Cordoba, Argentina ... At the age of 19, presumably fleeing from the law with a much older lover, he moved to the capital of that country, Buenos Aires. There, Tauber enrolled in the UBA (University of Buenos Aires) pursuing a degree in textile design ...
>
> (From Tardy, 2016, p. 156, excerpted from her Figure 5.4)

Later in this text, Juan, still in the narrator's voice, does indeed comment on his writing in Tardy's course, as was expected for the assignment. Also, as required, he includes samples of his course writing within his portfolio. Yet even here he mixes genres, "re-design[ing]" his writing samples to look like "crumpled artifacts rather than freshly submitted student papers" (Tardy, 2015, p. 340).

In terms of what possibly motivated Juan's genre play, Tardy (2015) tells us that throughout her course, Juan "was not one to write within the box" and that he "took an unconventional approach" on all of the class assignments (p. 340). Thus, his textual blends in the portfolio might be a way to express his personality, voice, and identity (in the spirit of "private intentions"

(Bhatia, 2014)). Simultaneously, however, Juan might be genre mixing in order to fulfill standard purposes of a first-year undergraduate writing portfolio. Tardy, in fact, observes that Juan's experimental prologue *enhances* the reflectiveness desired for this project. Or, as she writes, "Taking an outsider view to his own texts allows him a kind of critical distance that actually results in a more persuasive reflection on his writing than is typically found in this genre" (Tardy, 2016, p. 157).

Genre parody

Like genre stretching and mixing, parody is a kind of genre play with multiple potential motivations and effects. It is distinctive from these other genre play forms, however, in that it hyper-imitates—rather than deviates from—a genre's features, and through this exaggerated mimicry, mocks the genre and its purposes. In Bex's (1996) words, parody "uses the conventions appropriate to a particular genre to reveal and call into question the social functions served by that genre" (p. 226). Thus, in many if not most instances, parody actually creates a different genre with different purposes (i.e., critical exposé) than the genre it is imitating; as Hyland (2004b) writes, it "impersonate[s] the form of a genre while subverting its function" (p. 70).

Parodies have been performed of many genres—everything from news broadcasts to funerals to documentaries (a.k.a. 'mockumentaries') and others. Academic genres have also been parodied, including the ubiquitous RA. Bex (1996) refers to one such parody RA (which you may appreciate as a language teacher) entitled "The Use of Sensory Deprivation in Foreign Language Teaching" published by Swan and Walter (1982) in the long-running and well-regarded *ELT Journal*. At first skim, Swan and Walker's text appears to be a normal journal article, with the expected organizational moves. But a few paragraphs in, the reader registers the ridiculousness of the content in these moves, such as the following description of the experimental method in which language students are "taken to their individual SD [sensory deprivation] chambers ... each containing a bath in which the water is kept at a constant temperature of 37° C—blood heat" (p. 184). After 3–5 hours in their SD chambers, the 'article' tells us, the students begin to hallucinate in the second language (L2) input they heard in the half hour before entering the chamber. They then are "dried off and dressed" and allowed to meet each other and talk in the L2 (p. 184). However, they find it difficult to communicate because "each subject has attached his own private hallucination-generated meanings ('H-meanings') to the L2 elements that he has internalized" (p. 184).

This text caricatures the genre of the teaching methodology article, in addition to critiquing, as Bex (1996) points out, "the dangerous faddishness" that frequently invades English language teaching as a profession (p. 235), where eccentric, trendy methods often come and go. Swan and Walter's critique, however, seems to be delivered with more collegial fun than bite.

One imagines readers chuckling at the "worryingly high drop-out rate" of students in these classes (p. 185); and fellow researchers who have coined their own terms may laugh a bit at themselves when they read about the "H-meanings." In this way, Swan and Walter's text and other parodies, despite their taunting elements, can still entertain and build connection with their audiences.

Not all parodies, however, are delivered or received in a spirit of solidarity. Another case of a fake RA, now known as the "Sokal hoax," caused offense and consternation among some of its readers (Secor & Walsh, 2004). Physicist Alan Sokal submitted a manuscript, "Transgressing the Boundaries: Toward a Transformative Hermeneutics of Quantum Gravity," which was accepted in the journal *Social Text* (Sokal, 1996). Although Sokal's manuscript was meant as a critique of the journal's cultural studies bent and of what Sokal perceived as a general decline of academic rigor in the humanities, the journal editors did not recognize the text as parody and published it as a real article (Secor & Walsh, 2004; Tardy, 2016). Indeed, in their rhetorical analysis of this text, Secor and Walsh observe that Sokal so skillfully imitated the syntax and thematic focuses of *Social Text* articles that the editors missed his parodic exaggerations, such as the 20 pages of endnotes and references. When Sokal himself revealed, soon after publication, that his article was a fake, the revelation not only embarrassed the journal but angered those who felt his deception was harmful. Indeed, this type of genre play may be particularly painful when it intentionally exposes people as not having recognized its mockery. As Secor and Walsh point out, "[t]he Sokal hoax was all the more stinging because it duped sophisticated academic professionals" (pp. 72–73).

In other ways, as well, parody may not always be perceived as such. Some texts, for example, may both poke fun at a genre and fulfill some of its real purposes, making it unclear whether they are parodic or true genre exemplars. Instances of such 'in-between', semi-parodic texts are plentiful in comedic news programs such as the *The Daily Show*. This program has news mockery and humor as its core purposes, yet a number of viewers watch it as a main news source (Feldman, 2007). It has also been found to include as much substantive news content as mainstream broadcast news programs (Fox, Koloen, & Sahin, 2007) and has 'acted' like real news does, raising public awareness of issues and even influencing U.S. government legislation (Carter & Stelter, 2010). Task 7.1 below gives you a chance to explore the elements that contribute to both the parodic and real aspects of this show.

Task 7.1 Examining parody and reality in a comedic news show

1   Watch several episodes from *The Daily Show* www.cc.com/shows/the-daily-show-with-trevor-noah on topics of interest to you.

2   Select one of these episodes for closer analysis.

3   What aspects of a real news show does this episode imitate?

4   How does this episode critique these aspects of real news or its subject matter? For example, does it exaggerate them, caricature them in a particular way, and so on?

5   To what extent does the episode, even while making fun of the news, also function as real news? How so?

6   What might be the potential usefulness of examining a comedic news show in an ESP course?

What makes genre play work?

As the examples thus far have illustrated, speakers or writers engage in genre play with potentially multiple effects—some that serve idiosyncratic (often self-promotional) purposes of the individual 'genre players' and some that fulfill status quo purposes of the genres they are playing with. Whether individuals succeed in any of these purposes, however, depends not just on their skill in genre stretching, mixing, or parodying, but also on how their play is received by listeners and readers. Indeed, Tardy (2016) emphasizes audience *reception* as crucial in determining whether genre departures count as successful innovations or as deviant mishaps (p. 11). She and others have identified several factors influencing the likelihood of audience receptivity to genre play, including the flexibility of the genre, the authority of the genre 'player', and the perceived value of the play.

Flexibility of the genre

Speakers and writers are more likely to have their inventiveness accepted if they are playing with genres whose conventions are frequently stretched. These "baggy" (i.e., loose) genres, as Bawarshi (2003), after Medway (1998), has referred to them, "provide more room for transgression than others" (Bawarshi, p. 92). Of the genres discussed thus far in this chapter, advertisements, comedic news shows, and multimedia texts would fall toward the baggy end of the genre-flexibility continuum. By contrast, bureaucratic forms and legal texts would be on the tight, conservative end, given their strongly prescribed conventions and the likely negative consequences of breaking them.

Task 7.2 Baggy versus tight genres

This task gives you an opportunity to rank the relative bagginess of different genres in terms of the amount of creativity they readily allow, or not.

1   Place each of the following genres along the baggy–tight continuum below.

Baggy<=––––––––––––––––––––=>Tight
Birth certificates
University lectures
Online blog posts
Sympathy cards
Job advertisements
Novels
Eulogies
Restaurant menus
Job termination letters
Church newsletters
Laboratory reports
Conference papers
YouTube videos

2   From your continuum above, what factors do you notice determine whether a genre is baggy or tight?

3   Do either a or b.

   a   Select one of the genres above and find an example of a playful text within that genre (i.e., a text that stretches or mixes conventions in that genre).

   b   Parody is a form of genre play that may occur in even very tight genres, as we have seen with RA parodies. Find a parody of one of the genres above or another genre. Try searching the internet for "parody of _____" (fill in the blank with the genre of your choice). What aspects of this genre does the parody exaggerate or mock?

Authority of the genre player

Another factor determining whether genre play is viewed as effective is the perceived legitimacy of the genre player to innovate. Tardy (2016), drawing on Bourdieu's (1991) economic model of language use, points out that the right to innovate is earned over time as individuals produce texts (probably following genre conventions closely) that are accepted by others as appropriate and valuable. Their valued discourse then grants them the social "capital" to playfully break genre conventions (Tardy, 2016, p. 36). The influence of this accumulated capital is seen, among other places, in academic writing, where "many examples of innovation ... come from authors who have already established their linguistic and disciplinary competence and who hold relatively high status within their field" (Tardy, 2016, p. 36).

I recently came across an example of earned authority licensing genre play—this time in a spoken civic text. On June 26, 2015, U.S. president Barack Obama

Figure 7.1 "The President Honors the Life of Reverend Clementa Pinckney"
(screenshot)
Source: The Obama White House, YouTube (26 June 2015). Available at www.you
tube.com/watch?v=rRvBzzR5tdA.

delivered a eulogy for the Reverend Clementa Pinckney, a South Carolina state
senator and pastor, who was one of nine African Americans killed by a white
supremacist gunman at the Mother Emanuel African Methodist Episcopal
Church. President Obama's discourse, delivered at Reverend Pinckney's funeral
in South Carolina and televised nationally (see screenshot in Figure 7.1), was
very well received, even though (or maybe because) it was innovative in its
mixing of and playing with several genres, including the eulogy, the religious
sermon, and the presidential speech.

In eulogy-like sections of his address, such as in the following excerpt,
Obama described Pinckney's personal qualities, legacy, and contributions:

> Reverend Pinckney embodied a politics that was neither mean, nor
> small. He conducted himself quietly, and kindly, and diligently … He
> was full of empathy and fellow feeling, able to walk in somebody else's
> shoes and see through their eyes. No wonder one of his senate colleagues
> remembered Senator Pinckney as "the most gentle of the 46 of us—the best
> of the 46 of us."

Yet at other points, Obama uses sermon-like discourse. He opens his
remarks that day, for example, with a religious salutation and invokes the
Bible on hope and faith, to the approving applause of his audience: "Giving
all praise and honor to God. [Applause.] The Bible calls us to hope. To
persevere, and have faith in things not seen."

In other sections of his text as well, Obama, as a preacher might, calls his
listeners to live better lives in response to God's grace.

As a nation, out of this terrible tragedy, God has visited grace upon us, for he has allowed us to see where we've been blind. [Applause.] ... He's once more given us grace. But it is up to us now to make the most of it, to receive it with gratitude, and to prove ourselves worthy of this gift.

And then at other times, the president moves into the genre of political speech, as he connects the shooting to broad societal issues such as racism, voting rights, and gun control.

Maybe we now realize the way racial bias can infect us even when we don't realize it, so that we're guarding against not just racial slurs, but we're also guarding against the subtle impulse to call Johnny back for a job interview but not Jamal. [Applause.] So that we search our hearts when we consider laws to make it harder for some of our fellow citizens to vote. [Applause.]

For too long, we've been blind to the unique mayhem that gun violence inflicts upon this nation. [Applause.]

Finally, President Obama closes his address with still another genre—and a musical one: He sings the classic Christian hymn *Amazing Grace*. This final act of genre mixing surprises and delights the audience, who join him in singing. (For a complete video of President Obama's eulogy for Reverend Pinckney, please see www.c-span.org/video/?c4542228/president-obama-eulo gy-clementa-pinckney-funeral-service. All of the printed excerpts above are from https://obamawhitehouse.archives.gov/the-press-office/2015/06/26/ remarks-president-eulogy-honorable-reverend-clementa-pinckney.)

Obama's hybrid discourse was very well accepted, as evidenced not just by the immediate audience's frequent and enthusiastic applause but also by the follow-up press coverage, which indeed was not uniform in their naming of the genre of Obama's text. The *Wall Street Journal* called it "an impassioned eulogy" (Lee & Nelson, 2015, par. 1), the *Los Angeles Times* "a moving address" (Memoli, 2015, par. 2), and *Forbes* magazine "a standout speech" that "soared rhetorically and emotionally" (Morgan, 2015, par. 1–2). This successful reception was undoubtedly due in large part to the significant, in Bourdieu's terms, 'capital' Obama had that day to play with certain genres. As an African American Christian, he had authority to use the moves of a black church sermon in a national address—even in a country that values the separation of church and state—much more so than, say, a white and/or nonreligious president, whose mentioning of God's grace, use of black religious cadences, or singing of a hymn might be seen as strained or even offensive attempts at insider-ness. Obama was also in a space—a funeral attended by many black clergy—that licensed and encouraged him to invoke his religious identity. At the same time, his position as U.S. president legitimized his forays into the political speech genre at a funeral. In fact, it would have been surprising if, during this nationally televised event, Obama as president had not spoken on issues affecting the country. Thus, Obama's layers of discourse capital—connected to multiple aspects of his identity— allowed his hybrid text to work in a highly effective manner with a broad audience of listeners.

Value of the play products

Even when a genre is tight rather than baggy or when the speaker or writer lacks obvious capital to innovate, genre play may still be successful if the audience perceives it to produce something of value. Tardy's student Juan, for example, could 'get away with' being inventive for a serious final course project at least in part because of the intellectual and creative benefits his playfulness produced. Indeed, his portfolio won "a university-wide writing competition" (Tardy, 2016, p. 157). Tardy (2015, 2016) reports on a some- what similar case in the writing of Frank, an undergraduate in an environ- mental science research methods course. For this course, Frank composed an innovative research proposal (on the safety of produce grown on urban land), whose moves deviated from those that the professor recommended. Specifically, while the professor told the students that their proposals should begin with a "big idea" (Tardy, 2015, p. 350) laying out the importance of their topic, Frank opened his proposal with a specific scene "[o]n the south side of Chicago" where "unused plots of land are being transformed into small-scale urban farms" (Tardy, 2016, p. 114). And instead of closing his introduction with a hypothesis predicting a particular outcome (as the pro- fessor recommended), Frank indicated that his hypothesis about the safety of an urban farm's leafy greens might be incorrect and that, if so, he was "determined to understand why, and propose solutions to the problem" (p. 113). Interestingly, despite Frank's departures from the guidelines, the professor was very impressed with his proposal, noting that it was one of the best in the class, not just due its innovativeness but because it demon- strated a kind of creative thinking valued in science.

Task 7.3 Identifying what makes genre play successful

1   Look back at Task 7.2 and select one of the genres from the list or another genre.
2   Describe an example (an imaginary example is okay) of how someone might stretch or mix conventions of that genre. If you did 3a in this task, you should already have an example.
3   Explain how each of these factors could influence how well an audience would receive this instance of genre play:

- the bagginess of the genre;
- the speaker's or writer's capital to play with its conventions;
- the value of what is produced by the play.

The sections above have offered an overview of three strategies of genre play. Seeing these strategies in action reminds us that genres are more flexible than we often assume and that stretching, mixing, and parodying them can achieve multiple outcomes.

Possibilities for future genre play research

Genre play as a scholarly topic is in its relative genesis in ESP studies, and further research could yield insights of value to ESP practitioners and their students. One possible long-term project could involve building a public corpus of genre play exemplars, perhaps called the *Corpus of Innovative Texts* or *Corpus of Genre Play.* Scholars, teachers, and anyone else would be welcome (and invited) to submit examples they encounter of texts that depart from genre conventions, along with information about the texts' contexts. Such a corpus could serve as a great resource for ESP teachers seeking examples of innovative, genre-pushing texts to show their students. With these texts, students could also examine patterns in where and why genre play occurs, looking at, for example, textual dimensions most or least subject to convention-breaking or the demographic qualities of people who engage in genre play and how well their play is received and under what circumstances. Such analysis tasks could prepare students to interpret genre play in texts they read and listen to, as well as appreciate when they might engage in it themselves and to what effect. Using digital humanities technologies, it would also be interesting to create an interactive map of locations (geographical and/or online) of innovative texts in the corpus. Map-based projects could then track possible clustering of play texts and whether these clusters precede the standardization of previously innovative genre features.

What is genre learning transfer and why study it

Another area for future ESP research is genre learning transfer—that is, students' application of what they learn from a genre-based course to new contexts. Most studies on this topic have measured the impact of students' classroom-based genre learning in the short-term—for example, right after a course or lesson sequence. Relatively little is known about how much of this learning 'sticks' or if students are able to apply it to new situations. This question of the long-term transferability of classroom learning is important, for it asks us to consider whether our course designs and materials have lasting value for students. We hope that they do, but at present there is little documented evidence to that effect. In the research that does exist on this issue, two sub-questions have been central: 1) To what extent do students retain genre knowledge gained in a course? 2) How successfully do they transfer this knowledge to understanding or producing texts within new genres? The next section considers scholarship that addresses these questions.

Current observations of genre learning transfer

Retention of genre learning from instruction

In order for students to transfer genre knowledge or awareness, they first need to be able to hold it in memory, even if only on a subconscious level. Some research suggests that students are able to do this. In my own study of an ESL reading course, for instance, I found that students remembered, over an extended period of time, at least some of the course's genre-based material (Hyon, 2001). Eight of my students were interviewed one year after the course ended, and were prompted to describe genres taught in the course. Specifically, they were presented with four texts (which they had not seen before) that represented the four genres covered in class (hard news story, feature article, textbook, and research article), and for each text they were asked what they would call that "passage" and why (p. 423). Although students did not always remember the class names for these texts (particularly the news genres), they did mention specific genre features discussed in the course (e.g., the feature article's opening anecdote, the textbook's authoritative language, and the RA's introductory gap move), and they could point out these elements in the sample texts during the interview.

In another post-course follow-up study, Charles (2014) found that some students retained and continued to use specific genre analysis methods they learned from the course instruction. She surveyed 40 international graduate students one year after they completed an EAP course that taught them to build their own corpora of RAs (from their disciplines) and to use corpus tools like word frequency and collocation lists for examining lexicogrammatical features. Impressively, 70 percent of the students said that they had used their personal RA corpus sometime in the year following the course; and 38 percent of them were "regular users" of their corpus (consulting it once a week or more) (p. 34). Some users also found the corpus analysis tools particularly helpful for learning how to use English grammatical patterns and vocabulary in their own research writing. One enthusiastic student commented, "It's such fun to make different queries. It's like having a lovely friend with you who can advise you anytime you want" (Charles, 2014, p. 37). Some students also continued to build their corpora after the course; one, in fact, created a corpus with 640 research papers, and another who was conducting an interdisciplinary research investigation, developed three corpora of RAs from three fields in order to understand terminological differences across these disciplines. Thus, these students were able to retain and apply the course's genre analysis techniques (and specifically, corpus tools skills) over a substantial amount of time.

Transfer of genre learning to new texts and situations

Although it is helpful to see that, in at least these two studies, students held on to genre knowledge and text analysis strategies they had gained in a course, a still pressing question is whether students can transfer such course learning to navigating genres that are brand new to them. If the answer to this question is yes, then genre-based instruction has potentially long-lasting benefits for students, preparing them to understand and use many different kinds of texts in the future—way beyond those covered in the course.

High-road vs. low-road transfer

To explore the transferability of classroom-acquired genre knowledge, researchers in ESP and, even more so, Rhetorical Genre Studies (RGS) have returned to *transfer of learning* scholarship from the late 1980s, and particularly that of educational psychologists David Perkins and Gavriel Salomon (Beaufort, 2007; Brent, 2011, Johns, 2011; Reiff & Bawarshi, 2011). Perkins and Salomon's work is concerned not only with whether learners can transfer previous knowledge to novel contexts but also whether they can do it wisely and effectively. Specifically, they examine learners' engagement in *high-road transfer*, a process involving "deliberate mindful abstraction of skill or knowledge from one context for application in another" (Perkins & Salomon, 1988, p. 25). Although they developed this concept in relation to all types of learning (and not particularly genre learning), their "deliberate" and "mindful" descriptors allow us to envision someone, such as an ESP student, making conscious choices regarding if and when to transfer prior knowledge about one genre to another genre. For example, we might imagine a professor learning to give a TED Talk (see Chapter 2). This professor could make thoughtful, i.e., 'high-road', decisions about what she should or should not transfer from the university lecture genre that she already knows. She might mindfully decide to incorporate into her TED Talk anecdotes, as she does in her lectures, but at the same time to forgo her usual introductory outline of points, given the TED Talk time constraints and the importance of surprise in this genre.

Salomon and Perkins distinguish this conscious high-road transfer process from *low-road transfer*, or "the spontaneous, automatic transfer of highly practiced skills, with little need for reflective thinking" (Salomon & Perkins, 1989, p. 118). While low-road transfer is not necessarily bad transfer, as it facilitates quick, mindless application of skills across two similar situations (e.g., chopping a carrot and chopping a zucchini), reflective and selective high-road transfer is needed across distant contexts, such as across two different genres.

Adaptive transfer

A somewhat similar concept to high-road transfer is what DePalma and Ringer (2011) call *adaptive transfer*: the "conscious or intuitive process of applying *or reshaping* learned writing knowledge in new and potentially unfamiliar writing situations" (p. 141, emphasis added). (Their definition could apply to speaking situations as well.) Like high-road transfer, adaptive transfer is needed between two situations where the speaker or writer should apply some (but not all) skills and knowledge from one situation to another. However, unlike Perkins and Salomon's "mindful" descriptor of high-road transfer, adaptive transfer, as DePalma and Ringer describe it, may be either conscious *or* "intuitive" (p. 141). Thus, in this view, the university professor learning to give a TED Talk might have varying degrees of consciousness of how she is adapting her previous lecture genre knowledge to fit the new TED Talk genre. What is important to DePalma and Ringer is that adaptive transfer involves *transforming* previously learned knowledge for the new context, rather than just reusing this knowledge in the same form in which it was learned.

Investigations of high-road, adaptive transfer of genre knowledge

Although relatively little research has assessed students' abilities to transfer genre knowledge adaptively, a few studies have, and point to ways that ESP courses might prepare students to be effective genre knowledge 'transformers'. I offer brief snapshots of four such studies here—three of which explore how students transfer genre knowledge learned in academic contexts, like their university courses, to workplace contexts. Brent (2012) observes that this is transfer with "the most long-term consequences for students" (p. 561). These investigations also allow us to imagine how transfer may happen across other domains—such as from spoken to written communications, from the everyday to the academic, and from one workplace to another.

PARKS (2001): TWEAKING PRIOR GENRE KNOWLEDGE

Parks (2001) studied French Canadian nurses learning a new version of a genre they had learned before. As such, the transfer 'distance' was not radical: The new nurses were learning to write 'care plans' in Anglophone hospitals where they worked, after having previously written care plans in their Francophone university nursing programs. Still, because of differences between the two care plan varieties, they needed to adapt their prior knowledge and not just transfer it low-road style. What helped them to do this was observing the Anglophone hospital care plans while doing their rounds and collaborating on their plans with more experienced nurses. Through such activities, they recognized that the Anglophone hospital care plans allowed for, among other things, simpler diagnostic sections and use of medical diagnostic terms (e.g., *diabetes*) not permitted in their university nursing programs, where such language had been seen as the purview of the doctors.

SMART AND BROWN (2002): ADAPTING GENERAL GENRE PRINCIPLES

When the transfer distance between a course and an outside context is large, specific genre knowledge may not be transferable, though broad genre principles still can be. In their study of undergraduates completing workplace internships, for instance, Smart and Brown (2002) found that students successfully applied such principles and did so in a transformative, adaptive fashion. Specifically, their 24 undergraduate professional writing majors were able to apply concepts and skills they had learned in their writing coursework, such as "reader-centered writing" and research strategies, to new genres in their internships (p. 130). One intern noted, for example, that focusing on such ideas helped him to write to his expert readership, which included tech-savvy clients at a financial institution. In an interview for Smart and Brown's study, he said: "We're not writing to the everyday guy, Joe Day-Trader. So with the whole concept of reader-centered writing—we have to remember that we're writing for advanced to expert-level programmers and people like that" (from Smart & Brown, 2002, p. 130).

And students were able to adapt these rhetorical concepts for their worksites fairly quickly. As Smart and Brown note, "[t]ypically the interns were not given an opportunity to rehearse the genres in which they were working … ; rather, they were almost immediately placed in situations where they were expected to contribute as practitioners competent enough to accomplish significant work assignments" (p. 122). Similar to what Parks found with the nurses in the hospital setting, what helped the interns to apply and adapt previously learned genre principles were interactions with co-workers and time spent reviewing company documents to learn about their sites' cultural norms.

BRENT (2012): APPLYING GENRE SURVIVAL SKILLS FROM ALL OF LIFE

When faced with new genres, students may transfer a mix of different types of knowledge from both prior instruction and other life experiences. Brent (2012) found this to be the case in his study of Canadian undergraduates completing a workplace internship. Out of the six interns he studied (from a variety of disciplines), four of them had taken or were taking a professional communication course that focused on workplace genres. Interestingly, however, these four students, in their interviews with Brent, referenced this course as a source of only some of the genre knowledge and skills relevant to their internships, for which they wrote such varied texts as client surveys, news article summaries, church Sunday school lesson plans, control audits, and strategic marketing plans. In particular, the students, like those in Smart and Brown's study, indicated that from the professional communications course, they transferred broad abilities and knowledge, such as conciseness and awareness that workplace texts are organized hierarchically. Much of what the interns transferred, though, came not from just this single course but from the whole of their educational and other life experiences, which gave them what Brent calls "rhetorical survival instincts" (p. 586). For example, their experience with writing assignments in their degree programs primed them to seek out models for new genres in their workplaces, to tweak those models as needed, and to think about their audiences. One of the interns had also juggled school with work and other activities, giving her skills in personal organization and task management. Others also had experience with flexible maneuvering across multiple genres. In sum, says Brent, "the students seemed to be transferring not so much specific knowledge and skills as a general disposition to make rhetorical judgments" (p. 589)—a disposition developed out the totality of their experience.

REIFF AND BAWARSHI (2011): CROSSING GENRE BOUNDARIES LIKE A NOVICE

In the three studies above, all of the participants seemed able to transfer their previous genre knowledge or rhetorical strategies adaptively and effectively. Some individuals, though, may be better prepared (or naturally more inclined) to do this than others. Reiff and Bawarshi (2011) found this to be so among undergraduates in a first-year written composition (FYC) course. In studying how these students applied knowledge from secondary school, work, or everyday experiences to their FYC texts, they found that some engaged in high-road transfer where they selectively drew on strategies (such as analyzing a text, defending a stance, or using a quotation) from genres they had written before. These learners Reiff and Bawarshi called "boundary crossers," able to "repurpose" their antecedent genre knowledge so that it could cross over "for use in new contexts" (p. 325). Other students, however, did not adapt previously learned strategies and instead low-road transferred in whole genres, like the five-paragraph essay, even when these did not fit the FYC assignment. These "boundary guarders" seemed to hold on to their previous textual understandings "even in the face of new and disparate tasks" (p. 325).

Given that ideally our students would become nimble boundary crossers, it is interesting to note what Reiff and Bawarshi observed about these crossers as learners. Contrary to what we might expect, in their interviews these students "expressed a lack of confidence in approaching the [FYC] writing task based on their prior genre knowledge" and instead assumed the role of a beginner needing to figure out the new FYC genres (p. 325). Reflecting this humble orientation, the boundary crossers also used a lot of what Reiff and Bawarshi call "not talk" (p. 329) to describe their FYC texts—that is, commenting on what antecedent genres the FYC texts were *not* like (e.g., not like their high school term papers). In their cautious approach, these students were "mindful of the need for reinventing and reimagining [their prior] strategies" (p. 326). By contrast, the boundary-guarding students were much more confident in—and clung tightly to—their prior genres, making them more susceptible to low-road transfer that did not fit the FYC tasks. In light of these two learner profiles, Reiff and Bawarshi recommended that teachers encourage their students to adopt "the role of novice" so that they remain open to using, repurposing, and moving away from prior genre knowledge as the context demands (p. 330). They also suggest that teachers incorporate assignments "that invite students to mix genres and modalities ... and then to reflect afterward on the experience of crossing between genres and domains"—in other words, tasks that compel students to re-think and adapt their previous genre understandings (p. 332).

Taken together, the four studies above suggest that as students are faced with learning new genres, they *are* able to transfer and transform previous knowledge and skills (some specific and some general) gained through instruction. But what enables them to engage in high-road, adaptive transfer may go beyond a single course and include mentoring from experts in the new context, rhetorical 'street smarts' developed over time, and the orientation of a beginner.

Possibilities for future genre learning transfer research

Regarding future ESP research, several transfer-related topics could be usefully explored, with relevance for genre-based teaching. I consider two such topics below.

Over-transfer of genre knowledge

One interesting question for ESP researchers to take up is how *over-transfer* functions in students' development as genre users. Freedman (1994) has argued that genre-based instruction creates a potential "risk of overlearning or misapplication" of genre information (p. 195). And, indeed, such misapplication has been observed in students moving from secondary school to discipline-specific writing courses (Artemeva & Fox, 2010), from undergraduate to graduate coursework (Bangeni, 2013), and from academic programs to workplace contexts (Devitt, 2007; Hafner, 2013). In considering these transitional situations, one wonders whether students' over-transfer problematically interferes with them learning genres in the new context or is a natural (and even beneficial) part of that learning. Addressing this question, Devitt (2007) reflects on over-transfer she has observed among new law firm associates. Although the novice associates over-apply aspects of their law school genres (such as detailed law descriptions) when writing professional analytical memoranda, the *least* successful associates (interestingly) are not the over-transferers but those "who never mastered the genres of law school ... [and] do not control the genres upon which they might draw" for their professional legal writing (Devitt, 2007, p. 221). From this and other instances of mis-transfer, it would seem that having some relevant genre knowledge (even if it does not fit perfectly with the new situation) at least allows one an initial 'way into' learning a new genre. Future studies could investigate under what conditions over-transfer does or does not have these facilitative effects for genre learning, as well as how ESP instruction might be designed to encourage these effects while also helping students learn to notice and 'correct' their transfer errors over time.

Impact of genre play on transfer abilities

Future ESP studies might also examine connections between genre learning transfer and genre play. One question worth exploring here is whether integrating genre play into ESP courses develops students' skill in high-road adaptive transfer of prior genre knowledge. Below I discuss several reasons why it might.

Research indicates that play develops flexibility and an ability to adapt to new situations. Animal biologists, in fact, have found that young mammals that play (as seen in their exaggerated, mock-fighting movements) acquire survival skills. To take just a few examples of this phenomenon, juvenile ground squirrels show motor skill gains when they play (Nunes et al., 2004); young rats who wrestle have improved brain development and social skills acquisition (Pellis, Pellis, & Bell, 2010); and playful brown bear cubs boast a higher survival rate than their less playful counterparts (Fagen & Fagen, 2009). Offering insights into reasons behind such developmental benefits, biologists Spinka, Newberry, and Bekoff (2001) hypothesize that play gives animals practice with "atypical movements necessary for recovery from awkward positions" and with responding to being "surprised or temporarily disoriented or disabled" (p. 143). Similarly, Stuart Brown, founder of the National Institute of Play, says that through play, animals "explore options that they wouldn't otherwise explore if they hadn't played" and "take in novelty and newness, use it to adapt and become more flexible, and also have a good time in the process" (Brown, 2015). In other words, play prepares animals (including humans) to cope with unfamiliar situations.

Some scholarship also suggests that, for humans, play has benefits for language development (Cook, 2000). Breaking language rules for fun and entertainment, for example, may help second language learners stay open to growth in their 'interlanguage'—that is, their emerging grammar for the target language (Tardy, 2016; Tarone, 2002). And language play that involves 'double-voicing', a process by which learners engage in different language varieties of and identities in the second language (Broner & Tarone, 2001), could develop learners' sociolinguistic agility.

If play builds such skills and sensitivities, then classroom instruction that encourages genre play may help students become astute transferers and transformers of genre knowledge. Specifically, play could give them practice with how to respond flexibly and aptly with relevant prior knowledge when 'surprised or temporarily disoriented or disabled' by new genres or contexts. In my own first-year undergraduate writing course, I have seen how genre play assignments can accomplish this. In one assignment, designed by my colleague Parastou Feiz, students write a 'chemical love story' that requires them to mix different genre moves and writerly voices. Specifically, the assignment prompt tells them to compose a love story that views the lovers and their story from the perspective (i.e., paradigm) of a scientist, and while telling their story, to incorporate sources that address the neurobiological nature of love—but in a fun way in order to keep their audience entertained (see Hyon, 2015, p. 92 for Feiz's complete prompt). After they work through several scaffolding activities and drafts of their stories, I find that a number of the students are quite successful at transferring in and blending what they know about romantic narrative and research-based exposition to create their hybrid texts. Two excerpts below from a chemical love story by first-year undergraduate Kristy Plascencia illustrates some creative ways students respond to this task. A quick synopsis first of Kristy's story: The protagonists, Adam and Melinda, meet at a club, fall in love and get married, despite the meddling of Melinda's sister Belinda.

> Belinda noticed her sister's continuous staring ... Belinda walked up to her sister and told her, "Melinda, you are experiencing high levels of dopamine in your brain. Try to control your brain chemicals and snap out of it." ... Melinda said, "There you go again with your biological sayings. Are you going to tell me again that you read in a biology book some sort of theory relating brain chemicals and love?" "Indeed," Belinda began. "I once read a chapter called 'Chemistry of Love' by Helen Fisher and she said 'Elevated levels of Dopamine in the brain produce extremely focused attention'" (24). Belinda was a graduate student working on her biochemistry master's degree. It was common for her to read biology books under every circumstance.
> [...]
> ... Today they are now how Melinda hoped. Like a Prairie Vole, the couple "prefer[s] to spend time with each other" ... rather than going out to the club. They also "groom each other for hours on end and nest together" (I get a kick out of you, par. 3).

Other scholarship has also reported positive student response to playful tasks with genre parodies (Swales, 2004) and multimodal projects (Alexander & Rhodes, 2014; Ellis, 2013; Hafner, 2014; Tardy, 2016). Tardy (2016), for example, describes a successful unit in which her graduate students learned to create "video abstracts," an emerging research genre in which scholars present visual summaries of their work that both resemble and depart from traditional research abstracts (p. 153). Her students examine sample video abstracts alongside "other related and antecedent genres, such as print abstracts, video course descriptions, short TED Talks, animated journal articles, and video book summaries"; and discuss the "social actions" that video abstracts perform (p. 153). They then get a chance to create their own video abstracts, reflecting on both the challenges and advantages of "re-packag[ing]" their research with mixed media resources (pp. 153–154).

A delightful video abstract I viewed on the YouTube channel for Cell Press (see Figure 7.2) demonstrates mixing possibilities for this genre. In this abstract, the authors (Rao et al., 2014a) use an eight-minute live animation video with colorful origami objects to explain their findings about genome 'folds' in animal cells.

In terms of adaptive transfer, the researchers include some moves from their print article abstract (Rao et al., 2014b) while also adding non-verbal elements (like origami animals moving to ragtime music) that would appeal to the broad YouTube audience.

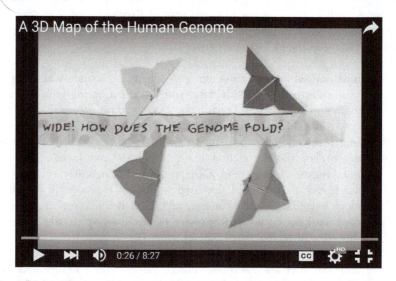

Figure 7.2 "A 3D Map of the Human Genome" (screenshot)
Source: cellvideoabstracts, S. Rao, et al., YouTube (11 Dec. 2014). Available at www.youtube.com/watch?v=dES-ozV65u4.

Student work on tasks like the chemical love story and video abstracts suggests that as students innovate with genres, they gain experience with transforming previous knowledge. Yet no scholarship to my knowledge has formally assessed the long-term benefits of this experience. Future investigations along these lines might compare groups of students who receive genre-based instruction with and without play activities. At the end of the instruction, the play and no-play groups could be evaluated on their performance in a task requiring adaptive high-road transfer to an unfamiliar genre. A more challenging but perhaps even more interesting investigation could follow the play and no-play students longitudinally after they leave the class, and observe how well they do adapting genre knowledge to new situations in their academic courses, workplaces, or other life contexts.

I hope that you have enjoyed this book and from it gained a sense of the evolution of ESP genre work, ESP approaches to genre analysis, and possibilities for incorporating genre into ESP course designs and materials. I also hope that, in working through various tasks in the chapters, you have developed confidence and inspiration for trying out your own genre analyses or creating your own teaching materials. Perhaps you will as well consider how to investigate students' genre learning in your classroom and beyond.

References

Ahmad, U. K. (1997). Research article introductions in Malay: Rhetoric in an emerging research community. In A. Duszak (ed.), *Culture and styles of academic discourse* (pp. 273–303). Berlin: Mouton de Gruyter.

Alexander, J., & Rhodes, J. (2014). *On multimodality: New media in composition studies*. Urbana, IL: CCCC/NCTE.

Angouri, J. (2010). Using textbook and real-life data to teach turn taking in business meetings. In N. Harwood (ed.), *English language teaching materials: Theory and practice* (pp. 373–394). Cambridge: Cambridge University Press.

Anthony, L. (2014). *AntConc* (Version 3.4.3). Computer software. Waseda University, Tokyo, Japan. Available from www.laurenceanthony.net.

Artemeva, N., & Fox, J. (2010). Awareness versus production: Probing students' antecedent genre knowledge. *Journal of Business and Technical Communication*, 24, 476–515.

Artemeva, N., & Freedman, A. (eds). (2015). *Genre studies around the globe: Beyond the three traditions* (pp. 31–79). Bloomington, IN: Trafford.

Ashmore, M. (1985). A question of reflexivity: Wrighting sociology of scientific knowledge. (Unpublished doctoral dissertation). University of York, York, UK.

Ashmore, M. (1989). *The reflexive thesis: Wrighting sociology of scientific knowledge*. Chicago: University of Chicago Press.

Askehave, I., & Swales, J. M. (2001). Genre identification and communicative purpose: A problem and a possible solution. *Applied Linguistics*, 22, 195–212.

Atkinson, D. (2004). Contrasting rhetorics/contrasting cultures: Why contrastive rhetoric needs a better conceptualization of culture. *Journal of English for Academic Purposes*, 3, 277–289.

Auerbach, E., & Wallerstein, N. (2004). *Problem-posing at work: English for action*. Edmonton, Canada: Grass Roots Press.

Badarneh, M. A., Al-Momani, K., & Migdadi, F. (2016). Between tradition and modernity: The bargaining genre in women's clothing stores in Jordan. *Journal of Pragmatics*, 101, 118–137.

Baker, P. (2006). *Using corpora in discourse analysis*. London: Continuum.

Bangeni, B. (2013). An exploration of the impact of students' prior genre knowledge on their constructions of 'audience' in a marketing course at postgraduate level. *English for Specific Purposes*, 32, 248–257.

Barber, C. L. (1962). Some measurable characteristics of modern scientific prose. In *Contributions to English syntax and phonology*. Stockholm: Almqvist & Wiksell.

Barton, E., Ariail, J., & Smith, T. (2004). The professional in the personal: The genre of personal statements in residency applications. *Issues in Writing*, 15, 76–124.

Basturkmen, H. (1999). Discourse in MBA seminars: Towards a description for pedagogical purposes. *English for Specific Purposes*, 18, 63–80.

Basturkmen, H. (2010). *Developing courses in English for specific purposes*. Basingstoke, UK: Palgrave Macmillan.

Bawarshi, A. (2003). *Genre and the invention of the writer: Reconsidering the place of invention in composition*. Logan, UT: Utah State University Press.

Bawarshi, A. S., & Reiff, M. J. (2010). *Genre: An introduction to history, theory, research, and pedagogy*. West Lafayette, IN: Parlor Press.

Bazerman, C. (1988). *Shaping written knowledge: The genre and activity of the experimental article in science*. Madison: University of Wisconsin Press.

Bazerman, C. (1994). Systems of genres and the enactment of social intentions. In A. Freedman & P. Medway (eds), *Genre and the new rhetoric* (pp. 79–101). London: Taylor & Francis.

Beaufort, A. (2007). *College writing and beyond: A new framework for university writing instruction*. Logan, UT: Utah State University Press.

Beckett, G. H., & Miller, P. C. (eds). (2006). *Project-based second and foreign language education: Past, present, and future*. Charlotte, NC: Information Age Publishing.

Bednarek, M. (2012). "Get us the hell out of here": Key words and trigrams in fictional television series. *International Journal of Corpus Linguistics*, 17, 35–63.

Belcher, D.D. (2006). English for specific purposes: Teaching to perceived needs and imagined futures in worlds of work, study, and everyday life. *TESOL Quarterly*, 40, 133–156.

Belcher, D.D. (2007). Seeking acceptance in an English-only research world. *Journal of Second Language Writing*, 16, 1–22.

Benesch, S. (1993). ESL, ideology, and the politics of pragmatism. *TESOL Quarterly*, 27, 705–717.

Benesch, S. (1996). Needs analysis and curriculum development in EAP: An example of a critical approach. *TESOL Quarterly*, 30, 723–738.

Benesch, S. (2001a). *Critical English for academic purposes: Theory, politics, and practice*. Mahwah, NJ: Lawrence Erlbaum.

Benesch, S. (2001b). Critical pragmatism: A politics of L2 composition. In T. Silva & P. K. Matsuda (eds), *On second language writing* (pp. 161–172). Mahwah, NJ: Lawrence Erlbaum.

Benesch, S. (2009). Theorizing and practicing critical English for academic purposes. *Journal of English for Academic Purposes*, 8, 81–85.

Bergsleithner, J. M., Frota, S. M., & Yoshioka, J. K. (eds) (2013). *Noticing and second language acquisition: Studies in honor of Richard Schmidt*. Honolulu, HI: National Foreign Language Resource Center, University of Hawai'i at Manoa.

Berkenkotter, C. (2001). Genre systems at work: DSM-IV and rhetorical recontextualization in psychotherapy paperwork. *Written Communication*, 18, 326–349.

Bex, T. (1996). Parody, genre and literary meaning. *Journal of Literary Semantics*, 25, 225–244.

Bhatia, V. K. (1993). *Analysing genre: Language use in professional settings*. London: Longman.

Bhatia, V. K. (2008). Creativity and accessibility in written professional discourse. *World Englishes*, 27, 319–326.

Bhatia, V. (2014). *Worlds of written discourse: A genre-based view*. London: Bloomsbury Academic (Bloomsbury Classics in Linguistics edition).

Bhatia, V. K., Langton, N. N., & Lung, J. (2004). Legal discourse: Opportunities and threats from corpus linguistics. In U. Connor & T. A. Upton (eds), *Discourse in the professions: Perspectives from corpus linguistics* (pp. 203–231). Amsterdam: John Benjamins.

Biber, D., Connor, U., & Upton, T. A. (eds). (2007a). *Discourse on the move: Using corpus analysis to describe discourse structure*. Amsterdam: John Benjamins.

Biber, D., Connor, U., & Upton, T. A. (2007b). Identifying and analyzing rhetorical moves in philanthropic discourse. In D. Biber, U. Connor, & T. A. Upton (eds), *Discourse on the move: Using corpus analysis to describe discourse structure* (pp. 43–78). Amsterdam: John Benjamins.

Biber, D., Johansson, S., Leech, G., Conrad, S., & Finegan, E. (1999). *Longman grammar of spoken and written English*. London: Pearson Education.

Bley-Vroman, R. (1978). Purpose, device, and level in rhetorical theory. In M. T. Trimble, L. Trimble, & K. Drobnic (eds), *English for specific purposes: Science and technology* (pp. 278–287). Corvallis, OR: English Language Institute, Oregon State University.

Bosher, S. (2010). English for nursing: Developing discipline-specific materials. In N. Harwood (ed.), *English language teaching materials: Theory and practice* (pp. 346–372). Cambridge: Cambridge University Press.

Bourdieu, P. (1991). *Language and symbolic power*, J. B. Thompson (ed.), G. Raymond & M. Adamson (trans.). Cambridge, MA: Harvard University Press.

Bowen, T., & Whithaus, C. (eds) (2013). *Multimodal literacies and emerging genres*. Pittsburgh, PA: University of Pittsburgh Press.

Brent, D. (2011). Transfer, transformation, and rhetorical knowledge: Insights from transfer theory. *Journal of Business and Technical Communication*, 25, 396–420.

Brent, D. (2012). Crossing boundaries: Co-op students relearning to write. *CCC*, 63, 558–592.

Broner, M., & Tarone, E. (2001). Is it fun? Language play in a fifth-grade Spanish immersion classroom. *Modern Language Journal*, 85, 363–379.

Brown, J. D. (2016). *Introducing needs analysis and English for specific purposes*. London: Routledge.

Brown, P., & Levinson, S. C. (1987). *Politeness: Some universals in language usage*. Cambridge: Cambridge University Press.

Brown, R. M. (2004). Self-composed: Rhetoric in psychology personal statements. *Written Communication*, 21, 242–260.

Brown, S. (2015). TED Radio Hour, interview by G. Raz. *NPR*, March 27. Retrieved from www.npr.org/templates/transcript/transcript.php?storyId=395065944.

Bruce, I. (2005). Syllabus design for general EAP writing courses: A cognitive approach. *Journal of English for Academic Purposes*, 4, 239–256.

Bruce, I. (2010). *Academic writing and genre: A systematic analysis*. London: Bloomsbury Academic.

Canagarajah, A. S. (2006). Toward a writing pedagogy of shuttling between languages: Learning from multilingual writers. *College English*, 68, 589–604.

Capps, T. (2013). *Cooking comically: Recipes so easy you'll actually make them.* New York: Perigee.

Carter, B., & Stelter, B. (2010). In 'Daily Show' role on 9/11 bill, echoes of Murrow. *New York Times*, December 26. Retrieved from www.nytimes.com/2010/12/27/business/media/27stewart.html.

Casanave, C. P. (1995). Local interactions: Constructing contexts for composing in a graduate sociology program. In D. Belcher & G. Braine (eds), *Academic writing in a second language: Essays on research and pedagogy* (pp. 83–110). Norwood, NJ: Ablex.

Charles, M. (2014). Getting the corpus habit: EAP students' long-term use of personal corpora. *English for Specific Purposes*, 35, 30–40.

Chen, R. (2001). Self-politeness: A proposal. *Journal of Pragmatics*, 33, 87–106.

Cheng, A. (2006). Understanding learners and learning in ESP genre-based writing instruction. *English for Specific Purposes*, 25, 76–89.

Cheng, A. (2007). Transferring generic features and recontextualizing genre awareness: Understanding writing performance in the ESP genre-based literacy framework. *English for Specific Purposes*, 26, 287–307.

Cheng, A. (2008). Analyzing genre exemplars in preparation for writing: The case of an L2 graduate student in the ESP genre-based instructional framework of academic literacy. *Applied Linguistics*, 29, 50–71.

Cherryholmes, C. (1988). *Power and criticism: Poststructural investigations in education.* New York: Teachers College Press.

Chiu, Y.-L. T. (2016). "Singing your tune": Genre structure and writer identity in personal statements for doctoral applications. *Journal of English for Academic Purposes*, 21, 48–59.

Chun, C. W. (2009). Contesting neoliberal discourses in EAP: Critical praxis in an IEP classroom. *Journal of English for Academic Purposes*, 8, 111–120.

Clark, I. L., & Hernandez, A. (2011). Genre awareness, academic argument, and transferability. *The WAC Journal*, 22, 65–78.

Coe, R. M. (1994). Teaching genre as process. In A. Freedman & P. Medway (eds), *Learning and teaching genre* (pp. 157–169). Portsmouth, NH: Boynton/Cook.

Cohen, M. A. (2007). Dear Birthmother: A linguistic analysis of letters written to expectant mothers considering adoption. Unpublished master's thesis. Indiana University, Indianapolis. Available from http://hdl.handle.net/1805/1114.

Collin, R. (2014). Activism, emotion, and genre: Young adults' composition of Urgent Action Letters. *Linguistics & Education*, 26, 18–30.

Connor, U. (2011). *Intercultural rhetoric in the writing classroom.* Ann Arbor, MI: University of Michigan Press.

Connor, U., & Gladkov, K. (2004). Rhetorical appeals in fundraising direct mail letters. In U. Connor & T. A. Upton (eds), *Discourse in the professions: Perspectives from corpus linguistics* (pp. 257–286). Amsterdam: John Benjamins.

Connor, U., & Rozycki, W. (2013). ESP and intercultural rhetoric. In B. Paltridge & S. Starfield (eds), *The handbook of English for specific purposes* (pp. 427–443). Malden, MA: Wiley-Blackwell.

Cook, G. (2000). *Language play, language learning.* Oxford: Oxford University Press.

Cope, B., Kalantzis, M., Kress, G., & Martin, J. (1993). Bibliographical essay: Developing the theory and practice of genre-based literacy. In B. Cope & M.

Kalantzis (eds), *The powers of literacy: A genre approach to teaching writing* (pp. 231–247). Bristol, PA: Falmer Press.

Cristovão, V. L. L. (2015). A genre-based approach underlying didactic sequences for the teaching of languages. In N. Artemeva & A. Freedman (eds), *Genre studies around the globe: Beyond the three traditions* (pp. 403–424). Bloomington, IN: Trafford.

Curry, M. J., & Lillis, T. (2010). Making professional academic writing practices visible: Designing research-based heuristics to support English-medium text production. In N. Harwood (ed.), *English language teaching materials: Theory and practice* (pp. 322–345). Cambridge: Cambridge University Press.

Davis, C. M. (2006). *Patient practitioner interaction: An experiential manual for developing the art of health care*, 4th ed. Thorofare, NJ: SLACK.

Denman, B. (2000). *In contact 1*, 2nd ed. White Plains, NY: Addison Wesley Longman.

DePalma, M.-S., & Ringer, J. M. (2011). Toward a theory of adaptive transfer: Expanding disciplinary discussions of "transfer" in second-language writing and composition studies. *Journal of Second Language Writing*, 20, 134–147.

Deroey, K. L. B. (2012). What they highlight is …: The discourse functions of basic wh-clefts in lectures. *Journal of English for Academic Purposes*, 11, 112–124.

Devitt, A. J. (2004). *Writing genres*. Carbondale, IL: Southern Illinois University Press.

Devitt, A. J. (2007). Transferability and genres. In C. J. Keller & C. Weisser (eds), *The locations of composition* (pp. 215–227). Albany, NY: State University of New York Press.

Devitt, A. J. (2009). Teaching critical genre awareness. In C. Bazerman, A. Bonini, & D. Figueiredo (eds), *Genre in a changing world* (pp. 337–351). West Lafayette, IN: Parlor Press.

Devitt, A. J. (2011). Creating within genres: How genre metaphors shape student innovation. Paper presented at the Conference on College Composition and Communication, Atlanta, GA, April.

Devitt, A. J. (2014). Genre pedagogies. In G. Tate, H. R. Taggart, K. Schick, & H. B. Hessler (eds), *A guide to composition pedagogies* (pp. 146–162). Oxford: Oxford University Press.

Devitt, A. J., Reiff, M. J., & Bawarshi, A. (2004). *Scenes of writing: Strategies for composing with genres*. New York: Pearson Education.

DeWalt, K. M., & DeWalt, B. R. (2011). *Participant observation: A guide for fieldworkers*, 2nd ed. Lanham, MD: Altamira Press.

Ding, H. (2007). Genre analysis of personal statements: Analysis of moves in application essays to medical and dental schools. *English for Specific Purposes*, 26, 368–392.

Dovey, T. (2010). Facilitating writing from sources: A focus on both process and product. *Journal of English for Academic Purposes*, 9, 45–60.

Downey Bartlett, N. J. (2005). A double shot 2% mocha latte, please, with whip: Service encounters in two coffee shops and at a coffee cart. In M. H. Long (ed.), *Second language needs analysis* (pp. 305–343). Cambridge: Cambridge University Press.

Dressen-Hammouda, D. (2013). Ethnographic approaches to ESP research. In B. Paltridge & S. Starfield (eds), *The handbook of English for specific purposes* (pp. 501–517). Malden, MA: Wiley-Blackwell.

Dudley-Evans, T., & St. John, M. J. (1998). *Developments in English for specific purposes: A multi-disciplinary approach*. Cambridge: Cambridge University Press.

Dunn, C. D. (2005). Genre conventions, speaker identities, and creativity: An analysis of Japanese wedding speeches. *Pragmatics*, 15, 205–228.

Dupuy, B. (2006). L'immeuble: French language and culture teaching and learning through projects in a global simulation. In G. H. Beckett & P. C. Miller (eds), *Project-based second and foreign language education: Past, present, and future* (pp. 195–214). Greenwich, CT: Information Age Publishing.

Ellis, E. (2013). Back to the future? The pedagogical promise of the (multimedia) essay. In T. Bowen & C. Whithaus (eds), *Multimodal literacies and emerging genres* (pp. 37–72). Pittsburgh: University of Pittsburgh Press.

Ellis, R. (2002). Grammar teaching: Practice or consciousness raising? In J. C. Richards & W. A. Renandya (eds), *Methodology in language teaching: An anthology of current practice* (pp. 167–174). Cambridge: Cambridge University Press.

Emerson, R. M., Fretz, R. I., & Shaw, L. L. (2011). *Writing ethnographic fieldnotes*, 2nd ed. Chicago: The University of Chicago Press.

Fagen, R., & Fagen, J. (2009). Play behaviour and multi-year juvenile survival in free-ranging brown bears, *Ursus arctos*. *Evolutionary Ecology Research*, 11, 1–15.

Feak, C. B., & Swales, J. M. (2009). *Telling a research story: Writing a literature review*. Ann Arbor, MI: University of Michigan Press.

Feak, C. B., & Swales, J. M. (2010). Writing for publication: Corpus-informed materials for postdoctoral fellows in perinatology. In N. Harwood (ed.), *English language teaching materials: Theory and practice* (pp. 279–300). Cambridge: Cambridge University Press.

Feak, C. B., Reinhart, S. M., & Rohlck. T. N. (2009). *Academic interactions: Communicating on campus*. Ann Arbor, MI: University of Michigan Press.

Feez, S. (2002). Heritage and innovation in second language education. In A. M. Johns (ed.), *Genre in the classroom: Multiple perspectives* (pp. 43–69). Mahwah, NJ: Lawrence Erlbaum.

Feldman, L. (2007). Young audiences, *The Daily Show*, and evolving notions of journalism. *Journalism*, 8, 406–427.

Fernández-Polo, F. J. (2014). The role of I mean in conference presentations by ELF speakers. *English for Specific Purposes*, 34, 58–67.

Fisher, H. (2004). *Why we love: The nature and chemistry of romantic love*. New York: Henry Holt & Co.

Fisher, H., Aron, A., & Brown, L. L. (2005). Romantic love: An fMRI study of a neural mechanism for mate choice. *Journal of Comparative Neurology*, 493, 58–62.

Flowerdew, J. (2002). Genre in the classroom: A linguistic approach. In A. M. Johns (ed.), *Genre in the classroom: Multiple perspectives* (pp. 91–102). Mahwah, NJ: Lawrence Erlbaum.

Flowerdew, J. (2009). Corpora in language teaching. In M. H. Long & C. J. Doughty (eds), *The handbook of language teaching* (pp. 327–350). Malden, MA: Wiley-Blackwell.

Flowerdew, J. (2011). Reconciling contrasting approaches to genre analysis: The whole can equal more than the sum of the parts. In D. Belcher, A. M. Johns, & B. Paltridge (eds), *New directions in English for Specific Purposes research* (pp. 119–144). Ann Arbor, MI: University of Michigan Press.

Flowerdew, J., & Wan, A. (2006). Genre analysis of tax computation letters: How and why tax accountants write the way they do. *English for Specific Purposes*, 25, 133–153.

Flowerdew, J., & Wan, A. (2010). The linguistic and the contextual in applied genre analysis: The case of the company audit report. *English for Specific Purposes*, 29, 78–93.

Fox, J. R., Koloen, G., & Sahin, V. (2007). No joke: A comparison of the substance in *The Daily Show with Jon Stewart* and broadcast network television coverage of the 2004 presidential election campaign. *Journal of Broadcasting and Electronic Media*, 51, 213–227.

Fredrickson, K. M., & Swales, J. M. (1994). Competition and discourse community: Introductions from Nysvenka Studier. In B.-L. Gunnarsson, P. Linnell, & B. Nordberg (eds), *Text and talk in professional contexts* (pp. 9–22). Uppsala: ASLA.

Freedman, A. (1993). Show and tell? The role of explicit teaching in the learning of new genres. *Research in the teaching of English*, 27, 222–251.

Freedman, A. (1994). "Do as I say?": The relationship between teaching and learning new genres. In A. Freedman & P. Medway (eds), *Genre and the new rhetoric* (pp. 191–210). London: Taylor & Francis.

Friginal, E., & Mustafa, S. S. (2017). A comparison of U.S.-based and Iraqi English research article abstracts using corpora. *Journal of English for Academic Purposes*, 25, 45–57.

Gallo, C. (2014). *Talk like TED: The 9 public-speaking secrets of the world's top minds*. New York: St. Martin's.

Gavioli, L. (2005). *Exploring corpora for ESP learning*. Amsterdam: John Benjamins.

Gimenez, J. (2011). *Writing for nursing and midwifery students*, 2nd ed. New York: Palgrave Macmillan.

Grujicic-Alatriste, L. (2013). A response to DePalma and Ringer's article "Toward a theory of adaptive transfer: Expanding disciplinary discussions of 'transfer' in second-language writing and composition studies". *Journal of Second Language Writing*, 22, 460–464.

Hafner, C. A. (2013). The discursive construction of professional expertise: Appeals to authority in barrister's opinions. *English for Specific Purposes*, 32, 131–143.

Hafner, C. A. (2014). Embedding digital literacies in English language teaching: Students' digital video projects as multimodal ensembles. *TESOL Quarterly*, 48, 655–685.

Handford, M. (2010). *The language of business meetings*. Cambridge: Cambridge University Press.

Harwood, N. (2010). Issues in materials development and design. In N. Harwood (ed.), *English language teaching materials: Theory and practice* (pp. 3–30). Cambridge: Cambridge University Press.

Harwood, N., & Hadley, G. (2004). Demystifying institutional practices: Critical pragmatism and the teaching of academic writing. *English for Specific Purposes*, 23, 355–377.

Helmer, K. A. (2013). Critical English for academic purposes: Building on learner, teacher, and program strengths. *Journal of English for Academic Purposes*, 12, 273–287.

Henry, A., & Roseberry, R. L. (1998). An evaluation of a genre-based approach to the teaching of EAP/ESP writing. *TESOL Quarterly*, 32, 147–156.

Herbert, A. J. (1965). *The structure of technical English*. London: Longman.

Herbolich, J. B. (1979). Box kites. *English for Specific Purposes*, 29. English Language Institute, Oregon State University, Corvallis, OR.

History of TED. (n.d.). Retrieved October 21, 2016 from www.ted.com/about/our-organization/history-of-ted.

Holliday, A. (1999). Small cultures. *Applied Linguistics*, 2, 237–264.

Hutchinson, T. & Waters, A. (1987). *English for specific purposes: A learning-centered approach*. Cambridge: Cambridge University Press.

Hyland, K. (1996). Writing without conviction? Hedging in science research articles. *Applied Linguistics*, 17, 433–454.

Hyland, K. (2002). Specificity revisited: How far should we go now? *English for Specific Purposes*, 21, 385–395.

Hyland, K. (2004a). *Disciplinary discourses: Social interactions in academic writing* (Michigan Classics edition). Ann Arbor, MI: University of Michigan Press.

Hyland, K. (2004b). *Genre and second language writing*. Ann Arbor, MI: University of Michigan Press.

Hyland, K. (2005). Stance and engagement: A model of interaction in academic discourse. *Discourse Studies*, 7, 173–192.

Hyland, K. (2006). *English for academic purposes: An advanced resource book*. London: Routledge.

Hyland, K. (2007). Genre pedagogy: Language, literacy and L2 writing instruction. *Journal of Second Language Writing*, 16, 148–164.

Hyland, K. (2012). *Disciplinary identities: Individuality and community in academic discourse*. Cambridge: Cambridge University Press.

Hyland, K. (2016a). General and specific EAP. In K. Hyland, & P. Shaw (eds), *The Routledge handbook of English for academic purposes* (pp. 17–29). London: Routledge.

Hyland, K. (2016b). *Teaching and researching writing*, 3rd ed. London: Routledge.

Hyon, S. (1996). Genre in three traditions: Implications for ESL. *TESOL Quarterly*, 30, 693–722.

Hyon, S. (2001). Long-term effects of genre-based instruction: A follow-up study of an EAP reading course. *English for Specific Purposes*, 20, 417–438.

Hyon, S. (2002). Genre and ESL reading: A classroom study. In A. M. Johns (ed.), *Genre in the classroom: Multiple perspectives* (pp. 121–141). Mahwah, NJ: Lawrence Erlbaum.

Hyon, S. (2008). Convention and inventiveness in an occluded academic genre: A case study of retention-promotion-tenure reports. *English for Specific Purposes*, 27, 175–192.

Hyon, S. (2011). Evaluation in tenure and promotion letters: Constructing faculty as communicators, stars and workers. *Applied Linguistics*, 32, 389–407.

Hyon, S. (2015). Genre play: Moving students from formulaic to complex academic writing. In M. Roberge, K. M. Losey, & M. Wald (eds), *Teaching US-educated multilingual writers: Pedagogical practices from and for the classroom* (pp. 70–107). Ann Arbor, MI: University of Michigan.

Itakura, H. (2013). Hedging praise in English and Japanese book reviews. *Journal of Pragmatics*, 45, 131–148.

Jasso-Aguilar, R. (2005). Sources, methods and triangulation in needs analysis: A critical perspective in a case study of Waikiki hotel maids. In M. H. Long (ed.),

Second language needs analysis (pp. 127–158). Cambridge: Cambridge University Press.

Johns, A. M. (1997). *Text, role, and context: Developing academic literacies.* Cambridge: Cambridge University Press.

Johns, A. M. (1999). Opening our doors: Applying socioliterate approaches (SA) to language minority classrooms. In L. Harklau, K. M. Losey, & M. Siegal (eds), *Generation 1.5 meets college composition: Issues in the teaching of writing to US-educated learners of ESL* (pp. 159–171). Mahwah, MJ: Lawrence Erlbaum.

Johns, A. M. (ed.). (2002). *Genre in the classroom: Multiple perspectives.* Mahwah, NJ: Lawrence Erlbaum.

Johns, A. M. (2008). Genre awareness for the novice academic student: An ongoing quest. *Language Teaching*, 41, 237–252.

Johns, A. M. (2011). The future of genre in L2 writing: Fundamental, but contested, instructional decisions. *Journal of Second Language Writing*, 20, 56–68.

Johns, A. M. (2013). The history of English for specific purposes research. In B. Paltridge & S. Starfield (eds), *The handbook of English for specific purposes* (pp. 5–30). Malden, MA: Wiley-Blackwell.

Johns, A. (2015a). Students as genre scholars: ESL/EFL classroom approaches. In N. Artemeva & A. Freedman (eds), *Genre studies around the globe: Beyond the three traditions* (pp. 364–385). Bloomington, IN: Trafford.

Johns, A. M. (2015b). Moving on from Genre Analysis: An update and tasks for the transitional student. *Journal of English for Academic Purposes*, 19, 113–124.

Johns, A. M., Bawarshi, A., Coe, R. M., Hyland, K., Paltridge, B., Reiff, M. J., Tardy, C. (2006). Crossing the boundaries of genre studies: Commentaries by experts. *Journal of Second Language Writing*, 15, 234–249.

Jolliffe, D. A. (2001). Writing across the curriculum and service learning: Kairos, genre, and collaboration. In S. H. McLeod, E. Miraglia, M. Soven, & C. Thaiss (eds), *WAC for the new millennium: Strategies for continuing writing-across-the-curriculum programs* (pp. 86–108). Urbana, IL: NCTE.

Kádár, D. Z., & Haugh, M. (2013). *Understanding politeness.* Cambridge: Cambridge University Press.

Koester, A. (2010). *Workplace discourse.* London: Continuum.

Lackstrom, J., Selinker, L., & Trimble, L. P. (1972). Grammar and technical English. *English Teaching Forum*, 10, 3–14.

Lackstrom, J., Selinker, L., & Trimble, L. (1973). Technical rhetorical principles and grammatical choice. *TESOL Quarterly*, 7, 127–136.

Lee, C. E., & Nelson, C. M. (2015). Obama calls for action in Charleston eulogy for Clementa Pinckney. *Wall Street Journal*, June 26. Retrieved from www.wsj.com/arti cles/obama-delivers-eulogy-at-clementa-pinckney-funeral-in-charleston-1435347261.

Lee, D., & Swales, J. (2006). A corpus-based EAP course for NNS doctoral students: Moving from available specialized corpora to self-compiled corpora. *English for Specific Purposes*, 25, 56–75.

Lee, J. J. (2009). Size matters: An exploratory comparison of small- and large-class university lecture introductions. *English for Specific Purposes*, 28, 42–57.

Leech, G. (2014). *The pragmatics of politeness.* Oxford: Oxford University Press.

Lillis, T. (2008). Ethnography as method, methodology, and "Deep Theorizing": Closing the gap between text and context in academic writing research. *Written Communication*, 25, 353–388.

Lillis, T., & Curry, M. J. (2010). *Academic writing in a global context: The politics and practices of publishing in English*. New York: Routledge.

Long, M. H. (2005). Methodological issues in learner needs analysis. In M. H. Long (ed.), *Second language needs analysis* (pp. 19–76). Cambridge: Cambridge University Press.

Louhiala-Salminen, L. (2002). The fly's perspective: Discourse in the daily routine of a business manager. *English for Specific Purposes*, 21, 211–231.

Macken-Horarik, M. (2002). "Something to shoot for": A systemic functional approach to teaching genre in secondary school science. In A. M. Johns (ed.), *Genre in the classroom: Multiple perspectives* (pp. 17–42). Mahwah, NJ: Lawrence Erlbaum.

Madison, D. S. (2012). *Critical ethnography: Method, ethics, and performance*. Thousand Oaks, CA: SAGE.

Malinowski, B. (1922). *Argonauts of the western Pacific: An account of native enterprise and adventure in the archipelagoes of Melanesian New Guinea*. London: Routledge & Kegan Paul.

Martin, J. R. (2015). One of three traditions: Genre, functional linguistics, and the 'Sydney School'. In N. Artemeva & A. Freedman (eds), *Genre studies around the globe: Beyond the three traditions* (pp. 31–79). Bloomington, IN: Trafford.

Martin, J. R., Christie, F., & Rothery, J. (1987). Social processes in education: A reply to Sawyer and Watson (and others). In I. Reid (ed.), *The place of genre in learning: Current debates* (pp. 58–82). Geelong, Australia: Deakin University.

Mauranen, A. (2006). A rich domain of ELF: The ELFA corpus of academic discourse. *Nordic Journal of English Studies*, 5, 145–160.

Medway, P. (1998). Understanding architects' notebooks. Does genre theory help? Symposium on genre: literacy and literature, Simon Fraser University, Burnaby, Canada, January.

Memoli, M. A. (2015). Obama embraces race, religion in moving address at Charleston funeral. *Los Angeles Times*, June 26. Retrieved from www.latimes.com/nation/la-na-obama-charleston-funeral-20150626-story.html.

Mendoza-Denton, N. (2008). *Homegirls: Language and cultural practice among Latina youth gangs*. Malden, MA: Wiley-Blackwell.

Mezek, S., & Swales, J. M. (2016). PhD defences and vivas. In K. Hyland, & P. Shaw (eds), *The Routledge handbook of English for academic purposes* (pp. 361–375). London: Routledge.

Michelson, K., & Dupuy, B. (2014). Multi-storied lives: Global simulation as an approach to developing multiliteracies in an intermediate French course. *L2 Journal*, 6, 21–49.

Miller, C. (1984). Genre as social action. *Quarterly Journal of Speech*, 70, 151–167.

Moder, C. L. (2013). Aviation English. In B. Paltridge & S. Starfield (eds), *The handbook of English for specific purposes* (pp. 227–242). Malden, MA: Wiley-Blackwell.

Molle, D., & Prior, P. (2008). Multimodal genre systems in EAP writing pedagogy: Reflecting on a needs analysis. *TESOL Quarterly*, 42, 541–566.

Morgan, B., & Ramanathan, V. (2005). Critical literacies and language education: Global and local perspectives. *Annual Review of Applied Linguistics*, 25, 151–169.

Morgan, N. (2015). What public speakers can learn from President Obama's eulogy for Reverend Pickney. *Forbes*, July 2. Retrieved from www.forbes.com/sites/nickm

organ/2015/07/02/what-public-speakers-can-learn-from-president-obamas-eulogy-for-reverend-pinckney/#dc3e5db35bf3.

Motta-Roth, D., & Heberle, V. M. (2015). A short cartography of genre studies in Brazil. *Journal of English for Academic Purposes*, 19, 22–31.

Myers, G. (1989). The pragmatics of politeness in scientific articles. *Applied Linguistics*, 10, 1–35.

Nation, I. S. P., & Macalister, J. (2010). *Language curriculum design*. New York: Routledge.

Negretti, R., & Kuteeva, M. (2011). Fostering metacognitive genre awareness in L2 academic reading and writing: A case study of pre-service English teachers. *Journal of Second Language Writing*, 20, 95–110.

Nesi, H. (2013). ESP and corpus studies. In B. Paltridge & S. Starfield (eds), *The handbook of English for specific purposes* (pp. 407–426). Malden, MA: Wiley-Blackwell.

Nesi, H., & Gardner, S. (2012). *Genres across the disciplines: Student writing in higher education*. Cambridge: Cambridge University Press.

Nickerson, C., & Planken, B. (2016). *Introducing business English*. London: Routledge.

Nunes, S., Muecke, E.–M., Lancaster, L., & Castro, L. (2004). Functions and consequences of play behaviour in juvenile Belding's ground squirrels. *Animal Behaviour*, 68, 27–37.

Nwoye, O. G. (1992). Obituary announcements as communicative events in Nigerian English. *World Englishes*, 11, 15–27.

Orr, W. W. F. (2007). The bargaining genre: A study of retail encounters in traditional Chinese local markets. *Language in Society*, 36, 73–103.

Pak, C.-S., & Acevedo, R. (2008). Spanish-language newspaper editorials from Mexico, Spain, and the US. In U. Connor, E. Nagelhout, & W. Rozycki (eds), *Contrastive rhetoric: Reaching to intercultural rhetoric* (pp. 123–145). Amsterdam: John Benjamins.

Paltridge, B. (2001). *Genre and the language learning classroom*. Ann Arbor, MI: University of Michigan Press.

Paltridge, B. (2008). Textographies and the researching and teaching of writing. *Iberica: Journal of the European Association of Languages for Specific Purposes*, 15, 9–23.

Paltridge, B. (2017). Context and the teaching of academic writing: Bringing together theory and practice. In J. Bitchener, N. Storch & R. Wette (eds), *Teaching writing for academic purposes to multilingual students: Instructional approaches* (pp. 9–23). New York: Routledge.

Paltridge, B., & Starfield, S. (eds). (2013). *The handbook of English for specific purposes*. Malden, MA: Wiley-Blackwell.

Paltridge, B., & Starfield, S. (2016). Ethnographic perspectives on English for academic purposes research. In K. Hyland & P. Shaw (eds), *The Routledge handbook of English for academic purposes* (pp. 219–230). Abingdon, UK: Routledge.

Paltridge, B., Starfield, S., & Tardy, C. M. (2016). *Ethnographic perspectives on academic writing*. Oxford: Oxford University Press.

Paltridge, B., Starfield, S., Ravelli, L. J., & Tuckwell, K. (2012). Change and stability: Examining the macrostructures of doctoral theses in the visual and performing arts. *Journal of English for Academic Purposes*, 11, 332–344.

Pang, T. T. T. (2002). Textual analysis and contextual awareness building: A comparison of two approaches to teaching genre. In A. M. Johns (ed.), *Genre in the classroom: Multiple perspectives* (pp. 145–161). Mahwah, NJ: Lawrence Erlbaum.

Parks, S. (2001). Moving from school to the workplace: Disciplinary innovation, border crossings, and the reshaping of a written genre. *Applied Linguistics*, 22, 405–438.

Partington, A. (2014). The marking of importance in 'Enlightentainment' talks. In M. Gotti & D. S. Giannoni (eds), *Corpus analysis for descriptive and pedagogical purposes: ESP perspectives* (pp. 143–165). Bern: Peter Lang.

Peck, W. C., Flower, L., & Higgins, L. (1995). Community literacy. *College Composition & Communication*, 46, 199–222.

Pecorari, D. (2006). Visible and occluded citation features in postgraduate second-language writing. *English for Specific Purposes*, 25, 4–29.

Pellis, S. M., Pellis, V. C., & Bell, H. C. (2010). The function of play in the development of the social brain. *American Journal of Play*, 2, 278–296.

Pennycook, A. (1997). Vulgar pragmatism, critical pragmatism, and EAP. *English for Specific Purposes*, 16, 253–269.

Perkins, D. N., & Salomon, G. (1988). Teaching for transfer. *Educational Leadership*, 46, 22–32.

Precht, K. (1998). A cross-cultural comparison of letters of recommendation. *English for Specific Purposes*, 17, 241–265.

Rao, S. S. P., et al. (2014a). A 3D map of the human genome. *YouTube*. Retrieved from www.youtube.com/watch?v=dES-ozV65u4.

Rao, S. S. P., et al. (2014b). A 3D map of the human genome at kilobase resolution reveals principles of chromatin looping. *Cell*, 159, 1665–1680.

Reiff, M. J., & Bawarshi, A. (2011). Tracing discursive resources: How students use prior genre knowledge to negotiate new writing contexts in first-year composition. *Written Communication*, 28, 312–337.

Rogers, P. S., Gunesekera, M., & Yang, M. L. (2007). Rhetorical tools for communicating strategic change: Dana's definitional statement. Working paper no. 1079, April. Ross School of Business, University of Michigan, Ann Arbor.

Rose, D. (2015). Genre, knowledge and pedagogy in the Sydney School. In N. Artemeva & A. Freedman (eds), *Genre studies around the globe: Beyond the three traditions* (pp. 299–338). Bloomington, IN: Trafford.

Rose, D., & Martin, J. R. (2012). *Learning to write, reading to learn: Genre, knowledge and pedagogy in the Sydney School*. Sheffield, UK: Equinox.

Russell, D. R., & Fisher, D. (2009). Online, multimedia case studies for professional education: Revisioning concepts of genre recognition. In J. Giltrow & D. Stein (eds), *Genres in the internet: Issues in the theory of genre* (pp. 163–191). Amsterdam: Benjamins.

Rutherford, W. E., & Sharwood Smith. M. (1988). *Grammar and second language teaching: A book of readings*. New York: Newbury House Publishers.

Salehzadeh, J. (2006). *Academic listening strategies: A guide to understanding lectures*. Ann Arbor, MI: University of Michigan Press.

Salomon, G., & Perkins, D. N. (1989). Rocky roads to transfer: Rethinking mechanisms of a neglected phenomenon. *Educational Psychologist*, 24, 113–142.

Samraj, B. (2002). Introductions in research articles: Variations across disciplines. *English for Specific Purposes*, 21, 1–17.

Samraj, B. (2013). Form and function of citations in discussion sections of master's theses and research articles. *Journal of English for Academic Purposes*, 12, 299–310.

Samraj, B. (2014). Move structure. In K. P. Schneider, & A. Barron (eds), *Pragmatics of discourse* (pp. 385–405). Berlin: De Gruyter Mouton.

Samraj, B., & Monk, L. (2008). The statement of purpose in graduate program applications: Genre structure and disciplinary variation. *English for Specific Purposes*, 27, 193–211.

Samraj, B., & Gawron, J. M. (2015). The suicide note as a genre: Implications for genre theory. *Journal of English for Academic Purposes*, 19, 88–101.

Santos, T. (2001). The place of politics in second language writing. In T. Silva & P. K. Matsuda (eds), *On second language writing* (pp. 173–190). Mahwah, NJ: Lawrence Erlbaum.

Schmidt, R. W. (1990). The role of consciousness in second language learning. *Applied Linguistics*, 11, 129–158.

Schmidt, R. W. (1993). Awareness and second language acquisition. *Annual Review of Applied Linguistics*, 13, 206–226.

Schryer, C. F. (1993). Records as genre. *Written Communication*, 10, 200–234.

Schryer, C. F. (2002). Walking a fine line: Writing negative letters in an insurance company. *Journal of Business and Technical Communication*, 14, 445–497.

Schryer, C. F. (2011). Genre as generative. Paper presented at the Writing and Rhetoric Across Borders conference, Fairfax, Virginia, February.

Schryer, C., McDougall, A., Tait, G. R., & Lingard, L. (2012). Creating discursive order at the end of life: The role of genres in palliative care settings. *Written Communication*, 29, 111–141.

Scott, M. (2017). *WordSmith Tools* (Version 7). Computer software. Stroud: Lexical Analysis Software.

Scott, M., & Tribble, C. (2006). *Textual patterns: Key words and corpus analysis in language education*. Amsterdam: John Benjamins.

Secor, M., & Walsh, L. (2004). A rhetorical perspective on the Sokal hoax: Genre, style, and context. *Written Communication*, 21, 69–91.

Seloni, L. (2014). "I'm an artist and a scholar who is trying to find a middle point": A textographic analysis of a Colombian art historian's thesis writing. *Journal of Second Language Writing*, 25, 79–99.

Shawcross, P. (2011). *Flightpath: Aviation English for pilots and ATCOs, student's book*. Cambridge: Cambridge University Press.

Shulman, M. (2006). *In focus: Strategies for business writers*. Ann Arbor, MI: University of Michigan Press.

Smart, G. (2006). *Writing the economy: Activity, genre and technology in the world of banking*. Sheffield, UK: Equinox.

Smart, G. (2012). Discourse-oriented ethnography. In J. P. Gee & M. Handford (eds), *Routledge handbook of discourse analysis* (pp. 147–159). New York: Routledge.

Smart, G., & Brown, N. (2002). Learning transfer or transforming learning?: Student interns reinventing expert writing practices in the workplace. *Technostyle*, 18, 117–141.

Sokal, A. D. (1996). Transgressing the boundaries: Toward a transformative hermeneutics of quantum gravity. *Social Text*, 14, 217–252.

Spinka, M., Newberry, R. C., & Bekoff, M. (2001). Mammalian play: Training for the unexpected. *Quarterly Review of Biology*, 76, 141–168.

Starfield, S. (2011). Doing critical ethnographic research into academic writing: The theory of the methodology. In D. Belcher, A. M. Johns, & B. Paltridge (eds), *New directions in English for specific purposes research* (pp. 174–196). Ann Arbor, MI: University of Michigan Press.

Starfield, S. (2013). Critical perspectives on ESP. In B. Paltridge & S. Starfield (Eds.), *The handbook of English for specific purposes* (pp. 461–479). Malden, MA: Wiley-Blackwell.

Starfield, S., Paltridge, B., & Ravelli, L. (2014). Researching academic writing: What textography affords. In J. Huisman & M. Tight (eds), *Theory and method in higher education research II* (pp. 103–120). Oxford: Emerald.

Stoller, F. (2002) Project work: A means to promote language and content. In J. C. Richards & W. A. Renandya (eds), *Methodology in language teaching: An anthology of current practice* (pp. 107–119) Cambridge: Cambridge University Press.

Stubbs, M., & Barth, I. (2003). Using recurrent phrases as text-type discriminators: A quantitative method and some findings. *Functions of Language*, 10, 61–104.

Sugimoto, C. R., & Thelwall, M. (2013). Scholars on soap boxes: Science communication and dissemination in TED videos. *Journal of the American Society for Information Science and Technology*, 64, 663–674.

Swales, J. (1971). *Writing scientific English: A textbook of English as a foreign language for students of physical and engineering sciences.* London: Nelson.

Swales, J. (1985a). *Episodes in ESP.* Oxford: Pergamon Institute of English.

Swales, J. (1985b). ESP: The heart of the matter or the end of the affair? In R. Quirk & H. G. Widdowson (eds), *English in the world: Teaching and learning the language and literatures* (pp. 212–223). Cambridge: Cambridge University Press.

Swales, J. M. (1990). *Genre analysis: English in academic and research settings.* Cambridge: Cambridge University Press.

Swales, J. M. (1993). Genre and engagement. *Revue Belge de philology et d'histoire*, 71, 687–698.

Swales, J. M. (1996). Occluded genres in the academy: The case of the submission letter. In E. Ventola & A. Mauranen (eds), *Academic writing: Intercultural and textual issues* (pp. 45–58). Amsterdam: John Benjamins.

Swales, J. M. (1998). *Other floors, other voices: A textography of a small university building.* Mahwah, NJ: Lawrence Erlbaum.

Swales, J. M. (2004). *Research genres: Explorations and applications.* Cambridge: Cambridge University Press.

Swales, J. M. (2009a). When there is no perfect text: Approaches to the EAP practitioner's dilemma. *Journal of English for Academic Purposes*, 8, 5–13.

Swales, J. M. (2009b). Worlds of genre: Metaphors of genre. In C. Bazerman, A. Bonini, & D. Figueiredo (Eds.), *Genre in a changing world* (pp. 3–16). West Lafayette, IN: Parlor.

Swales, J. M. (2011/1981). *Aspects of article introductions: A reissue of Aston ESP research reports No. 1* (1981). Ann Arbor: University of Michigan Press.

Swales, J. M. (2016). Reflections on the concept of discourse community. *ASp: la revue du Geras*, 69, 1–12.

Swales, J. M., & Rogers, P. S. (1995). Discourse and the projection of corporate culture: The mission statement. *Discourse & Society*, 6, 223–242.

Swales, J. M., & Feak, C. B. (2011). *Navigating academia: Writing supporting genres.* Ann Arbor, MI: University of Michigan Press.

Swales, J. M., & Feak, C. B. (2012). *Academic writing for graduate students: Essential tasks and skills*, 3rd ed. Ann Arbor, MI: University of Michigan Press.

Swales, J. M., Barks, D., Ostermann, A.C., & Simpson, R. C. (2001). Between critique and accommodation: Reflections on an EAP course for Masters of Architecture students. *English for Specific Purposes*, 20, 439–458.

Swan, M., & Walter, C. (1982). The use of sensory deprivation in foreign language teaching. *ELT Journal*, 36, 183–185.

Tardy, C. M. (2003). A genre system view of the funding of academic research. *Written Communication*, 20, 7–36.

Tardy, C. M. (2006). Researching first and second language genre learning: A comparative review and a look ahead. *Journal of Second Language Writing*, 15, 79–101.

Tardy, C. M. (2009). *Building genre knowledge*. West Lafayette, IN: Parlor Press.

Tardy, C. M. (2015). Bending genres, or when is a deviation an innovation? In N. Artemeva & A. Freedman (eds), *Genre studies around the globe: Beyond the three traditions* (pp. 339–363). Bloomington, IN: Trafford.

Tardy, C. M. (2016). *Beyond convention: Genre innovation in academic writing*. Ann Arbor, MI: University of Michigan Press.

Tardy, C. M., & Swales, J. M. (2014). Genre analysis. In K. P. Schneider & A. Barron (eds), *Pragmatics of discourse* (pp. 165–188). Berlin: De Gruyter Mouton.

Tarone, E. (2002). Frequency effects, noticing, and creativity: Factors in a variationist interlanguage framework. *SSLA*, 24, 287–296.

Tarone, E., Dwyer, S., Gillette, S., & Icke, V. (1981). On the use of the passive in two astrophysics journal papers. *The ESP Journal*, 1, 123–140.

Tessuto, G. (2011). Legal problem question answer genre across jurisdictions and cultures. *English for Specific Purposes*, 30, 298–309.

Thompson, G., & Hunston, S. (2000). Evaluation: An introduction. In S. Hunston & G. Thompson (eds), *Evaluation in text: Authorial stance and the construction of discourse* (pp. 1–27). Oxford: Oxford University Press.

Thompson, S. (1994). Frameworks and contexts: A genre-based approach to analysing lecture introductions. *English for Specific Purposes*, 13, 171–186.

Tomlinson, B. (2010). Principles of effective materials development. In N. Harwood (ed.), *English language teaching materials: Theory and practice* (pp. 81–108). Cambridge: Cambridge University Press.

Tracy, S. J. (2013). *Qualitative research methods: Collecting evidence, crafting analysis, and communicating impact*. Malden, MA: Wiley-Blackwell.

Upton, T. A., & Cohen, M. A. (2009). An approach to corpus-based discourse analysis: The move analysis as example. *Discourse Studies*, 11, 585–605.

van der Bom, I. & Mills, S. (2015). A discursive approach to the analysis of politeness data. *Journal of Politeness Research*, 11, 179–206.

van Willigen, J. (1989). *Gettin' some age on me: Social organization of older people in a rural American community*. Lexington, KY: University Press of Kentucky.

Vergaro, C. (2002). "Dear sirs, what would you do if you were in our position?": Discourse strategies in Italian and English money chasing letters. *Journal of Pragmatics*, 34, 1211–1233.

Wardle, E. (2007). Understanding "transfer" from FYC: Preliminary results of a longitudinal study. *Writing Program Administration*, 31, 65–85.

Wardle, E. (2009). "Mutt genres" and the goal of FYC: Can we help students write the genres of the university? *College Composition and Communication*, 60, 765–789.

Wardle, E., & Downs, D. (2017). *Writing about writing: A college reader*, 3rd ed. Boston: Bedford/St. Martin's.

Widdowson, H. G. (1983). *Language purpose and language use.* Oxford: Oxford University Press.

Winsor, D. A. (2000). Ordering work: Blue-collar literacy and the political nature of genre. *Written Communication*, 17, 155–184.

Witte, S. (1992). Context, text and intertext: Toward a constructionist semiotic of writing. *Written Communication*, 9, 237–308.

Woodrow, L. (2018). *Introducing course design and English for specific purposes.* London: Routledge.

Yasuda, S. (2011). Genre-based tasks in foreign language writing: Developing writers' genre awareness, linguistic knowledge, and writing competence. *Journal of Second Language Writing*, 20, 111–133.

Yayli, D. (2011). From genre awareness to cross-genre awareness: A study in an EFL context. *Journal of English for Academic Purposes*, 10, 121–129.

Zare, J., & Keivanloo-Shahrestanaki, Z. (2017). Genre awareness and academic lecture comprehension: The impact of teaching importance markers. *Journal of English for Academic Purpose*, 27, 31–41.

Index